All American

THE RISE AND FALL OF JIM THORPE

Bill Crawford

WILEY

John Wiley & Sons, Inc.

*Dedicated to Diana, Amelia, Joe, and all other
athletes, amateur and professional*

Illustration credits: pages 145, 147 (top), 149, 150 (bottom), 152 (top), 153 (bottom), 154, 155, 156 (top), 157 (bottom), 158, 159, and 160 (top) from the Cumberland County Historical Society, Carlisle, Pa.; page 146 courtesy of the Harry Ransom Humanities Research Center, The University of Texas at Austin; pages 147 (bottom), 148 (top), and 151 (top) courtesy of Fred Wardecker and Wardecker's Men's Wear, Carlisle, Pa.; pages 148 (bottom), 152 (bottom), 153 (top), 156 (bottom), and 157 (top) courtesy of the Carlisle Indian Industrial School, U.S. Army Military History Institute; page 150 (top) courtesy of the Concord Historical Society and the Warner Museum, Springville, N.Y.; page 151 (bottom) courtesy of the National Archives and Records Administration, Washington, D.C.; and page 160 (bottom) from Photofest.

This book is printed on acid-free paper. ∞

Published by John Wiley & Sons, Inc., Hoboken, New Jersey
Published simultaneously in Canada

Design and production by Navta Associates, Inc.

For general information about our other products and services, please contact our Customer Care Department within the United States at (800) 762-2974, outside the United States at (317) 572-3993 or fax (317) 572-4002.

Wiley also publishes its books in a variety of electronic formats. Some content that appears in print may not be available in electronic books. For more information about Wiley products, visit our web site at www.wiley.com.

Library of Congress Cataloging-in-Publication Data:
Crawford, Bill.
  All American : the rise and fall of Jim Thorpe / Bill Crawford
    p. cm.
  Includes bibliographical references and index.
  ISBN 0-471-55732-3 (cloth : alk. paper)
  1. Thorpe, Jim, 1887-1953. 2. Athletes—United States—Biography. 3. Indian athletes—United States—Biography. I. Title.
  GV697.T5.C73 2004
  796'.092—dc222   004014376

Printed in the United States of America

10 9 8 7 6 5 4 3 2 1

Contents

Introduction

This is a story of blood and honor. *Blood* as the term was used at the dawn of the twentieth century, the time of Jim Thorpe's emergence as America's first international sports megastar. Blood as race. For it was blood and percentage of blood that determined Jim Thorpe's place of birth, his educational path, and his position in the rigid, blood-soaked hierarchy of American society.

This is also a story of honor. Honor won on the athletic field, and honor tested in the corporate conference room. Jim Thorpe brought unprecedented honor to himself and those around him. In 1912, Thorpe was the greatest sports celebrity in the world. He was a combination Jim Brown, Jesse Owens, Emmitt Smith, and Deion Sanders, the highest-scoring American football running back, and the world's most celebrated Olympic hero.

In the days before pro football, Thorpe filled America's largest stadiums with tens of thousands of cheering fans who watched him run for touchdowns, hurl passes, flatten ball carriers, boot field goals, and almost single-handedly drop-kick football into the modern era.

"Watching him turn the ends, slash off tackle, kick and pass and tackle," Harvard's coach Percy Haughton recalled, "I realized that here was the theoretical superplayer in flesh and blood."

Thorpe's mastery of the gridiron brought honor to himself and to his teammates at the Carlisle Indian Industrial School in Carlisle,

Pennsylvania. The Indians, as they called themselves, defeated Harvard, the University of Pennsylvania, and the other mighty elite white sports powerhouses of the time. Fewer than twenty-five years after the massacre at Wounded Knee, Thorpe and his teammates proved that they could beat the white man at his own game and honored the blood of all Indians across the country.

In addition to being America's number one football hero, Thorpe was a dazzling international track superstar, the only athlete ever to win Olympic gold medals in the pentathlon and the decathlon. The veteran sports scribe Al Stump described Thorpe as "the most formidable running, jumping, smashing, heaving, plunging, and all-around bedazzling sports superhuman of them all." Sweden's king, Gustav V, host of the Fifth Olympiad in Stockholm, described Thorpe simply as "the world's greatest athlete."

Born in 1887 to an Indian ranching family on the Sac and Fox Reservation in Indian Territory, Jim Thorpe would never have realized his athletic potential if not for the efforts of his coach and mentor, Glenn Scobey Warner. Warner, the first modern king-coach, rose to prominence along with Thorpe at the Carlisle Indian Industrial School. Pop, as he was called, was one of the most successful and innovative football coaches in history, and one of the most contradictory characters in American sports. He was a burly amateur boxer, a penny-pincher, and a compulsive gambler. He was a brutal football lineman who enjoyed painting watercolors and writing poetry. He was a drinker, a smoker, a blasphemer, and a jokester who once nailed the shoes of his assistant coach to the floor of the locker room. He was a caring, sensitive coach who was not afraid of kicking, punching, or beating his players when he felt they deserved it.

If Jim Thorpe was the Elvis Presley of twentieth-century American sports, Pop Warner was his Colonel Parker. It was Warner who provided the money, the publicity, and the managerial acumen that molded Jim Thorpe into an athletic superstar. Under Warner's tobacco-stained hands, Thorpe became the biggest name in sports. Media outlets around the world celebrated his whalebone toughness; his quiet self-confidence; his calm, brown-eyed gaze; and the strength of his rock-hard jaw, raised slightly with the pride of his blood. According to Warner, Thorpe was "the most remarkable physical machine in the annals of athletics."

Along with the honor that Thorpe won on the athletic field came money, big money. Not for Thorpe, but for Warner and the sports establishment that emerged in the wake of Thorpe's phenomenal triumphs, for Thorpe's rise to glory came at the moment when the business of American sports took its modern form. As Thorpe struggled on the athletic field, businessmen, politicians, and educators struggled to control the flow of money though American sports. During Thorpe's rise to glory, professional baseball came of age. The National Collegiate Athletic Association (NCAA) emerged as America's preeminent collegiate sports business management organization. College football expanded from the rugby scrum of its early years into the fast-moving, crowd-pleasing, open-field game we know today. The U.S. Olympic Committee helped transform the Olympic Games into one of the world's most lucrative sporting events. At the same time, American sports bureaucrats institutionalized the concept of the "amateur" athlete to tighten their control over young athletes and the money they generated.

The toughest test of Jim Thorpe's honor came not on the athletic field, but in the conference rooms of the American sports establishment, for it was here that Pop Warner and others dealt with the issue of Jim Thorpe's status as an "amateur" and first struggled with the questions of honor and money that continue to bedevil American collegiate and Olympic sports.

How was Pop Warner able to take a young Oklahoman of mixed Indian blood and mold him into one of the first international sports celebrities? What forces colluded to dishonor Thorpe and transform him from an American hero into an American disgrace? How did Thorpe's teammates defend his honor and the honor of all Indians? During the course of the controversy, who lied and who acted honorably?

Newly uncovered information and the redefinition of "amateur" sports have made it possible to reveal the real story of Jim Thorpe and Pop Warner. In this tale of blood and honor, we can see many of the best attributes of the American character: loyalty, pugnacity, competitiveness, independence, brashness, sincerity, courage, resourcefulness, and talent. We also can see many of America's failings: greed, hypocrisy, violence, and addiction. Through it all, Thorpe and Warner survived as legends. In many ways, their story is the story of us all.

I

American Airedale

A late-summer Allegheny sun warmed the maples, elms, and pines surrounding the green turfed playing field as Jim Thorpe approached the varsity football tryouts for the Carlisle Indian Industrial School. His knee-length moleskin football pants were cinched like a padded flour sack around his waist. His narrow chest did not quite fill his oversized cotton practice jersey. His socks bunched inside the battered pair of leather and metal cleats the trainer had let him borrow. At five feet, ten inches and 148 pounds, twenty-year-old Thorpe was not as big as many of the other Indian athletes. Still, as he loped onto the field, he was confident that he could kick farther and run better than any of them.

In a faded gray sweatshirt and knickers, a Turkish Trophy cigarette burning in his hand, the beefy-jawed Coach Glenn "Pop" Warner paced up and down the sidelines, evaluating the prospects for his 1907 football squad with canny intensity. At a trim six feet, two inches and two hundred pounds, the thirty-five-year-old Warner wore his curly brown hair in the current long cut of a football player and still had the toughness to match any player on the field, slug for slug.

"What do you think you're doing out here?" Pop barked at Thorpe when he noticed him on the gridiron. Thorpe was one of Warner's top prospects for the Carlisle track team, an all-around performer who could run, jump, and throw.

Thorpe turned to his coach, his chin raised. "I want to play football."

Warner shook his head. "I'm only going to tell you once, Jim," he ordered. "Go back to the locker room and take that uniform off! You're my most valuable track man, and I don't want you to get hurt playing football."

Thorpe stood his ground. "I want to play football."

"All right, if that's the way you want it." Just to humor the boy, Pop relented and sent Jim over to take a few kicks.

Thorpe studied the other players practicing their punts, as he had for many years. He had played football before, pickup games with his friends back home on the Sac and Fox Reservation, and with his classmates at the Haskell Institute, an all-Indian boarding school in Lawrence, Kansas. Thorpe had even scrimmaged with the "tailoring team" in the Carlisle subvarsity league. But when a player finally threw him a varsity football, he held it gingerly. It was one of the first times he had actually touched a real football, made of leather, slightly wider than today's ball, but the same length, between 11 and 11¼ inches. Thorpe held the ball out at arm's length, took a step with his right leg, a step with his left leg, swung his right leg, and connected. His knee almost grazed his forehead with the straight-legged follow-through.

The ball sailed high and arced down the field. Standing on the sidelines, Warner nodded. Not bad. Thorpe seemed to have a knack for sports. When Warner had first come to Carlisle in 1899, Captain Richard Henry Pratt, the school's founder and superintendent, had told him that Indians were natural athletes. Warner had found it to be true. From a talent pool of only 250 male students who were old enough to play athletics, Warner had managed to build a nationally recognized athletic program that generated substantial income as well as the publicity needed to maintain congressional and private support for the Carlisle Indian school. Now, in the fall of 1907, Warner was more determined than ever to build a winning football squad.

Thorpe soon tired of kicking practice. He went up to Warner and asked for a chance to run with the ball. Warner refused. Thorpe persisted. Warner still refused. He did not want his track man hurt by his hard-hitting football players. When Thorpe still refused to take no for an answer, Warner decided to teach him a lesson.

"All right!" Warner said. "If this is what you want, go out there and give my varsity boys a little tackling practice. And believe me, kid, that's all you'll be to them."

The entire varsity squad and "the hot shots," as the second team was called, lined up on the gridiron, spaced out over the field at five-yard intervals. The forty or so players stood at ease, smiling and joking, waiting to get a crack at the skinny ball carrier. Thorpe stood behind the goal line, cradling the ball in his arms. This was his chance. He was ready.

Thorpe took off, running up the field. He kept his head up and cut left and right, avoiding the first few tacklers with tremendous acceleration and deceptive speed. When a tackler managed to grab him, his hard-pumping legs nonetheless drove him forward. Others who came close to him were knocked over by his high-jutting knees, or sheered off by the force of his steel-spring stiff-arm. From the sidelines, Warner watched what he described as Thorpe's "magical run through the Carlisle defense." Thorpe ran one hundred yards, crossed the goal line, and touched the ball down.

The triumphant Thorpe trotted over to the sidelines with a big grin. "I gave them some good practice? Right, Pop?"

Warner was not smiling. He had just seen the humiliation of his entire football squad. According to different versions of the story, either Warner or one of his assistants lectured Thorpe, "You're supposed to let them tackle you, Jim. You're not supposed to run through them."

Frustrated by the response from the coaching staff, Thorpe fumed, "Nobody is going to tackle Jim!"

"By now my face was flush[ed] with anger at being shown up by this young Indian and his display of cockiness," Warner later recalled. "I took the football and slapped it into his midsection and told him, 'Well, let's see if you can do it again, kid!'"

As Jim took his place on the goal line, Warner shouted to his players, "This isn't a track meet. Who does this kid think he is? Get mean! Smack him down! Hit him down so hard he doesn't get up and try it again!"

Once again, Jim took off. Once again, he sliced through Carlisle's entire team before gracefully striding across the goal line. Smiling, Thorpe circled back to Warner, tossed his coach the ball, and proudly said, "Sorry, Pop. Nobody is going to tackle Jim!"

Warner cussed Thorpe for his insolence and his team for their incompetence. Then he turned to his trainer, Wallace Denny, and observed, "He certainly is a wild Indian, isn't he?"

According to Warner, Denny answered, "Yeah, untamed, and one of a kind."

"Now, after a lifetime of football coaching," Pop Warner later wrote, "I must admit that Jim's performance at practice that afternoon on the Carlisle varsity playing field was an exhibition of athletic talent that I had never before witnessed, nor was I ever to again see anything similar which might compare to it."

Jim Thorpe had been running through interference of one sort or another for his whole life. According to baptismal records at Sacred Heart Church near the town of Konawa in Pottawatomie County, Oklahoma, James Francis Thorpe and his twin brother, Charles, were born on May 22, 1887. Charlotte Vieux Thorpe, their sturdy, full-faced mother, was a devout Catholic of mixed French, Potawatomi, Menominee, and Kickapoo blood. Her ancestors included successful French Canadian businessmen who built trading posts on the site of present-day Green Bay and Milwaukee, Wisconsin, and were later forced by the U.S. government to move from the Great Lakes region to reservation land in Iowa, and then to Kansas.

Charlotte Thorpe's grandfather, Louis Vieux, built a successful ranch, mill, and ferry service on the banks of the Vermilion River in Kansas and catered to travelers along the Oregon Trail. When American authorities announced that they were going to remove the tribe to the Indian Territory, Louis Vieux successfully petitioned the government for citizenship and a patent on his lands within the new reservation. More than a thousand others followed Vieux's example, and the group that moved south became known as the Citizen Potawatomi Band.

Charlotte was about four years old in 1867 when her parents, Jacob Vieux and Elizabeth Goeslin (also spelled Gosselin, Goselin, or Gosland), settled with others of the Citizen Potawatomi Band in the Indian Territory. Within a short time of their move, Charlotte's family donated land, money, and labor to the Order of St. Benedict, a French Catholic denomination. With the support of Charlotte's tribe, the Benedictines established the Sacred Heart Mission, which included a church and a school to serve the Citizen Potawatomi Band and other residents of the Indian Territory.

Charlotte Vieux met her future husband, Hiram P. Thorpe, in about 1880, probably at a powwow, one of the Indian gatherings for dancing, gift giving, and trading that are still a central part of life in Oklahoma, the former Indian Territory. Hiram was hard to miss, even in a crowd. At six feet, two inches tall, and weighing more than two hundred pounds, Hiram wore rough leather boots; a tall, broad-brimmed black hat; and a white man's business suit. With a handlebar mustache; a strong jaw; and an aggressive, almost haughty glance, Hiram was known as one of the toughest men in the Indian Territory.

Born in 1852, Hiram was seventeen when he moved to the Indian Territory along with his family and other members of the Sac and Fox tribe. His father was Hiram G. Thorpe. Or Thorp. The final *e* appears and disappears from Jim Thorpe's family name in government documents over the decades. Jim Thorpe's grandfather, Hiram G. Thorpe, was a man of Irish or perhaps English descent. He was born in Connecticut and may or may not have abandoned a family when he moved west. He settled in Iowa on a reservation inhabited by the Sac and Fox tribe. The Sac and Fox was actually a combination of two closely allied tribes from the Great Lakes region who came to be treated as one.

Jim Thorpe's grandfather took a wife, Notenoquah, Wind before a Rain or Storm, a full-blooded member of the Sac tribe. Notenoquah belonged to the Thunder Clan, the same clan as Black Hawk, the famous warrior whose opposition to white encroachment on his people's lands led to the tragic slaughter known as the Black Hawk War. Hiram G. secured a position on the federal payroll as the tribal blacksmith, moved with the tribe when they were resettled to Kansas, and raised a family with Notenoquah.

In 1869, the Thorpes were among the 387 members of the Sac and Fox tribe who settled on a new reservation—a seventeen-mile-wide, thirty-mile-long rectangle of thickly wooded rolling hills that stretched from the Cimarron River in the north to the North Canadian River in the south. The Sac and Fox reservation was just north of the Potawatomi reservation and near the reservations of the Kickapoo, the Shawnee, and other tribes originally from the Great Lakes region. These tribes, who had been in close contact for centuries, inhabited the patchwork of reservations known as the Indian Territory that would eventually become the state of Oklahoma.

According to Jim Thorpe's daughter Grace Thorpe, "Grandpa was a horse breeder, a wife-beater and the strongest guy in the county. He was a polygamist and had two wives. My understanding was he kicked them out when he met Charlotte, my grandmother."

At the time he met Charlotte Vieux, Hiram Thorpe did indeed have two wives, Mary James and Sarah LaBlanche, and three children. According to family legend as recounted by Jim's son, Jack Thorpe, "Hiram walked in the front door with Charlotte, pointed to each of the women and said, 'You can stay. You can go. You can stay. You can go. You can stay. You can go. I don't give a damn, I'm going to bed.'"

In later probate court testimony, a witness named Alexander Connelly recalled the day in 1880 when Charlotte Vieux moved in with Hiram. "I was with Hiram the night he brought Charlotte back to live with him, and then the other two women he was living with picked up and left him," Connelly testified. "I drove them to Okmulgee myself."

Some say that Hiram Thorpe and Charlotte Vieux were actually married in a Catholic ceremony at the Sacred Heart Mission, but no record of such a marriage exists. Charlotte moved into her husband's home, a cedar log cabin, near the North Canadian River. The cabin was about sixteen feet long and ten feet wide, with two small glass windows on one wall, doors at either end, and an upstairs sleeping loft for the children. Serving as a kitchen, a workroom, and a bedroom, the one-room dirt-floor cabin was crowded, hot, and noisy.

Children soon came to Charlotte and Hiram. George was born in 1882. Rosetta, born late that same year, lived only to see her seventh birthday. In the winter of 1883, Charlotte gave birth to twin daughters, Mary and Margaret. Mary died in the summer of 1884, and Margaret died fewer than three years later. In 1887 Charlotte gave birth to twin sons, James Francis and Charles. Mary was born in 1891. A son, Jesse, was born later that same year, but died just before his first birthday. In about 1893, Charlotte and Hiram separated for a time. Hiram fathered a son, William Lasley, by a woman named Fannie Groinhorn (or McClellan), before rejoining Charlotte in about 1894. Adaline Thorpe was born to Hiram and Charlotte in 1895, and Edward in 1898. Hiram and Charlotte's last child, Henry, was born in November 1901 and died a few days later. Shortly after Charlotte's death, Hiram married Julia Mixon, a white woman, and fathered two sons by her,

Ernest, who died in infancy, and Roscoe, born July 5, 1904. By the time of his death at age fifty-two, Hiram P. Thorpe had fathered at least eleven surviving children by at least five different women.

Throughout his life, Jim Thorpe shrugged off discussions of his ancestry with typical offhand humor. "My father, Hiram Thorpe, was half Sac and Fox and half Irish. My mother was three-fourths Sac and Fox and one-fourth French," he explained to an inquisitive reporter. "That makes me five-eighths Indian, one-fourth Irish, and one-eighth French. Guess you'd call me American Airedale."

2

An Incorrigible
Youngster

Jim and his twin brother, Charlie, grew up as Oklahoma farm
boys. By no means wealthy, they were more prosperous and
Westernized than most on the Sac and Fox reservation. According
to an 1887 report by the Sac and Fox Indian agent, the Thorpes
were among the 15 percent of the tribe who wore "civilized clothes"
and lived in a log farmhouse. Most members of the tribe wore breech-
clouts or other traditional clothing and lived in bark-covered shelters
for much of the year.

Although the Thorpe twins learned enough of the Sac and Fox language to get along with others on the reservation, they grew up speaking English, the only language that their mother and father had in
common. The modest government annuities that the Thorpes
received as members of the Sac and Fox tribe were higher than those
received by the Shawnee or Potawatomi. With passage of the Dawes
Allotment Act of 1887, the Thorpe family received some twelve hundred acres of land. They built a new cedar log cabin not far from the
site of their first home and settled down on some of the reservation's
best farmland—relatively flat and well watered, with good grazing for
livestock along the North Canadian River. Even today, what was once
the Thorpe homestead is a productive farm.

Jim Thorpe spent his first years in the constant company of his twin
brother. Together, black-haired Jim and brown-haired Charlie

explored the elm and black oak woodlands surrounding their family cabin. They hunted for blackberries, wild plums, and grapes among the wildflowers that bloomed in the sandy fields along the river bottom. They wrestled. They grabbed onto a rope swing hung by their father and launched themselves into the river. Some days they helped Frank, their older half brother, haul twenty-pound catfish out from the rapids down by the falls. When they were feeling lazy, the boys fished from a wagon parked in the river.

They snared quail in a figure-four trap made from cornstalks, and they stalked wild turkey in the pecan groves down by the river. They hunted squirrels and birds with bows and arrows. With a small-gauge rifle they took potshots at rabbits, opossums, and almost anything else that moved. They relished their mother's country cooking—fried squirrel, with cream gravy and baking powder biscuits—a meal that would remain Jim Thorpe's favorite even after he had dined at the finest restaurants in New York City, Paris, and Tokyo. "Our lives were lived out in the open, winter, and summer," Thorpe later recalled. "We were never in the house when we could be out of it. And we played hard."

Charlotte Thorpe tended fields of wheat and other crops, and grew corn, pumpkins, beans, squash, and melons in a large fenced-in garden near the cabin. She did this farmwork in addition to the housework— an endless cycle of washing and mending clothes, scrubbing floors, and cooking all the family's meals. Of course, she also took care of the children.

Her husband, Hiram, built corrals and let his livestock range freely during the day. He traded the products of his farm for salt, sugar, cloth, and other goods at the settlement of Econtuchka, a few miles west of their home. "We raised hogs, cattle, and horses and the regular farm eating stuff," Jim recalled. "We always had plenty to eat at our house." That was saying a lot in 1890 Indian Territory.

Hiram Thorpe did not really care for farming. Horses were his real love. He liked to trade them, race them, and bet on them. He also enjoyed sports. The Thorpe home was the site of regular wrestling matches and running races, events that were enlivened by wagers and lubricated with alcohol. "He was a big fellow, about six feet two and 230 pounds," Thorpe later said of his father. "He was strong as hell. I know he could lick any man in our county in wrestling."

On September 22, 1891, twenty thousand non-Indians rushed in to the Sac and Fox reservation to claim seven thousand 160-acre tracts opened up for settlement by the U.S. government. Overnight, Indian Territory was cut into two sections. The land where the Thorpes lived became Oklahoma Territory, while the Creek and Seminole reservations, just a few miles to the east and south of the Thorpe homestead, remained in Indian Territory.

The land run opened up the Sac and Fox reservation to whites of all kinds, from hardworking Bohemian settlers to the most notorious outlaws on the American frontier. Rustlers drove off herds of valuable horseflesh. Thieves butchered cattle in the fields. Hiram Thorpe kept his livestock penned up at night in an effort to protect them. Some of Hiram's neighbors stood guard over their livestock all night, every night. One neighbor shot only at the arms and legs of would-be thieves because he did not believe in killing.

Almost as soon as the dust had settled from the land run, clusters of saloons, known as "whiskey towns," sprang up along the border between Oklahoma and Indian Territory. One of the most notorious of these towns was Keokuk Falls. Location was the key to success in the whiskey business, and Keokuk Falls was located just right. The town was on a sliver of Oklahoma Territory that jutted four miles to the east, into Indian Territory, just across the North Canadian River from the Seminole Reservation and just south and west of the Creek Reservation. The location made Keokuk Falls a convenient spot for reservation Indians seeking alcohol and for bootleggers seeking quick access to Indian lands where they could escape arrest by U.S. lawmen for the illegal manufacture and sale of alcoholic beverages.

Hiram Thorpe often made the ten-mile trip west from his homestead to "the seven deadly saloons" of Keokuk Falls along a road that is still marked as "Moccasin Trail." According to a story that has been told and retold among the Sac and Fox, Hiram Thorpe was drinking in a saloon when an argument erupted between two of his fellow patrons. Gunfire left one man on the floor, the other waving his gun in the air challenging anyone to take him on. Hiram Thorpe walked over to the inert victim, stuck his finger in the bullet hole, held up the finger dripping with blood, stuck it in his mouth, sucked it clean, and told the killer, "Yeah, I'm ready. Let's go outside." The killer backed off.

"He was a big, ornery guy," Hiram's granddaughter Grace recalled. "He liked to drink and fight. When Grandpa would come along in his wagon along Moccasin Trail, folks would turn off their lights, 'cause he liked to shoot them out as he came down the road."

Hiram's grandson Jack Thorpe, who later served as the principal chief of the Sac and Fox tribe of Indians in Oklahoma, recalled seeing many letters in the tribal archives complaining of Hiram's behavior. One of those who complained was Superintendent Samuel Lee Patrick, the senior U.S. government official in charge of maintaining order on the reservation, who lodged a formal complaint about Thorpe's bootlegging activities with the U.S. Attorney's office: "Hiram Thorpe, a Sac and Fox Indian, did on the fifth of November 1895 introduce onto this reservation one gallon of whisky and gave same to Naw-mil-wah, Henry Miller, Parkinson, Sam Brown, Sac and Fox Indians." Hiram Thorpe's style particularly irked the federal representative. He was not just "introducing whisky." He was selling it at the Sac and Fox Agency headquarters at the time of payment to tribal members. Patrick went on, "He is very defiant in the matter and I respectfully request that you have him immediately apprehended and prosecute him to the full extent of the law."

There is no record of Hiram Thorpe's arrest or further prosecution, although it is believed that he continued his bootlegging activities and certainly maintained his defiance of authority.

Even as a young boy, Jim Thorpe exhibited his father's defiant attitude. On one trip into town with his mother, Jim was fooling around with his twin brother, Charlie, and his older half brother, Frank. When Jim showed Frank a coin their mother had given Jim, Frank asked, "Why didn't I get one?"

Jim yelled, "Because you can't do this!" He then farted loudly, ran a few steps, leaped into the air, somersaulted, and landed back on his feet.

Although Hiram Thorpe was a hell-raiser and a bootlegger, he was one of the few literate men in the area. He had attended a mission school in Kansas, one of only a handful of Sac and Fox children, mainly mixed-bloods, who had done so. Charlotte Vieux, Jim Thorpe's mother, also was literate. She had studied with Catholic nuns at a different mission school in Kansas and could speak French as well as English and Potawatomi. The Thorpes believed in education for their children, especially education that was provided free by the government along with free room and board.

The school closest to the Thorpe ranch was the Sac and Fox mission school, a vocational boarding school founded by Quakers in 1872 at the Sac and Fox Agency, the town that grew up around the Sac and Fox Indian agent's office. More than a hundred residents lived in bark houses, tepees, and frame houses at the agency, which also boasted doctors' offices, a church, several stores, a blacksmith shop, and the substantial brick home of the Sac and Fox tribal chief.

American religious reformists had promoted Indian schools for centuries. French Jesuit missionaries established an Indian boarding school in 1611. Harvard College opened an institution of higher education for Indians in 1654. The Sac and Fox school was one of many founded in the 1870s by church and reform organizations in the wake of the Indian wars. The Boston Indian Citizenship Committee, the Indian Rights Association, and other groups, founded in some instances by former abolitionists, believed that segregating Indians on reservations was wrong. They believed that education was the best way to Americanize the Indians and integrate them into the rest of the U.S. population as equals. Many officials with the Bureau of Indian Affairs agreed with this position and the bureau began establishing day schools for Indian students in about 1873.

In the summer of 1893, Hiram loaded his six-year-old twin boys into his wagon, drove them north twenty-three miles to the agency, and enrolled them in school. Jim Thorpe would spend most of the next twenty years in such institutions and never earn a diploma, a certificate, or any type of degree.

Perhaps marital turmoil had as much to do with the decision to send Jim and Charlie to boarding school as anything else. Just before he took his twin boys away, Hiram broke with Charlotte and took up with another woman, Fannie Groinhorn (or McLellan). They had a son, William Lasley Thorpe. Charlotte was furious and filed for divorce. The divorce was never granted, however, and Hiram eventually moved back in with Charlotte. They were listed on the Sac and Fox annuity rolls of 1896, "reunited under Indian custom."

At the agency school, the Thorpe twins joined a group of about ninety students ranging in age from five to twenty. Most of their classmates were Sac and Fox, although there were some students from the

Ottawa, Potawatomi, Iowa, and Kickapoo tribes. It was a homecoming of sorts for Jim and Charlie. Their half brother Frank; their half sister, Minnie; and their older brother George also were boarding at the school.

No doubt, their siblings and half siblings helped the six-year-old twins settle into the school. They slept, ate, and attended dances and other gatherings along with the other students in the large three-story brick main building. To the east of the main building stood the brick classroom building. The laundry, the storeroom, and the tool shed stood nearby.

"In contrast to the inadequate rural schools," recalled veteran Indian school teacher Walter White, "the government provided a school for Indian children that was up to date in every way, with modern buildings, dormitories, and the very best equipment available." At the time, no other American ethnic group enjoyed such well-endowed educational facilities funded by the federal government.

The teachers at the school were a mixed lot. Some had been hired by the Quakers. Most were women. Many had been educated in the East and had little knowledge of reservation life. By the standards of the day, their salary was adequate—$50 every three months, from which they paid a small amount for their room and board. According to one veteran teacher of the time, Thomas Wildcat Alford, teachers and other employees of the Indian Service had a tough time hanging onto their jobs. "Many were transferred or fired through a political spoils system."

The teachers were responsible for "civilizing" the Indians. According to the contemporary government policy, the quickest way to accomplish the civilization process was by separating children from their tribal homes. "You go to an Indian school, and you are taken away from your traditional society," recalled Jack Thorpe, who, like his father, also attended Indian boarding schools. "There's no going home."

The Sac and Fox school was run on a strict all-English basis. Students were forbidden to speak any non-English words, even their names. Those who did not have English names were given them on registering. For example, Chi-ki-ka, a full-blood Sac and Fox, was registered under the name Shelah Guthrie. Other students were assigned names chosen from a list of outstanding Americans. Thus John Brown, Jesse James, and Tecumseh Sherman all attended the Sac and Fox boarding school.

The Thorpe boys learned to make their beds, polish their shoes, comb their hair properly, and use good table manners. Dressed in government-issued cheviot shirts, dark suits, vests, and hats—black felt in winter, straw in summer—they marched in step to their classes, where they received instruction in elementary reading, writing, and arithmetic. When they were not reciting their ABCs, the Thorpe twins and their schoolmates did chores. Girls learned sewing, cooking, and other domestic skills. A government farmer taught the other boys their most important lesson: how to use farm tools. Not only did the male students need to raise crops to help feed themselves at the school, they were also preparing for the future. Government policy insisted that Indians put their allotment lands to good agricultural use, even if that land was not particularly suited to agriculture.

There were no organized team sports at the agency school. Teachers supervised students as they played horseshoes and other games recommended by government regulations. Whenever they could, the Thorpe twins and their friends made up their own games. Jim fondly remembered playing follow the leader, "climbing hickory or tall cedar trees, getting to the top, swinging there and leaping to the ground, ready for the next 'follow.'" The most fun Jim recalled having at the school was when he brought a pocket full of marbles out to the school yard, tossed them in the air, and watched the other kids scramble for them.

Since the Thorpe boys usually spoke English at home, they had less difficulty than others in adapting to the English-based education system. "We got a licking many times when we could not spell a simple word," recalled one student. "As a result, we could not learn very much, because most of us were afraid of our teacher."

The school days were tightly structured, strictly disciplined, and tedious. "Our lives were just one bell after another," one student remembered. "We got up by bells, ate by bells, went to class by bells. Everything was routine work and much different than our free life on the reservation. That is why so many children hated the school."

According to the school reports for the summer of 1896, Jim's behavior was "fair," while Charlie's was "good." Teacher Harriet Patrick remembered Charlie as "a sweet gentle little boy" and Jim as "an incorrigible youngster."

The "incorrigible youngster" hated school so much that he ran away. He was not, however, the only one. Runaways were so common in 1896 that the school superintendent requested federal troops to help round up missing students.

As the story goes, Jim was picked up by truant officers and hauled home in a wagon. Jim was wailing so loudly that many of the neighbors thought he was a crybaby. Jim received a beating from his father, who promptly returned him to school.

In early 1897, a typhoid epidemic swept through the Sac and Fox Agency. Harriet Patrick and the other teachers and staff members did their best to nurse their stricken students. As Patrick told the story:

> The superintendent was very ill. Many of the pupils were ill, too, and I took care of them, giving them medicine every hour but by the time that I had made the rounds, it was time to begin again. Charlie Thorpe had also contracted pneumonia. I took care of him at night with the other children. Mr. and Mrs. Thorpe came one night to relieve me, and I tried to get a little rest. At 5:00 A.M., word came that Charlie was worse. I went to him and took him in my arms, put his little feet in mustard water, and sent for the doctor. But the poor little fellow just lay back and died. That was in 1897.

Charlie's death devastated Jim. The incorrigible youngster was to become more incorrigible and a loner. "Up to the time that little Charlie died," Jim Thorpe later recalled, "we roamed the prairies and swam and played together always. After Charlie's death, I used to go out by myself with an old dog and hunt coon when I was only nine years old. Often I would make camp and stay out all night."

"I'm a twin," he later told a reporter, typically evading the truth about his twin brother's death, as he did at one time or another about almost every aspect of his life story. "My twin brother died when we were five . . . or six."

"How did it happen?" the reporter asked.

"We were raised on canned condensed milk and we ran out of cans."

After Charlie's death, Jim lived at home for some time. He also spent time with his older brother George, but most of the time Jim was alone, hunting or fishing. Sometimes he was able to sell his pelts, collecting as much as $2.85 for a skunk skin. But he really hunted because he loved to, running for miles behind his favorite hunting dogs.

Jim Thorpe also enjoyed hunting with his father. "I have never known a man with so much energy as my father," said Thorpe, who shot his first deer when he was ten. "He could walk, ride, or run for days without ever showing the least sign of fatigue. Once, when we didn't have enough horses to carry our kill, my father slung a buck deer over each shoulder and carried them twenty miles to our home."

Sometimes Thorpe attended powwows. Walter White, a white man who grew up on a homestead in the former Sac and Fox reservation, recalled selling watermelons at one such gathering. An Indian boy walked up to him, held out a small jackknife, and asked, "Will you trade a melon for this knife?"

"Two cowpokes on their way to ranch in the Creek Nation had just bought a melon," White recalled in an oral history preserved at the Sac and Fox National Library. "One of them drawled, 'If that boy ever grows to fit his mouth he will be the biggest Injun in the Sac tribe.'"

"He was a handsome boy, as boys go, with a tendency to legginess," White remembered. "The most striking thing about Jim was the way he handled himself. The easy hip action when he walked marked him as a runner, his movements, catlike in lightness."

White traded Thorpe the watermelon and then tried to engage the boy in conversation. Thorpe remained silent. "He evidently did not regard talking as being part of the bargain," White recalled.

Jim returned to the Sac and Fox school, but he ran away again in the early spring of 1898, one of fifteen runaways that season. When he arrived home, his father beat him, took him back to school, and left him. According to legend, Jim immediately ran away again. He took a shortcut and met his father at the door of their cabin.

Hiram was irate and laid into his stubborn eleven-year-old son.

Thorpe took the beating but did not break. "I talked with my uncles," Jack Thorpe recalled, "and they all said everyone was afraid of Hiram. The only one that could stand up to him was Jim. Hiram could scare anyone in the county, but he couldn't control Dad."

A furious Hiram swore at his obstinate son, "I'm going to send you so far you will never find your way back home."

3

Men Born Shaggy

While Jim Thorpe was toddling across the beaten earth floor of his family's cabin on the North Canadian River, a white Yankee teenager was sharpening plows, building fences, and driving teams of horses across his family's wheat ranch three hundred miles to the southwest.

Glenn Scobey Warner was born on April 5, 1871, on a farm outside the town of Springville, New York, about thirty miles southeast of Buffalo. His father, William H. Warner, signed up as an enlisted man to fight for the Union in the Civil War and mustered out as a captain with the Fourth Regiment, Arkansas Cavalry. Adeline Scobey, Warner's mother, was the daughter of a local miller. The oldest of three boys with two older sisters, Glenn was nicknamed "Butter" because he was a heavy child with a taste for butter and apple pie.

He attended Griffith Institute in Springville, an elementary and secondary school established by a local philanthropist. Warner enjoyed sports, especially baseball, and played as a pitcher and catcher on a local Springville team. The only football he played as a child was in neighborhood pickup games. Their goals were two streets, their ball was an inflated cow's bladder, and the game they played looked a lot more like soccer than football.

After graduating from Griffith Institute in 1889, eighteen-year-old Butter Warner took the entrance exam to West Point but failed to gain admission. In the fall of that year he set out for the little town of Iowa Park near Wichita Falls, Texas, where his family had acquired a wheat ranch. Warner enjoyed the work, riding beside his father and his younger brothers, Fred and Bill, tinkering with horse-drawn harvesters and water-pumping windmills. Even more than the ranchwork, Warner enjoyed camping and hunting in the wide-open country. "There were no game laws or at least none that were enforced," Warner later recalled. "I have chased many a bunch of antelope over the rolling Red River banks, which are now covered with oil derricks and farmhouses. . . . Quail, prairie chicken, plover, curlew, wild turkeys and in winter ducks and geese were plentiful."

Warner liked the ranch life but did not care for the low pay. He accepted an offer to become the apprentice of a local tinsmith. With a natural flair for drawing and painting, Warner took to the work and quickly became a full-fledged "tinner" and the manager of a shop at the salary of $15 per week, at a time when laborers earned only $1.25 a day.

The money was good, but not good enough for Butter. Ambitious, athletic, and a risk taker, he wagered $20 that his fastest cow pony could beat one of his friend's mustangs. "I [was] my own jockey and I weighed 200 pounds," Warner explained after he lost the race and the money. "My opponent weighed only 140."

Warner's real dream was not to race horses or punch cows. He wanted to be part of the new sporting craze that was sweeping the country: professional baseball. With his size and strength, Warner believed that he had what it took to be the next Cap Anson or Dan Brouthers, and to play someday for the Brooklyn Bridegrooms (later known as the Dodgers) or the Cincinnati Reds.

He was good enough to pitch for a North Texas team in 1890. The fact that Warner and his teammates played in an "amateur" league did not prevent them from picking up a few dollars every now and then when attendance was good and the manager generous. They were a decent ball club and wound up playing a series of games against Waxahatchie for what Warner called the "amateur championship of Texas."

Riding the range, working tin, and playing baseball, Warner thoroughly enjoyed the Lone Star State. He later recalled, "Those three years that I lived in Wichita Falls were perhaps the happiest of my life."

Warner headed back to New York in the summer of 1892 for what he claimed was a "vacation," though it might have had something to do with his mother's ill health. He got the chance to play in a series of five "amateur" baseball games for Springville against a team from Gowanda, New York. As the competition heated up and the betting became serious, Warner found that he was competing with "ringers," gypsy athletes who played for whatever team was willing to meet their price. One of these ringers was a shortstop named John McGraw, from a semipro league in western Pennsylvania. "Mugsy" McGraw later would become a major-league ballplayer, the manager of the New York Giants, and a key figure in the professional career of Warner's greatest athletic discovery, Jim Thorpe.

After the baseball series, Warner traveled to nearby Buffalo to do some sightseeing. The sight that he found most interesting was the track where the Grand Circuit harness races were running. Warner took his money, bet it, and won $50. He followed the Grand Circuit to its next stop, Rochester, where his luck turned cold. As Warner later told the story, "Leaving the park, I bucked a 'wheel of fortune' in a desperate effort to recoup and ended up with nothing left but my return ticket to Springville."

According to Warner, he could not face telling his father that he had gambled away all his money. He knew that his father wanted him to go to law school, and he knew that many law schools then did not require an undergraduate degree. So Warner sent his father a letter saying that he had decided to go to law school and asking for registration money. To make the letter convincing, Warner enclosed a catalog from the Cornell University Law School. Warner's father sent back a check for $100, and Warner caught the next train for Ithaca, New York. On the train, Warner met Carl Johanson. Johanson was a journeyman athlete who had played football at Williams College for several years and was currently the captain and the coach of the Cornell football team. Johanson's position was not unique at the time. Many talented football players hopped from college to college, and player/captains often served as coaches for the football teams that were springing up on college campuses across the country.

Despite football's popularity with students and alumni, many faculty members were opposed to the sport. Almost twenty years before Warner met Johanson, Cornell's president, Andrew D. White, had emphatically turned down a challenge to play football against the University of

Michigan, declaring, "I will not permit thirty men to travel four hundred miles merely to agitate a bag of wind." Johanson invited the stocky Warner to come out to football practice and to try his hand at "agitating windbags."

Warner's version of the story may be somewhat fanciful. According to his boyhood friend Dr. Ralph W. Waite, Warner had lost all his money and was on the train back to Springville when "Johanson took one look at Pop, who was a sturdy six-foot, two-hundred-pounder, felt his bicep, and said, 'Boy, you are coming to Cornell.' "

In any event, Warner accepted Johanson's invitation to be on the team and wandered out to the Cornell football field, which he later described as "little more than a corner lot."

"Get on a suit right away," Johanson told Warner. "We need a left guard."

"Wait a minute," Warner hesitated. "I don't know anything about the game at all."

"Never mind. All you've got to do is to keep 'em from going through you and spoiling the play when we've got the ball, and when they've got the ball, knock the tar out of your man and tackle the runner. Perfectly simple!"

Warner threw on a borrowed uniform in the makeshift locker room under the old wooden grandstand. During the scrimmage, Warner played with the varsity team against the scrubs. When his team punted, he chased the high kick downfield and batted the ball on a bounce over the goal line. Sure it incurred a penalty. Warner was not supposed to touch the ball, and it was illegal to knock it forward. Still, Johanson appreciated his new recruit's "elephantine enthusiasm."

"Good work, Pop!" Johanson said, slapping the recruit on the back.

"There has to be a Pop on every team," Warner explained, "and being big, good-natured, and several years older than the rest, I was elected to carry a nickname that has stayed with me ever since."

That evening, as Pop sat "trying to get my chin loose from the nape of my neck" and preparing for school registration, he learned that the Cornell football squad was scheduled to play Syracuse the very next afternoon. "Registration Day, being an idle time for the student body, was then looked on as a good chance for football."

Warner played the entire game at left guard as Cornell won, 58–0.

He was elated about his performance—until he shook hands with one of his opponents. "This is my first game," Warner bragged.

"You've got nothing on me," the opposing guard said with a gasp. "It's my first, too."

In 1892, Pop's first year of play, football bore little resemblance to the multibillion-dollar, high-speed, high-impact, video-enhanced athletic ballet of today. "Football is about the oldest sport of which we have any record, dating back to the great days of Greece and Rome," Warner wrote, referring to the game Americans call soccer. "The English began to carry the ball, rugby," Warner continued. A plaque on the campus of the Rugby School in Rugby, England, commemorates the "exploit of William Webb Ellis who . . . first took the ball into his arms and ran with it thus originating the distinctive feature of the rugby game A.D. 1823."

"As near as I can make out," Warner wrote, "the American version [of rugby] started rough and got rougher. Harvard's annual class game was known as 'Bloody Monday' as early as 1827."

"Bloody Monday" and other early collegiate football games were little more than glorified hazing, pitting freshmen against upperclassmen in a giant wrestling match. Over the decades, hazing developed into a more formal game in which players attempted to kick or carry a ball over a goal line. What is generally accepted as the first intercollegiate football game took place on November 6, 1869, in New Brunswick, New Jersey, between Rutgers and Princeton. In 1876, Princeton, Harvard, and Columbia formed the Intercollegiate Football Association. Three years later, Yale joined. Walter Camp was the captain and coach of the Yale squad, where he played for five years.

In 1892, *Harper's Weekly* declared Camp the "Father of American Football," a title he truly deserved. After leaving Yale, Camp took a position at the New Haven Clock Company that he held for the rest of his life. While working at the clock company, his real business was running Yale's football program. He was never paid by Yale for his services or even publicly acknowledged. Camp ran Yale's football operation through his own athletic association, a private organization that collected gate receipts, covered team expenses, and secretly distributed cash to Camp and whomever else Camp wanted to pay. At the end of the 1889 season, Camp and the sportswriter Caspar Whitney began choosing the best players of the year, the All-Americans, a tradition that continues to the present. Camp's Yale organization was the prototype of the modern alumni booster club, and the model that Pop Warner eventually copied at Carlisle. According to Walter Camp, "The organizer wins in athletics as he does in business."

When Warner began playing football for Cornell in 1892, players participated in the entire game—on offense, defense, and special teams. Coaches were not allowed to coach from the sidelines. There was no forward pass, and there were few breakaway runs as we know them today. There was no NCAA. Players, many of whom were only nominally college men, won glory on the gridiron by bunching in tight formations, bashing their opponents, and muscling or booting the football across the goal line.

As Warner put it, "football was a game to be played only by men born shaggy." Why shaggy? According to Warner, "Headgear had not been invented, and the player's one hope was to mattress his skull with the thickest possible hirsute growth. This sometimes had its disadvantages . . . a man [would make] his tackle by simply knotting both hands in the opponent's hair."

Many games were little more than free-for-all combat. "The average coach's idea of psychology was a sock on the nose or a kick in the shin [delivered to one of his own players]," Warner recalled, "and when an official's back was turned everything went, from slugging, to kneeing, to mayhem." Linemen sparred across the line of scrimmage before the snap. Warner saw linemen pick up handfuls of dirt and throw them into an opponent's eyes at the snap of the ball. Substitutes were often put in at the start of a game to pick fights with stars on the other team and get them out of the game by crippling or disqualification. Once a referee saw a player kick another and threw him out of the game. "But you can't do that," the ejected player complained. "I didn't kick the guy until after the whistle blew."

There were no rules against pushing or pulling. Players wore belts with handles so that ball carriers could hang on to them as they beat their way through the opposing lines, lines that Warner described as resembling "a herd of hairy mammoths." Warner described one early Harvard–University of Pennsylvania contest as a "carnivorous game when it was claimed that the Penn players free-lunched off the legs of the Crimson players."

With only five yards to gain in three downs, teams needed nothing but a slam-bang ground attack. There were no rules against starting a play with any number of players back from the line of scrimmage. The best college teams relied on the flying wedge, the turtleback, and other mass formations in which the interference locked themselves together around the ball carrier and plunged forward in a mass with "the crushing drive of a giant tractor."

The only possible defense against this type of play was for the defensive center and guards to throw themselves under the feet of the opposition to try and trip them up while the tackles dove from the sides into the churning mass. The defensive ends and backs closed onto the fringes of the formation, ready, in Warner's words, to "nail the runner if he managed to break away."

As Warner recalled, "Substitutions were few, for an ability to 'take it' was demanded of every man and all shrank from seeming to show the white feather." One Yale player fought through a game with two smashed ribs, a sprained shoulder, and a cracked collarbone. The 1894 Harvard-Yale game resulted in a broken leg, a broken collarbone, a broken nose, and several players hospitalized with head injuries.

According to one popular shaggy football story, a back once said with a groan, "I've got to quit. My left leg's gone."

"Well, what of it?" his captain replied with a snarl. "You've got your right one, haven't you?"

Warner played the entire 1892 season with the Cornell football team, a season in which Cornell compiled an outstanding record of ten wins and one loss. Cornell even defeated the football powerhouse Harvard. The game was played in Springfield, Massachusetts, which Warner described as "a red-hot town in those days, sometimes drawing crowds of ten or fifteen thousand people who rode out to the field in traps, surreys and victorias and who were sporty enough to pay a whole dollar for a seat." In the stands watching the Harvard-Cornell game was Mike "King" Kelly, a well-known major-league baseball player. When a reporter asked him if he would like to join the boys on the football field, Kelly replied, "Not me! When I want to get knocked out, I'll go up against [boxers James J.] Corbett or John L. [Sullivan]. They'll do it quick and easy."

At the end of football season, Warner played other sports. He boxed well enough to become Cornell's heavyweight champion. He competed in track, threw the hammer, and put the shot. He continued to play baseball until he damaged his arm by throwing too hard in an attempt to impress a Cornell coach. Warner later constructed a special harness, hoping to return to the pitcher's mound, but to no avail. For the rest of his life, football was his game.

According to Warner, the 1893 season was "one of the most disastrous in Cornell's gridiron history." As the Redmen won only two games, Warner learned "how easily good players could be ruined by overworking them."

Warner completed his law courses in the spring of 1893 but was invited to stay on as the captain of the 1894 Cornell football squad. He signed up for a few postgraduate courses, but spent most of his time on the gridiron. It was hard for the twenty-three-year-old New York farm boy to earn his tuition money, room, and board. "I worked my way through Cornell, waiting on table, organizing boarding clubs, and even peddling water-color landscapes that I turned out in spare moments," Warner commented, "but there were days during the football season when I couldn't hold a brush or carry a tray."

The 1894 Cornell squad was coached by Marshall Newell. Newell, who had been an All-American at Harvard, believed that to get the best performance from his team, the coach had to develop the total player. Newell not only conditioned his team on the field, he also kept them on a strict diet; no sweets or even apples. Newell reserved Sundays for rest and inspiration. He led his players on walks through the woods, "talking of trees and flowers, books, sportsmanship, ideals, standards, and values." Warner would use Newell's physiological and psychological training techniques extensively in his own coaching career.

When Newell returned to Harvard for two weeks to help his alma mater get ready for the big game against Yale, Cornell football captain Warner got his first chance at coaching. "I remember well the first play I ever doped out," Warner later recalled of the play he designed for the game against Williams College. In the second half, the Cornell backfield faked an end run to the left, while the quarterback handed the ball off to the left guard, who was, not coincidentally, Warner. Warner took the ball and gained twenty-five yards before he was tackled from behind and fumbled. Warner's first coaching assignment ended in a 0–0 tie.

Warner left Cornell in the fall of 1894, passed the New York bar, and took a job with a Buffalo law firm in January 1895. The following spring, he received a letter from the Cornell football team business manager. The letter included a query from Iowa Agricultural College (now Iowa State University of Science and Technology) at Ames, Iowa, looking for a football coach. The Cornell man thought that Warner would be perfect for the job.

Warner was intrigued by the offer. His law practice was rather dull and not particularly lucrative. At the time, college football was just moving west of the Alleghenies, and newly formed state colleges there, which would eventually come to dominate the sport, were struggling to attract enough students to fill their classrooms. The salary of $25 per week to coach at Iowa sounded pretty good to Warner, who recalled that "a dollar then looked as large as a balloon tire does today."

Warner and others believed that there was money to be made in football. On Thanksgiving Day, 1893, forty thousand football fans paid up to $5 a seat to watch the Yale-Princeton football game on New York City's Manhattan Field (later the site of the Polo Grounds). "Thanksgiving Day is no longer a solemn festival to thank God for mercies given," declared the *New York Herald* in 1893. "It is a holiday granted by the State and the nation to see a game of football."

According to the president of Lafayette College in Pennsylvania, "The Thanksgiving game in football for a big team brings in revenue greater than the total expenditure of the trustees supporting twenty-five professors and educating three hundred men." By 1894, Harvard's football club was taking in as much as $42,000 a season.

Warner accepted the job at Iowa, then leveraged his position by applying for coaching jobs at other schools. He landed an offer from the University of Georgia for $35 per week, $10 more than his offer from Iowa. Warner told Iowa that he was going to take the job in Georgia but offered to coach the Iowa team for five weeks in the late summer, before the season started at Georgia. Iowa agreed to hire Warner for $150 for five weeks, and Warner began his formal coaching career at Ames in July 1895. Warner later claimed, "I learned more football in five weeks at Iowa than in three years at Cornell."

In addition to leading his Iowa players in drills and scrimmages, Warner decided to arrange preseason games for his team. The Butte Athletic Club in Butte, Montana, proposed a game with Warner's Iowa boys to be played on a Sunday, when they could be certain of attracting a large crowd. The guarantee was substantial enough to attract Warner's attention. Since the Iowa faculty would certainly have objected to breaking the Sabbath, Warner told his superiors that the game was to be played on Saturday, then took his team west by rail.

"At that time," Warner recalled, "Butte was the toughest and sportiest town in the United States; everything was wide open both night and day, for the mines ran three eight hour shifts."

There was considerable betting on the game. "I even let my youthful gambling spirit get the better of my judgment," Warner admitted. He bet $150, his entire Iowa coaching salary, on his boys.

As soon at the game began, Warner realized that he was in trouble. The Butte team was comprised of former college stars, among the toughest characters Warner had ever seen. The fumes of the ore smelters had killed off all the vegetation, leaving the playing field nothing but hardened, sun-dried clay, "bare and hard as an iron griddle." Warner's center was used to snapping the ball and letting it bounce or roll back to the quarterback, a strategy that worked well on the grassy fields of the East Coast but led to numerous fumbles in Butte.

The crowd was as much of a hindrance to play as the field conditions. Gangs of screaming fans moved up and down the sidelines, interfering whenever they could and occasionally swarming onto the field, ready for a fight. In Butte, Montana, the fans were not merely rabid, they were also armed.

"The Butte cheerleaders were whiskered gentlemen who kept up a continuous fusillade with six-shooters," Warner recalled. "Almost every man in the crowd had a large gun at his belt, and any time Butte pulled off a ground-gaining play, out came those guns and barked their applause."

The officials also were against them. If Iowa managed to make a good play, the referee or other game officials took it back. When Warner threatened to leave the field, the promoters of the game reminded him that he would not get his guarantee unless his team played to the last whistle.

Warner was so desperate that he played guard for the second half of the game. Even this effort proved futile. "We not only lost the game," Warner later joked, "but also our uniforms, for every man on the team came out of the game half naked." Warner lost his salary as well. He later reflected philosophically, "Since that day, I always made sure I knew a lot more about my competition before betting on one of my teams."

Warner coached at the University of Georgia in the fall of 1895. In the game against North Carolina, a North Carolina player threw the football instead of kicking it, scoring a touchdown. Warner protested that passing was illegal, which it was then, but the referee claimed that he had not seen the pass so the touchdown stood, marking one of the first forward passes ever thrown in football history.

After the season, Warner returned to his law practice in Buffalo. In 1896 he repeated the routine, coaching at Iowa and Georgia Tech before returning to Buffalo to practice law. He earned a reputation as a good, solid coach, although he suffered some serious losses, as in the 1895 Georgia defeat at the hands of the Alabama Polytechnical Institute (later known as Auburn University).

"In my strong desire to turn out a winning team," Warner later admitted, "I had brought the boys up to their final game in an over-trained condition. . . . They were overconfident and self-satisfied, and they hadn't scouted the opposition." The Auburn coach who defeated Warner's Georgia squad was John Heisman. Today, Heisman's name adorns the most prestigious award in college football.

In the fall of 1897, Warner gave up his coaching jobs in Georgia to coach at his alma mater, Cornell, for what he described as "a sweetened salary offer of $600 for the season." He continued to coach preseason at Iowa State. Although Warner personally broke the collarbone of a promising young player when he participated in a practice scrimmage, the Cornell Redmen performed well enough so that Warner received a raise to $800 for the 1898 season, during which he led the team to a 10-and-2 record. The most bitter defeat of the season was to archrival Penn, a game played in rain and snow. Warner attributed the loss to the fact that the Penn team was able to change uniforms at halftime, while he had neglected to bring a change of uniform for his Cornell players.

One of Cornell's most intriguing opponents in 1898 was a team from the Carlisle Indian Industrial School. As had become his practice, Warner had done a thorough job of scouting the team before the game. The Indians had begun playing football and baseball in the early

1890s. W. G. Thompson, the school disciplinarian in charge of the older boys, was the first coach at Carlisle; he was followed by a series of Yale football men, Vance C. McCormick, W. O. Hickock, William T. Bull, and John A. Hall. McCormick worked for free, but after his tenure, the coaches received a salary. The first big Carlisle football game was arranged in 1896 against Yale. The Yale team, the best in the country, expected an easy practice game, but instead fought a bruising battle against the Indians. According to Pop Warner, "I understand that only some official's decisions most favorable to Yale enabled the Elis to defeat them in a very close game."

It was true. When a Carlisle touchdown was called back by the official, a former Yale man, the Indians threatened to walk off the field. Captain Richard Henry Pratt, the founder and superintendent of the school, rushed out onto the field and talked with his students. "You must fight the battle out," he explained. "If you leave you will be called quitters and will probably lose future opportunities." The Carlisle team finished the game, and Pratt became an outspoken football enthusiast. "If it was in my power to bring every Indian into the game of football," he later wrote, "I would do it, and feel that I was doing them an act of the greatest Christian kindness, and elevating them from the hell of their home life and reservation degradation into paradise."

In 1896, the Carlisle Indians defeated the University of Cincinnati, Penn State, and Brown. At a game played in Chicago, Carlisle defeated the University of Wisconsin in one of the first illuminated night games in the history of American sports. Sportswriters could not get enough of the Indians and gave their games extensive coverage in the sports sections that began appearing in newspapers across the country in the 1890s. Football news filled a hole in the Sunday editions, the slowest day of the week. Although Joseph Pulitzer and other editors at first scorned football as a rich college man's sport, the Carlisle Indians helped prove to the media that football was a game with broad appeal across class barriers. Each Carlisle game was a classic, almost mythic, contest. White against red. Brawn against speed. "The career of the lads from Carlisle has not been the least amazing feature of this amazing year of 1896," wrote Stephen Crane in the *New York Journal*. "How Geronimo would have loved it!"

The 1898 Carlisle Indian team was equally strong, led by the impressive kicking ability of the team captain and quarterback, Frank Hudson. In front of a hometown Ithaca crowd, Warner's Cornell Redmen fought the Carlisle Indians in a game where slugging was almost as common as tackling. Cornell managed to move the ball well with "double pass" plays, or double handoffs, around each end, but Warner was taking no chances. The bowler-hatted referee had been the captain of the Cornell team the year before, and called back not one, but two Carlisle touchdowns for mysterious reasons. "Slugging was indulged in openly by the Ithacans," reported the *Carlisle Daily Herald* after the game, "and all attempts at protestation on the part of the Indians were promptly rejected by the umpire, whom Captain Hudson, of the Indians, styles quite honestly, 'the twelfth member of the Cornell team.'"

"We outscored 'em but we didn't defeat 'em," Warner said of the 23–6 Cornell victory, "if you follow me."

Although his team had done well during the 1898 season, Warner got caught up in a political struggle that eventually cost him his job. Every year, the captain of the Cornell football team, who was elected by the players, was responsible for appointing the football coach. An assistant coach was gunning for Warner's job and was lobbying to have his own man elected captain. Warner postponed the election but saw the handwriting on the locker room wall. Realizing that the faculty would try to hire a coach who had not been involved in the controversy, Warner began "shopping around for the best opening."

One of the schools he thought about was Carlisle. "The Indian boys appealed to my football imagination," Warner recalled, "and I decided to apply for the job at Carlisle."

Captain Pratt of Carlisle approached Warner with a job offer on the recommendation of Walter Camp, who admired the Cornell coach. When Warner met with Pratt in Carlisle, the two got right down to business. Captain Pratt asked Warner to name his salary requirements. Warner said, "$1,200 plus expenses." It was a high salary, but the twenty-eight-year-old Warner needed the money. He wanted to get married. He was ready to coach at one school and give up his preseason coaching position at Iowa State.

Pratt did not hesitate. He offered the Cornell coach the job at

Carlisle at the salary he demanded. Warner married Tibb Lorraine Smith, his childhood sweetheart, and the newlywed couple moved from Springville, New York, into one of the small cottages on the campus of the Carlisle Indian Industrial School in Carlisle, Pennsylvania.

4

Oklahoma Buckaroo

With his substantial salary of $1,200, Warner was under considerable pressure to create a winning football team at Carlisle, and he immediately got down to work. "My first view of Carlisle's football material was anything but favorable," he later wrote, recalling the fall of 1899, "for the boys who reported to practice were listless and scrawny, many looking as if they had been drawn through a knot-hole."

"They have been on farms all summer," his boss, Captain Pratt, assured him, "and these Pennsylvania farmers insist on getting their money's worth. The youngsters will soon begin to pick up weight, so don't worry."

Though they were scrawny, Warner soon learned that the Carlisle Indian athletes were smart, fast, tough, dedicated, and talented. "When I went to the Carlisle school in 1899 as football coach," he later recalled, "I had all of the prejudices of the average white, but after fourteen years of intimate association, I came to hold a deep admiration for the Indian and a very high regard for his character and capacities."

Warner quickly learned that he could best communicate with his Indian athletes by demonstration, in part because some of his players had only limited command of the English language. "Nik," Warner asked the lineman Nikifer Shouchuk during the 1901 season, "what do you do on 15–25–36?"

"Me run," the Eskimo athlete answered. "Yes, sirree, Pop. Me run most fast."

The one thing that all the Indians understood and were particularly sensitive to was swearing, which caused problems for Warner. "Having been coached by some rather hard-boiled gents during my years as a player," he later wrote, "I took a fairly extensive vocabulary with me to Carlisle and made full use of it.

"A week went by, and then many of the best players turned in their suits and announced that they were not coming out for practice anymore. It took some time to get at the trouble, but I finally learned that they 'didn't like to be cussed at.' I apologized, profoundly and sincerely, and [I] should have thanked them too, for the rebuke made me do some hard, helpful thinking."

"I also found the Indian boys to be very sensitive and this trait could not be driven or abused," Warner observed. "Above all, they hated to be ridiculed. To get results, I used to kid with them, pat them on the back, and praise them when they did things well. I only criticized them in a friendly way when they made mistakes." When Warner first patted a player on the back, the Indian misunderstood the gesture and started slapping Warner on the back, thinking that was what Warner wanted him to do.

Warner discovered that Carlisle, which was created to destroy Indian culture, actually strengthened the ethnic identity of his athletes. Once on the team, they were no longer Cheyenne, Sioux, Chippewa, or mixed-bloods. They were Indians, Carlisle Indians, who took pride in winning honor for their teammates and their race.

Warner's first season at Carlisle was so succcessful that the team played the University of California in San Francisco and won. On the journey home, Warner and the Carlisle Indians stopped at Lawrence, Kansas, for a visit to the Haskell Institute, an all-Indian boarding school founded in 1884 and modeled after Carlisle. On January 12, 1900, the Indian students at Haskell thrilled at the sight of the handsome Carlisle players in their blue military-style uniforms and their yellow-lined military capes, turned back ever so smartly on one shoulder. The Carlisle players, accompanied by Pop Warner and the Carlisle school physician Dr. Carlos Montezuma, entered the domestic science rooms for a breakfast prepared and served by Haskell students. Later the Carlisle students inspected the campus, and Dr.

Montezuma addressed the students assembled in the chapel. "Work," Montezuma lectured, "is the most necessary thing to learn." Haskell supervisor R. P. Wright welcomed the visitors from the East and declared, "Carlisle and Haskell, the two best schools in the Indian service, the two best schools in the United States!"

In some ways it was a recruiting trip for Warner and for the Haskell athletic administrators as well. Pop later recruited several Haskell players for Carlisle. After Thaddeus Redwater was expelled from Carlisle in 1901 for unruly behavior, he played for Haskell. Captain Pratt approved of Warner's recruiting efforts. Pratt, who kept strict control over Warner and his athletic activities, was always on the lookout for good students to bring to Carlisle. Before the Carlisle school first opened in 1879, federal officials had ordered Pratt to recruit the children of hostile Sioux chiefs as students, with the intention of holding the children as hostages to ensure good behavior by the Sioux. Twenty years later, Pratt was recruiting athletes instead of hostages. "If you should by chance have a sturdy young man anxious for an education who is especially swift of foot or qualified for athletics," Pratt wrote to the Sac and Fox Indian agent in 1899, "send him and help Carlisle to compete with the great universities on those lines and to now and then overcome the best." In effect, the Haskell Institute, other Indian schools, and the entire reservation system became an informal minor league for Warner, as he recruited the best Indian athletes in the country for Carlisle.

One of the Haskell students who would later play for coach Pop Warner was thirteen-year-old Jim Thorpe. Hiram Thorpe had sent his defiant son Jim to Haskell, three hundred miles north of his home on the Sac and Fox Reservation, so that Jim would not be able to run away as he had from the Sac and Fox Mission School.

A large, open campus with imposing gray stone building, Haskell in 1900 was home to about five hundred Indian students from ninety different tribes, ranging in age from five to the midtwenties. At Haskell, Jim Thorpe and his fellow students lived a life of strict military discipline that mixed elementary education with vocational training, military drills, and athletics in an all English-speaking environment. For Jim Thorpe, the training at Haskell was similar in many ways to the training he had received at the Sac and Fox Agency school—highly structured, highly supervised, and extremely tedious. Not only that, but the social life among the students was often brutal, especially for a boy of mixed blood, such as Jim Thorpe. Jim's son Jack Thorpe, who also grew up in the Indian boarding school system, later recalled, "When someone insulted you and called you a white boy or a 'goddam breed (a mixed blood),' you had no choice. You had to fight."

After arriving at Haskell on September 17, 1898, Thorpe showed little interest in academic work or in his vocational major, electricity. The only thing that piqued his interest was sports. Like Carlisle, Haskell had a strong sports program, one that brought it a good deal of publicity. Dr. James Naismith, who had invented basketball in 1891, was a teacher at Haskell and coached the Haskell basketball squad to victories over the University of Kansas and other tough rivals. The Haskell baseball team was so good that is made a summer tour of Kansas and Nebraska in 1901, winning eighteen of thirty-two games against semiprofessional ball clubs throughout the region.

In 1900, the Haskell football team was undefeated against such rivals as Missouri State University and defeated the University of Texas at Austin in 1902. The team tried to arrange a football game against the University of Kansas, but according to the *Indian Leader*, the school publication, on November 9, 1900, "Heretofore K.U. has used professional men. This season the faculty decided not to do this, so K.U. was not able to get a team together at this time that could play with the Haskell team."

Thorpe spent most of his free time hanging around the athletic fields, watching the athletic stars practice their moves. The most accomplished of the Haskell athletes was Chauncey Archiquette. Archiquette played on the basketball squad, was the leading batter on the baseball squad, and was a hard-hitting end and the captain of the football squad. Thorpe later described Chauncey Archiquette as his first football hero. Legend has it that Archiquette noticed a group of young boys running along the sidelines of the practice field. One kid in particular caught Archiquette's eye. The kid was scrawny but very fast. Archiquette introduced himself to the young boy and asked him if he wanted to play football. When Jim Thorpe responded with an enthusiastic yes, Archiquette helped his young friend construct a practice football from pieces of leather stuffed with rags and showed him a few football moves.

According to Henry Roberts, who was one of Thorpe's friends at Haskell, the boys had first played football among themselves with a grass-stuffed stocking. "One of the [school] disciplinarians took us aside and taught us a few basics of the game," Roberts recalled. "We played in our regular hickory-cloth work shirts, jeans, and heavy shoes."

At age thirteen, Thorpe was a slender, timid youth who looked nothing like the powerful, confident champion he would eventually become. According to fellow Haskell student George Washington, "He was small for his age, so the football recruiters ignored him. It is ironic that they let the greatest of them all slip right through their fingers."

Thorpe felt the same way about Haskell as he had felt about the Sac and Fox Agency School. He hated it. He wanted to hunt. He wanted to ride horses. He wanted to relax with his family and friends. In the late summer of 1901, Thorpe got word that a letter had come for him from Oklahoma saying that his father had been seriously injured in a hunting accident. "I never did find out why they didn't give the letter to me," Thorpe said. He made up his mind. He did not give a damn how far it was to Oklahoma. To a reporter he later explained, "Word came that my dad was sick, so I ran away from Haskell and went to him."

Thorpe hopped a freight train, only to realize that it was headed north instead of south. He left the train and walked home, occasionally cadging rides on horse-drawn farm wagons and ox-hauled freighters.

Thorpe arrived home after traveling for two weeks. Hiram Thorpe had recovered from his injury and was not at all happy to see his son. His son had defied him. Nobody defied Hiram Thorpe without paying for it. Once again, Jim Thorpe faced off against his old man, defiant and unafraid. He was not going to go back to Haskell no matter how hard the beating. "One character of the Thorpe clan is that we're all bullheaded as hell," Jack Thorpe says. "We rub the fur the wrong way and get sparks. Dad liked to get those sparks flying."

Jim Thorpe, then fourteen, accepted his beating and settled into the ranch routine. He hunted deer, quail, squirrel, and rabbits and became a dead-eye shot. He tended the cattle and hogs and worked with his father's horses. He added to the stock, roping, riding, and breaking the occasional wild pony that wandered through their land.

According to Sam Morris, a Sac and Fox elder, Jim was a hard-headed and fearless outdoorsman. When they went bow-hunting, Morris, Thorpe, and their friends had to cross a field in which a farmer kept a mean bull. Every time the boys crossed the field, they had to run away from the bull until Thorpe finally got fed up. As the others ran away, Thorpe stood his ground, pulled back on his bow, and shot the bull, dropping it dead. Jack Thorpe, who later read a letter from the farmer wanting to get paid for the bull, said, "Dad wasn't afraid of anything."

Though he enjoyed being home, Thorpe still had a defiant attitude. One afternoon, Jim and his brother George went fishing instead of feeding and corralling the livestock. When Hiram Thorpe found his horses and cattle scattered all over the ranch, he gave his boys a serious thrashing. "I deserved it," Jim confessed, "but I didn't feel like taking it. So I ran away from home to the Texas panhandle and worked for a year fixing fences on a ranch and taming wild horses."

The whalebone-tough fifteen-year-old went to work on the High Plains of Texas, the location of some of the biggest cattle ranches in the world. Thorpe found his niche breaking horses. To do the job, he herded the wild animals one at a time into a small, round corral. In the center of the corral was a thick post, the "nubbing" post. Thorpe lassoed the horse and looped his lariat around the nubbing post. As the horse jumped, snorted, kicked, and bucked, Thorpe pulled on the lariat, reeling in the horse like a twelve-hundred-pound trout until it was pulled up tight to the nubbing post. Thorpe then put a sack over the horse's head as a blindfold and slipped a lead around the horse's neck. He climbed up on the back of the horse and rode the fight out of it.

Thorpe learned to anticipate a horse's moves from the blink of an eye or the flick of a mane. Breaking horses was a great game of power and strength, of dominance and submission, of man against horse. Riding in a daily private rodeo, the teenaged Thorpe developed an iron grip, quick reflexes, strong legs, a fearless attitude, and the ability to withstand the pain of hard falls, horse bites, and vicious kicks. It was bareback bronc riding but not for show. Breaking horses was all business in the Texas panhandle in 1901.

"Of all my activities as a boy I liked best catching wild horses on the range," Jim later recalled. "At fifteen I had never met a wild one that I could not catch, saddle and ride. That is one achievement of my boy-hood days that I do not hesitate to feel proud about."

When Jim worked in Texas for part of 1901 and 1902, he managed to buy himself a team of horses. "When I came home," the Oklahoma buckaroo later explained, "my father took a look at the horses and decided to let me stay."

Things had changed at the Thorpe home. His mother, Charlotte, had given birth to her eleventh child—a boy, Henry, who died in infancy. She herself passed away on November 17, 1901, a short time after that birth. On November 20, Charlotte was buried at the Sacred Heart Catholic Church Cemetery. At the time of her death, Jim Thorpe's mother was thirty-nine years old.

Hiram Thorpe recorded January 28, 1902, as the date of Charlotte's death with the Indian Agency, probably so he could pocket her spring 1902 tribal annuity payment. On February 6, 1902, Hiram took a fifth wife "according to the white man's law," a white woman named Julia Mixon. The couple had two sons: Ernest, born April 10, 1903, who died a few months later; and Roscoe, born July 5, 1904, who survived.

Jim Thorpe's older brother George had moved west and his half brother Frank had married and moved to a place of his own. Jim was the eldest son in the one-room cabin he shared with his father, his stepmother, and his younger siblings Mary, Adaline, Edward, and his infant stepbrother Roscoe. The house was crowded and chaotic. Still, Hiram insisted that his son Jim attend school. Hiram took Jim to enroll in the Garden Grove School, a public, non-Indian school opened by a teacher, Walter White, just a few miles up the Moccasin Trail from the Thorpe home.

White recalled that he arrived at the small clapboard building one morning to find the Thorpes standing at the door waiting for him. White knew of Jim's reputation as a runaway. As the boy stood there with "a sort of hangdog look," Hiram came straight to the point. Hiram asked White, "Can you teach the boy anything?" and explained to the teacher, "I take him [Jim] to Agency School, he come back. I take him again, he come back. Five, six, ten times I take him, all time he come back."

White turned to Jim and asked, "Why did you leave the Agency School, Jim?" According to White,

Jim looked down at his toes and said, "I don't like it."

"Did they do things to you, punish you or things like that?"

"No. Agency school not good for Indians. Indian boys, all, don't like it."

I doubted if Jim was capable of putting into words why he disliked the Agency school, and asked, "Will you run away from this school?"

The question surprised Jim. Perhaps the thought crossed his mind; since this was his home community, there would be no place he could run. He said, "I will not run away."

I am sure that it was not any burning desire to get an education which caused him to choose the Garden Grove School. He was just choosing the lesser of two evils.

5

The "Hunchback" Play

Whice Jim was once more living with his turbulent family, Pop Warner was taking on new responsibilities at Carlisle. After the end of the 1899 season, Pratt had been so pleased with Warner's performance that he offered him the position of the director of athletics, at a starting salary of $2,500. "I did like athletics," Warner later wrote, "and the $2,500 salary I was offered was more than I could make at my law business and therefore I finally decided to accept the position." For the first time in his life, Warner was relying on athletics as his sole means of support.

In the spring of 1900, Warner coached baseball and formed the first Carlisle track team. "I knew less than nothing about track and field," Warner admitted, although he had competed in track at Cornell. He read every book on track and field he could get his hands on and visited with other coaches, including Michael Murphy and Jack Monkley. One of Warner's closest advisers was George Connors, who had been a famous long-distance runner in England and America and had coached track at Cornell for several years. After leaving Cornell, Connors became the track coach at Phillips Exeter Academy in New Hampshire and traveled to Carlisle for several years to help Warner develop his athletic programs.

Warner found that one of his biggest obstacles to developing a track team was the attitude of his Indian athletes. "[The Carlisle students] were natural runners and jumpers, of course, but everything else was not only viewed indifferently but sometimes actively resisted. Putting the shot and hurling the discus struck them as a silly waste of effort, entirely lacking in sense, and as for hurdling, they looked on it as a form of insanity."

"Run one thing and jump, one other thing," said a Sioux boy according to Warner. "No can do two together same time." Still, Warner found that track provided excellent training for his Indian athletes once they overcame their objections to the sport.

Warner's football squads performed well in 1900 and 1901. After the 1902 football season, Warner had a lot to be proud of—an 8-and-3 record, and the honor of being picked by Walter Camp as the line coach for Camp's All-American team. Pop even found time to earn some extra money by playing football himself. "In the early 1900s," Warner said, "sometimes as much as a million dollars was bet on a game." Hoping to get in on some of the big money, Bill Warner approached his brother with a proposition: the chance to play in a professional football tournament at Madison Square Garden.

According to Warner, "Tom O'Rourke, the old prize-fight promoter, was handling the affair on a cooperative basis . . . and each player received explicit assurance that his share would amount to $300 at least. . . . I had not played since leaving Cornell in 1894, but my coaching [had] kept me in fair condition, and $300 looked mighty good to a man on a small salary; besides, I wanted a vacation."

The Warner brothers played on a team representing Syracuse. Both played on the line, along with Jack Wright, an All-American center from Columbia, and two Carlisle players, Hawley Pierce and Bemus Pierce. "While I managed to play the whole game," Warner recalled, "the next morning found me a total wreck, and my brother Bill had to help me dress. To add to the pain, the tournament proved a financial flop, and at the end I found that I had died for dear old Madison Square for exactly $23."

Warner healed from his professional football experience and led the Carlisle team into the 1903 season, which would prove to be one of the most memorable in college football history. Quarterback Jimmie Johnson led the Carlisle squad to a record of eleven wins, one tie, and two losses—the first loss was to Princeton in a game played on a muddy field in a pouring rain, conditions in which the lightweight Indians were at a disadvantage against the heavier Princeton squad.

"If the field was a sea of mud, or if snow fell, or if an icy wind was blowing, the redskins had a tendency to play listlessly and half-heartedly," Warner later commented. "A big center once said to me, 'Football no good fun in mud and snow.'"

But it was the 1903 loss against Harvard that made Pop Warner and the Carlisle Indians a legend. Carlisle managed to score first, near the end of the first half, when Jimmie Johnson booted a field goal from twelve yards out for five points. (At the time, field goals scored the same as touchdowns, five points.) But Warner knew that his team could not keep Harvard scoreless for long. He had only two reserve players, and Percy Haughton, the Harvard coach, "could pour in a flood of fresh bodies" from the huge Crimson bench. Warner had to do something dramatic.

"The fury of their attack tore heavier lines to pieces and their tack-ling had the force of a catapult," Warner said. "Trick plays, however, were what the redskins loved best. Nothing delighted them more than outsmarting the palefaces. There was never a time when they wouldn't rather have won by an eyelash with some wily stratagem than by a large score with straight football." Thus came the "hidden ball" or "hunchback" play.

Warner told what happened after Harvard kicked off in the second half and Carlisle's Jimmie Johnson caught the kick on the first yard line.

> The Indians gathered at once in what now would be called a huddle, but facing outward, and Johnson quickly slipped the ball under the back of Charlie Dillon's jersey. Charlie was picked as the "hunchback" because he stood six feet and could do a hundred yards in ten seconds. Besides, being a guard, he was less likely to be suspected of carrying the ball. "Go!" yelled Johnson. And the Carlisle players scattered and fanned out toward the sidelines, each back hugging his helmet to his breast [pretending it was the ball], while Dillon charged straight down the center of the field.
>
> Talk about excitement and uproar! The Indian backs were chased and slammed, but when the tacklers saw that it was only

headgear they were cuddling, not the ball, they began to leap here and there, yelping like hounds off the scent. Nobody paid any attention to Dillon, for he was running with both arms free, and when he came to Carl Marshall, safety man, the Harvard captain actually sidestepped what he thought was an attempt to block and dashed up the field to join the rest of the team in a frantic search for the ball.

The fans in the stands could see the bulge in the back of Dillon's jersey and screamed at the Harvard players, but it was no use. Dillon crossed the goal line. One of his teammates jerked the ball out of his jersey and touched it down on the turf.

When the referee signaled a touchdown, the Harvard team exploded in protest. But Warner had briefed the officials before the game and had received their okay. It wasn't even the first time Warner had used the play. He had run it against Penn State in 1898 while coaching at Cornell. That game had not been very important, so few people had taken note of the incident.

Although Carlisle lost to Harvard 12–11, there was no mourning on the Indian bench. Warner claimed that he employed the play "as a good joke on the haughty Crimson players."

"Some plays you make up to fool a smart man," he observed, "some to fool a stupid one."

The 1903 season was a triumph for Warner and his team. Their fast, tough style, the "hunchback" play at Harvard, and their tough schedules against teams across the county had earned the Indians a reputation as the most colorful team in football. The "nomads of the gridiron" had become one of the most exciting athletic phenomena of the age.

Word of the Carlisle Indians' success spread across the country, even to the sandy hills along the North Canadian River, where Jim Thorpe was sporadically attending the Garden Grove School. Thorpe's teacher Walter White knew that he faced a challenge just in keeping his students in the classroom. "The teachers at the Agency School found the Indian children very uncooperative," he said. "Not that they resisted the authority of the teachers, they just ran away. . . . They ran away at every opportunity and were quite adept at finding opportunities. When the Agent sent his deputies to bring them back, they hid like quail."

Jim seemed to like Garden Grove better than the Sac and Fox mission school or Haskell, perhaps because he was living at home and had the freedom to hunt and be with his family. One of the events that Thorpe recalled with great fondness were weekly "amateur" track meets his father held on the family ranch. At these events, Hiram, Jim, and other local folks competed in running races, in wrestling, and probably in horse racing. Gambling and drinking likely enhanced the competition.

Jim also enjoyed playing a game he had learned from his older brother George. They called it "prairie baseball," baseball played on a diamond stamped out in the middle of a field of harvested wheat. The biggest problem with the game was that they lost an awful lot of balls.

"When I was a kid, I didn't ever expect to get very far in sports," Thorpe said. "I wasn't big enough, for one thing. And the way we lived—way off from everything—made it hard to learn. We didn't have a coach and most of the time we played barefoot. We made our own balls out of whatever was handy, used sticks for bats, flat rocks for bases, and made up our own rules."

At the Garden Grove School, Walter White understood the importance of athletics for his students and did his best to encourage them. "The boys and I laid out a track and rigged bars for the high jump and the pole vault. We bought baseball equipment with proceeds from a box supper. Our homemade track equipment was a bit crude, but I doubt if the boys appreciated it any less because of that. It was their first introduction to organized athletics, and they were all enthusiastic about it. . . . All, that is, except Jim Thorpe. Jim wandered about, apparently indifferent."

White told a story about Jim that would be retold in many other versions through the years. According to White, "The boys were practicing the high jump. Some of them were getting quite good at it. Jim was standing nearby, seemingly not interested, just watching."

"Jim," White encouraged, "why don't you try that?"

"Jim trotted over and cleared it with apparent ease. They raised the bar and Jim cleared it again and again, until he was jumping higher than any of the other, older boys. With little show of effort."

Whether White's version of the story is true will never be known. But there is no doubt that Jim played all kinds of sports around the

Garden Grove School yard, running, jumping, vaulting, and playing "prairie baseball."

When the school was closed during the summer, White and the other folks in the community organized a baseball team that played other small-time area teams on Saturday afternoons. Some money probably changed hands among players, managers, and the people who bet on the games. White remembered Jim as the best player around. He recalled that folks began talking admiringly about "that young Indian."

The Garden Grove teacher Walter White claimed that he mentioned the Carlisle School to Jim Thorpe. According to White, Jim did not want to go to Carlisle at first, but others encouraged him, saying that Carlisle was a great place for an athlete. Thorpe himself told the reporter Al Stump in 1949 that a Carlisle assistant superintendent had traveled out to Oklahoma Territory looking for candidates and that a crowd of students had met with him. When the recruiter asked Thorpe what he wanted to be, he replied that he wanted to get into the electrical trade. "We have no electrical department," the Carlisle recruiter answered, "but you can learn to be a painter, a carpenter, or a tailor."

Though it will never be known exactly how Jim decided to attend Carlisle, the following letter is in Jim Thorpe's official file from the Sac and Fox archives now maintained by the Oklahoma Historical Society Research Library. The letter, written in pencil on a small, lined sheet of school paper, reads as follows:

Bellmont OT
Dec 13th 1903

U.S. Indian Agent
Sac and Fox Agency OT

Dear Sir—I have a boy that I Wish you could Make rangements to Send of to School Some Ware Caryle or Hampton I don't Care ware He went to Haskill but I Think it better one of the former plases so he Cannot run a way—he is 19 years old and I Cannot do any thing with him So plese at your Earlest Convence atend to this for he is getting worse very day—and I want him to go and make somthing of him Self for he cannot do it hear—

> Respectfully yours
> Hairm Thrope
> Bellmont OT

His Name is James Thrope

Like so much in the story of Jim Thorpe, the letter is curious. If Hiram actually did write the letter, surely he would have known how to spell his own name. If Hiram didn't write the letter, who did? Did Hiram dictate the letter to a friend, even though he was literate? Or was it dictated at the suggestion of a Carlisle recruiter to someone else who submitted the letter to Carlisle? Or was the letter written years after the fact and added to Jim Thorpe's file by some historical revisionist?

No matter how the connection was made, in early 1904, Jim Thorpe set off by rail to attend the Carlisle Indian Industrial School in Carlisle, Pennsylvania.

6

"White Man Bathed in Red"

The air was relatively warm on February 6, 1904, when sixteen-year-old Jim Thorpe stepped off the train in Carlisle, Pennsylvania. The terminal was near the center of the colonial town, founded in 1751 by white settlers and platted according to a plan drawn up by the family of William Penn. Benjamin Franklin, General George Washington, and General J. E. B. Stuart all had passed through Carlisle on the Appalachian Ridge just west of the Susquehanna River. In 1879, Richard Henry Pratt, then a captain in the U.S. cavalry, had transformed the town's abandoned military outpost, known as the Carlisle Barracks, into the first federally operated boarding school created for the education and the assimilation of American Indians.

Pratt, a decorated Civil War veteran who fought at Nashville, Pittsburgh Landing, and Chickamauga, began serving at Fort Sill in the Indian Territory in 1867. He commanded a unit of African American "buffalo soldiers" and Indian scouts who worked as warriors, jailers, and diplomats, trying to keep the Kiowa, the Cheyenne, and other tribes on their reservations and away from white settlers. "Their intelligence, civilization, and common sense was a revelation," Pratt later recalled of his Indian troops, some of whom, like himself, were veterans of the Civil War, "because I had concluded that as an army officer I was there to deal with atrocious aborigines."

Given responsibility for the Indian prisoners held at Fort Sill, Pratt became known for his understanding treatment. Pratt was a forward-thinking individual, a man who believed that assimilation rather than extermination was the answer to the Indian question. In April 1875, Pratt transported a group of seventy-two Indian warriors to St. Augustine, Florida, to oversee their incarceration in what one historian described as "the dungeons of Marion Prison."

Away from his superiors, Pratt experimented with the rehabilitation of his prisoners. He treated his Indian captives like military recruits, recruits who had to earn their way into the ranks of white society. Pratt came to believe that nurture trumped nature and that Indians, even the most hostile Indians, could be successfully integrated into white society.

Pratt decided to start a vocational boarding school for young American Indians. He experimented by sending Indians to the Hampton Normal and Agricultural Institute in Hampton, Virginia, an institution founded in 1868 to educate freed slaves. Pratt garnered support for his own institution from politicians in Washington, former Quaker abolitionists, philanthropists such as Mrs. Walter Baker of the Baker Chocolate Company, and liberal journalists who agreed with Pratt that the Indian was nothing more evil than a "white man bathed in red." In mid-1879, just three years after General George Custer died in the Battle of the Little Big Horn, Pratt secured permission from the Department of the Interior to use the Carlisle Barracks for his proposed Indian school and opened the Carlisle Indian Industrial School, in Carlisle, Pennsylvania, later called the U.S. Indian School.

The officials in the Department of the Interior were willing to go along with the Carlisle experiment in part because they viewed Pratt's boarding school as a useful way to maintain hostagelike control over the sons and the daughters of restive Indians. Knowing that his funding depended on this, Pratt managed to convince powerful Indian leaders such as American Horse, Red Cloud, and Spotted Tail to send their children or grandchildren to Carlisle. Twenty-five years after Pratt founded his school, the U.S. government was operating more than two dozen boarding schools based on the Carlisle model.

By 1904, the people of Carlisle were used to seeing young Indians such as Jim Thorpe arrive in town, chilled and confused, wondering how to get to the Indian school. Thorpe, like so many others before him, was directed to the trolley, which stopped near the entrance of the school, northeast of the town square.

Thorpe walked from the train depot and turned up Garrison Street. He made his way along the six-foot-high picket fence that surrounded the school toward a large wooden entrance gate. He passed Flickinger's store and paused, perhaps, to look at the Carlisle souvenirs in the window. There were pennants in the school colors, crimson and gold, as well as postcards, "before and after" shots of various students, transformed from long-haired Native Americans into clean-cut students in well-tailored business suits. The photo postcards were an important part of Pratt's "propaganda," as he called his public relations efforts. In the summertime, as many as three hundred tourists a day visited the Carlisle school and later described for their friends the well-manicured campus with its picturesque student body of civilized Indians.

Thorpe reported to the "guardhouse," a former powder magazine constructed by Hessian prisoners during the Revolutionary War. He then walked south along a cleared path covered with wooden slats to the school hospital, where he presented the medical staff with a medical form filled out by the Sac and Fox physician, Dr. F. W. Wyman.

Like all incoming students, Thorpe stripped and washed before being examined by the Carlisle medical staff. He was given a haircut and presented with a suit of black jeans, a uniform, underwear, shoes, red flannel long johns, nightshirts, and a hat. Thorpe's discorded Western-style clothing was probably of little interest to the enterprising Carlisle administrators, who confiscated and sold more traditional Indian apparel. Thorpe also received a set of towels and bedding and a trunk in which to store his clothing and personal items. Laundry was done once a week, washed and ironed by Carlisle students.

Thorpe carried his newly issued gear to his room in the boys' dormitory, a room that he probably shared with two or three others. At the sound of a bugle, Cadet Thorpe, as he was then to be formally known, took his position outside the dormitory with his assigned student company and stood at attention, ready to follow orders.

The routine was familiar to Jim. He had experienced life strictly regimented by the bugle and bell during his years at the Sac and Fox

Agency School and at the Haskell Institute in Lawrence, Kansas, a school modeled after Carlisle.

Carlisle was run according to a strictly regimented hierarchy. Thorpe belonged to a company of students who marched together to and from classes, the dining hall, and all other organized programs. "We keep them moving," Pratt explained, "and they have no time for homesickness—none for mischief—none for regret." Students rose at 5:30 A.M. and marched to breakfast at 6:15. In the dining hall, Thorpe sat on a bench at a long table and ate from white china bearing the red letters CIIS, the Carlisle logo. Female students in white caps and aprons served him. A monitor supervised his table manners. Outside of the dining hall, student officers were responsible for company behavior, both on the march and at rest. Student-run courts, closely supervised by the administration, handed out punishments for misconduct. At the top of the hierarchy was the school supervisor, Captain Pratt.

Since founding the school, Pratt had relied on strict discipline, academic work, and vocational training to detach Indians from their native "savagery" and integrate them into the white world. Pratt led his students and teachers in repeating his motto "There is only one way; to civilize the Indian get him into civilization, to keep him civilized, let him stay." Pratt later reduced this slogan to an even simpler message: "Kill the Indian, save the man." Self-righteous, intolerant, and unwavering in his belief in "acculturation under duress," Pratt understood the importance of creating a respect and a need for private property in his students. "Education," he declared, "consists in creating wants and imparting the ability to supply them." When his own wants exceeded his federal funding, Pratt did not hesitate to use "off-the-books" financing, raising money from outside donors and using it as he saw fit without turning the money over to the Department of the Interior. Supporters hailed Pratt as "the best educational friend the Indians ever had" and "the Red Man's Moses." Opponents considered him to be an obsessive social reformer, "an honest lunatic."

Pratt closely monitored the progress of each student, making notes to himself—"indifferent, drinks," "ne'er do well," "married white man, doing remarkably well." He continually recruited new students, rejecting some as too young, too old, too white, or "too much Negro."

Every Saturday he gathered all his other students to review the past week's proceedings and to expose them to his own oratorical skills. "You have to S-T-I-C-K T-O I-T if you want to make something of yourself," Pratt was fond of saying. "Sticking," as he called it, was one of his favorite themes. "My son, observe the postage stamp," Pratt once wrote in the Carlisle student paper. "Its usefulness depends upon its ability to stick to one thing 'til it gets there."

The school claimed that it offered students a variety of other subjects, including chemistry, physics, government, geography, history, advanced mathematics, and biology. In reality, classes appear to have been informal at best, and certainly not demanding. In 1901, Estelle Reel, the superintendent of Indian schools with the federal government, presented the *Uniform Course of Study* for Indian schools, which was supposed to be followed by all educators of Indians.

Reel firmly believed that Indians did not have the same intellectual capacities as whites and set out a course of vocational training for the Indian as an "inferior" race.

Superintendent Pratt, who believed that Indians were not inferior to whites, ignored much of the U.S. government's official curriculum and tried to offer his students a liberal arts education complete with music lessons, which were required for all students. The Carlisle marching band played at the 1893 World's Columbian Exposition in Chicago and marched across the Brooklyn Bridge on its opening day in 1883. Carlisle students also took art classes, in which they were forbidden to practice their native crafts but were encouraged instead to create Western-style watercolors and oil paintings of fruit bowls, landscapes, and overstuffed pillows. Colorful Indian marching bands and delicate oil paintings provided dramatic testimony to Carlisle's "civilizing" influence.

A mastery of academic skills was more difficult to demonstrate. Pratt attracted loyal and dedicated teachers, most of them single women with some experience in teaching Indians, and he paid them well for the time, augmenting their salaries with funds raised from private donations.

To complete the full course of study, students had to sign up for two five-year terms. With such a lengthy and tedious curriculum, it is not surprising that only a few students actually graduated from the academic course to receive their Carlisle diploma. Many of the students who did not manage to complete the academic course received industrial certificates. Most of the students who attended Carlisle left the institution without any certificate at all. Of the more than 8,000 students who attended Carlisle from 1879 to 1918, only 761 graduated. More than twice that many simply ran away. Several hundred died—either at the school or after being sent home with a serious illness. Still, even being in high school was exceptional for the times. In 1900, only one out of ten Americans aged fourteen to seventeen attended school beyond the elementary grades.

Following a morning in academic classes, students received vocational training. Both male and female students received two ungraded lessons a week in "sloyd," a Swedish system of manual training. Jim Thorpe and other male students at Carlisle practiced trades: they took up carpentry, blacksmithing, tinsmithing, shoemaking, tailoring, and business. Jim Thorpe was enrolled in the tailoring shop. Female students focused on the homemaking arts—dressmaking, cooking, nursing, and childcare. Students were supposed to make their own uniforms, kitchen utensils, furniture, harnesses, and wagons, and to grow much of their own food. But production was inefficient and by the time of Thorpe's arrival at Carlisle, even the bureaucrats in charge of Indian affairs had come to realize that the ideal of training the Native American to be a self-sufficient farmer was unrealistic. Later on in Thorpe's Carlisle career, farm work was treated as a punishment rather than a vocation.

Mingling of the sexes was kept to the absolute minimum, lest students be tempted to acts of immorality. Male and female students were strictly forbidden from socializing in dormitories or common areas. Students were permitted to ride the trolley to downtown Carlisle, but males and females traveled separately, on alternate Saturdays. On Sundays, female students attended chapel on campus, while male students marched to church in Carlisle. Thorpe and many others chose to attend St. Patrick's Church, the church located closest to the campus. All students, both male and female, were required to participate in athletic activities. While Estelle Reel wrote in her curriculum that Indian pupils needed physical conditioning to "counteract the influences of unfortunate heredity," Pratt believed in sports for all students, white or red, and understood the importance of athletics from a revenue-generating and publicity standpoint. He encouraged Jim Thorpe and the younger Carlisle boys to play shinny, an Indian ball game, on the playground next to the Hessian guard-house.

Just as Thorpe was carving a place for himself at Carlisle, he got bad news from home. Hiram Thorpe, his father, passed away on April 24, 1904, at the age of about fifty-two. The cause of his death was said to be "blood poisoning" or "septicemia." Another report had it that he died in a hunting accident. Others claimed his death was caused by a snake bite. Hiram was buried in the Garden Grove Ceme-tery, across the road from the Garden Grove School, which Jim had attended, and only a few miles from their home on the North Cana-dian River.

Thorpe received the news of his father's death so late that he was unable to attend the funeral. The loss hit him hard. He was now an orphan. According to some accounts, Thorpe became withdrawn and sullen. Perhaps an observant teacher thought it would be good for Jim to get away from school for a while, or perhaps it was just his turn. For whatever reason, on June 17, 1904, just four months after arriving at Carlisle, Jim Thorpe was sent off campus to participate in "the outing system."

Established by Pratt in 1880, the outing system was the most renowned aspect of the Carlisle educational experiment. Under this system, the school placed students in the homes of farmers and other middle-class families in the Northeast for a work-study experience "to learn English and the customs of civilized life." Typically, Carlisle stu-dents stayed with the families for the three months of the summer break, although many remained for an extended stay.

The system was popular with federal bureaucrats as well as the Carlisle faculty, since it was such an economical way of training Indian students. Half of the wages that Carlisle students earned on their "out-ings" were put into trust for them in an interest-bearing account. A portion of the remainder was paid to Carlisle. In addition, Carlisle continued to receive a federal subsidy for each student who was out "in the country," despite the fact that Carlisle had obtained special permission from Pennsylvania state authorities for Carlisle students to attend public school while participating in the outing system during the winter months. Any fees incurred were paid by the outing family or from the student's wages.

"When you boys and girls go out on jobs, you don't go as employees," Pratt explained to the students. "You go and become part of the family." Jim traveled to Somerton, Pennsylvania, and moved into the home of A. E. Buchholz. Far from imbibing the best of civilization, Thorpe found himself mopping floors, boiling laundry, and peeling potatoes, for which he was paid $5 per month, only half of which he was permitted to keep. As household help, Jim was not permitted to dine with the family but took his meals in the kitchen.

Thorpe hated the housework and resented his low wages. Frustrated, he did what he had done so many times before: he ran away. He did not run back to Oklahoma, since it was too far for a young man to go with no money in his pocket; he ran back to Carlisle.

The exact date when he returned to Carlisle is not recorded in the "Carlisle Indian Industrial School Descriptive and Historical Record of Student," one of the few extant records of Thorpe's Carlisle career. Recordkeeping at Carlisle was slipshod at best, especially records of runaways, student deaths, or any other incidents that did not reflect positively on the school.

There is no record of what Thorpe did right after his return to Carlisle. He probably continued with his tailoring program and began to get involved in athletics. Carlisle had an intramural organization that pitted students from different courses against one another—the blacksmiths vs. the tailors, etc. Thorpe earned a spot playing guard on the tailoring football squad. In addition to helping him get in shape, playing for the tailoring team introduced him to the intricate system of plays that Pop Warner had devised. Thorpe enjoyed football, and he knew that if he proved himself, he had a chance of making the Carlisle varsity.

Thorpe stayed at Carlisle through the fall of 1904 and into 1905. On March 31, 1905, his record indicates that he went on another outing, this time to the farm of James L. Cadwallader in Dolington, Pennsylvania. Thorpe returned to Carlisle on July 1, 1905. On September 15, 1905, he was sent out on yet another outing, this time to the farm of Harby Rozarth in Robbinsville, New Jersey.

It appears that Thorpe enjoyed the Rozarth farm well enough. He worked in the fields and soon was promoted to foreman. Records show that Thorpe remained with Rozarth until March 9, 1907. From February 6, 1904, until March 9, 1907, Thorpe spent approximately fourteen months on campus and twenty-one months in the country.

In April 1907, Sadie Ingalls, a full-blood Sac and Fox girl who was a student at Carlisle and who had attended the Sac and Fox Agency school with Jim, mentioned in a letter home, "I am sorry to say that Jim Thorpe is in the guard house for running away from his country home."

According to his Carlisle record, Jim returned to Carlisle from the Rozarth farm on March 9, 1907. Two days later he left again for the Rozarth farm but returned to the campus once more on April 8, 1907. It is possible that he ran away from the farm. Carlisle teachers did not tolerate insubordination, and reluctance to go on the outing program provoked stern discipline, even beatings.

There is no record of why he ran away from the job he had held since September 1905, but if Jim Thorpe did not like a situation, he simply left it. And there were many parts of the job to dislike. The pay was terrible, and the work was hard and boring. For Thorpe, getting away from indentured servitude in New Jersey probably was well worth time spent in the cold, damp, century-old guardhouse.

While Thorpe was on the outing, Warner also was away from Carlisle. Warner left Carlisle on July 8, 1904, to take a job coaching at his alma mater, Cornell. Warner said that he took the job to help out his brother Bill, who had coached the Cornell team through the 1903 season. "It was not a flattering salary offer which had turned my head," Warner later maintained. "Instead it was the fact that I sincerely didn't want to see my brother Bill get caught in the middle of any tug-of-war match with the Cornell alumni and administration over the football team's direction." Warner also claimed that his decision to take the position at Cornell was made easier "knowing that Major Pratt was probably gonna be forced to retire from his post . . . by certain federal officials and Congressmen who didn't agree with his continued success at the Indian School."

Though Warner expressed support for Pratt in public, in private he clashed with his Carlisle superior on a number of occasions. Pratt did not support all of Warner's attempts to recruit players for the Carlisle football program. When one of Warner's recruits, Frank Beaver, requested that he be allowed to come back to Carlisle to play more football for Warner, Pratt advised him not to return to his alma mater and wrote, "Take my advice and let football go." Addressing Warner about the same matter, Pratt said, "I do not think it is well to let Frank Beaver come back to Carlisle just for football purposes, and I wish you would not ask me to do that." Despite Pratt's reservation, Beaver did indeed return to play for Warner. While Warner coached at Cornell, he kept a close eye on developments at Carlisle.

7

"Athletocracy"

In many ways, Pratt brought about his own removal from the school he had created. An educational crusader, Pratt ignored the changing political winds in Washington that favored increased funding for Indian schools located on or near the reservations over funding for distant boarding schools. He loudly criticized the administration of President Theodore Roosevelt and what he described as White House efforts to "farm" Carlisle, handing out jobs to political appointees. In addition, Pratt refused to change with the shifting philosophical winds. He maintained his belief in total assimilation rather than adopting the separate-but-equal approach to Indian education supported by "progressive" government employees such as Francis E. Leupp, the man President Roosevelt chose as his commissioner of Indian Affairs in 1905.

Leupp was a journalist and a newspaperman from New York whose lifelong interest in Indian affairs sprang from youthful visits to New York tribes. A trusted adviser to President Grover Cleveland and President Roosevelt, Leupp served as the Washington agent for the Indian Rights Association before taking his post as the Indian Affairs commissioner.

Leupp considered the Indian to be "a natural warrior, a natural logician, and a natural artist." His appreciation was tempered by the belief that Indians were not the intellectual equals of whites, a belief that probably was informed by the writings of Francis Galton, Charles Davenport, and other social Darwinists. "By force of both ancestry and environment they [Indian students] are not in a condition to absorb and assimilate, much less utilize effectively, the higher learning of the books," Leupp wrote, "and it is unwise to promote an impractical at the expense of an obviously practical course of instruction." Rather than challenge Indians with the curriculum of white prep school students, Leupp suggested, "Give him [the Indian] simple nature books—the life story of a wolf, a description of a family of prairie dogs, the wonderful adventures of Mr. Bear and Mrs. Bear and the three juvenile Bears."

Leupp openly opposed the way Pratt ran Carlisle. "Every Commissioner and Secretary had been terrorized by Pratt," Leupp wrote in 1896, "on the theory that to dismiss him would be to call down upon the administration a storm of abuse from well-meaning but misguided champions of Carlisle." In 1910 Leupp published a book titled *The Indian and His Problem*. Pratt titled his unpublished memoir, "The Indian No Problem."

The harder Washington insiders fought to change Carlisle, the harder Pratt fought to preserve it. In 1903, the War Department promoted Pratt to full colonel and attempted to retire him from the military and thus remove him from Carlisle. A furious Pratt submitted a letter of resignation, which he withdrew a few days later. On May 9, 1904, Pratt finally stepped over the line when he addressed the Baptist Ministers' Conference in New York City and declared, "I believe that nothing better could happen to the Indians than the complete destruction of the [Indian] Bureau." This statement and other similar comments by Pratt touched off a storm of protest in Washington that reached all the way to the White House. On June 15, 1904, the War Department issued Special Order No. 137, relieving Pratt from all duty at Carlisle. Fifteen days later, Pratt left the school he had founded more than thirty years earlier. For the rest of his life, Pratt continued to promote his fierce doctrine of cultural extinction, the only solution he thought possible for the "Indian non-problem."

Captain William A. Mercer took Pratt's position as the new superintendent of the U.S. Indian School. Standing six feet tall and weighing over 250 pounds, Mercer constantly complained of severe headaches, and even the slightest exertion exhausted him. Like Pratt, he was a soldier. He had served as an officer in the Sioux Campaign of 1890 and 1891 and in the massacre at Wounded Knee in 1890. After the Indian wars, Mercer had worked as an Indian agent for thirteen years.

Unlike Pratt, Mercer was not an ideologue. He was a realist, a down-to-earth military man with solid political connections, including the Secretary of the Interior, who was his wife's cousin. Mercer appreciated Indian culture and even claimed to speak a little Chippewa and Ute. While serving in Nebraska, he had helped arrange "the last gathering of tribes" at the Trans-Mississippi International Exposition at Omaha in 1898, an exhibition that Pratt described as "a Wild West show of the most degenerate sort."

After arriving at Carlisle, Mercer downplayed the importance of academic pursuits in favor of vocational training and military drills. He loosened Pratt's tight social restrictions and allowed male and female students to mingle and enjoy themselves at dances two or three times a week. Above all, Mercer was a sports fanatic. He hired the former Carlisle players Bemus Pierce and Frank Hudson as well as George Woodruff, the former head coach at the University of Pennsylvania, to coach the Carlisle football team for the 1904, 1905, and 1906 seasons, respectively. Mercer later bragged about his years at Carlisle, "I developed the most wonderful athletes and the best football team in the country."

While the Carlisle Indian football program continued to thrive during those years, the game of football as a whole did not. In the spring and summer of 1905, investigative journalists turned their attention from the evils of big oil, meatpacking, and other scandal-plagued "trusts" to the abuses of college sports.

"If dishonorable practice is necessary to the building of honorable prestige, then we must find some new definition for 'college honor' or some university must confess to a lie," Edward S. Jordan wrote in a series of articles titled "Buying Football Victories" for *Collier's* magazine. "Football as an amateur sport in the colleges of the Middle West has almost passed out of existence. Football as a business, highly organized and calculated to derive enormous profits through furnishing spectacular entertainment to the general public has taken its place."

Jordan quoted Coach George Huff of the University of Illinois, who claimed that there are "more liars and hypocrites than amateurs" made by efforts to hide the money that was flowing to players and coaches in college sports.

Other exposés were equally revealing. *Outlook* published a series of articles in which the reporter Clarence Deming revealed that Walter Camp ran a secret athletic slush fund, the Yale Financial Union, which took in more than $100,000 per year. From this fund, Camp paid salaries to a number of people, including Yale's athletic trainer, Mike Murphy, and himself.

"Between you and me it [the Yale Financial Union] has proven wonderfully successful both from an economical standpoint and a standpoint when measured by athletic victories," Camp explained to a Stanford administrator. To a different audience, Camp expressed outrage at the notion of sports professionalism: "A gentleman does not make his living from his athletic prowess," Camp asserted. "He does not earn anything from his victories except glory and satisfaction. . . . A gentleman never competes for money, directly or indirectly."

Added to these reports of financial shenanigans were sobering statistics about football violence. Reporters claimed that in 1905, 18 players were killed on the football playing field and 159 seriously injured.

The negative press grabbed the attention of America's most prominent sports enthusiast, President Theodore Roosevelt. The president was torn by two conflicting impulses. On the one hand, he felt that college sports had become a corrupt business. On the other hand, he was an ardent Harvard football fan who helped hire good coaches, wrote letters of encouragement to the team, and did as much as he could to help his beloved alma mater win football games.

In the summer of 1905, Roosevelt, who had named the crusading journalists "muckrakers," met with leading muckraker Henry Beech Needham to discuss the situation in college sports. The president was not overly concerned with the violence of football. "I do not in the least object to the sport because it is rough," the president later observed. "We cannot afford to turn out of college men who shrink from physical effort or a little physical pain." What concerned Roosevelt most were the financial improprieties.

On October 9, 1905, the president called a meeting of Ivy League administrators at the White House and asked them to clean up the game of football. The assembled athletic administrators murmured their agreement but took no action.

On December 8, 1905, representatives from thirteen colleges met to vote on the question "Ought the present game of football be abolished?" The representatives from five institutions voted yes. Shortly after this vote, Columbia, Northwestern, MIT, University of California, Duke, and several other colleges voluntarily banned football. Stanford and the University of California substituted English rugby for American-style football.

Under increased pressure from President Roosevelt to stop the evils of what some called the American "athletocracy," a group of educators from sixty-eight institutions met at the Murray Hill Hotel in New York City on December 28, 1905, and agreed to form the Intercollegiate Athletic Association of the United States. On January 12, 1906, this organization held a meeting at the Hotel Netherland in New York City. At the same time, in the same hotel, the International Football Rules Committee, controlled by its secretary Walter Camp, also held a meeting. The two groups joined together to form the organization that would eventually become the National Collegiate Athletic Association (NCAA).

The newly formed NCAA did little to address the issue of financial irregularities. What the organization did do was to change the rules of football in 1906 to open up the game and make it less dangerous. Committee members passed rules that increased the distance required for a first down from five to ten yards, thereby forcing teams into a more open style of play. The rulemakers required seven men to be on the line of scrimmage, effectively ending flying wedges and other purely "beef" plays. They established a neutral zone between the two opposing teams at the line of scrimmage to cut down on slugging. The number of officials required to be present at every game was increased to four, and new rules were added to cut down on the most vicious hits. As Warner noted, "Severe penalties stopped the practice of meeting a runner in the face with the heel of the hand."

Over the objections of Walter Camp and Pop Warner, a forward pass of more than ten yards was legalized. The rules stipulated that the pass had to be thrown from five yards behind the line of scrimmage and had to be thrown at least five yards to the side of the center. To allow for referees to judge the distance from center, the rules committee mandated that football fields be marked out in five-foot-square boxes, thus turning the gridiron into a grid. An incomplete pass on the first or second down resulted in a fifteen-yard penalty for the offensive team. An incomplete pass on the third down was a turnover. Any pass that hit the ground without being touched also was ruled a turnover.

While football boosters and reformers butted heads, Warner was having his own troubles at Cornell. He led the team to good seasons in 1904 and 1905 but had to discipline a star player and drop him from the lineup. When protesting students challenged his action, Warner claimed, "I did what any coach would have done, if he has any *backbone* to him."

Warner also felt pressure from "gangs of alumni" who were "openly offering inducements in the shape of sinecures at good wages. The number of miners, blacksmiths, and plumber's helpers taking art courses was a standing joke." Warner particularly resented those Cornell alumni who found their way onto the sidelines as assistant coaches. "Not having anything else to do but get out on the football field every afternoon, many of them spent their time in carousing riotous living while on these temporary vacations," Warner complained. "Frequently they appeared on the football fields in no condition to coach." When asked by other coaches how Carlisle could turn out such great teams with such a small student body, Warner often replied, "Because the school's alumni players were all too far west to return and try to dictate how the team should be handled."

In September 1906, the Carlisle superintendent, Mercer, invited Warner back to Carlisle for a couple of weeks before the beginning of Cornell's season to familiarize the Carlisle coaching staff and players with the revised rules of the game. According to Warner, "I was delighted to put in a couple of weeks at 'my old stamping grounds.'"

At the end of the 1906 season, Warner ran into Mercer and a Carlisle athlete named Albert Exendine at the Army-Navy football game in Philadelphia. Mercer pulled Warner aside and urged him to come back to Carlisle. Warner did not need much persuasion. At the end of the game, a smiling Pop went up to Exendine, stuck out his hand, and said, "I want you to meet the new football coach."

8

"Run Fast Good"

By the spring of 1907, Jim Thorpe had changed almost as much as the situation at Carlisle. Two years of farm labor had tempered his natural athleticism into a powerful physical machine. Muscles bulged in sinewy bands along his legs, arms, and back. At twenty years of age, Jim Thorpe, horsebreaker, farmer, and prairie baseball player, was ready to become one of Pop Warner's select athletes, known as the "athletic boys."

Thorpe was walking across the upper track field one evening in the summer of 1907 on his way to play a pick-up football game with one of the scrub teams, when he noticed some of Carlisle's varsity track athletes practicing the high jump. He later told reporters the story of how he first caught the attention of the man who would become his greatest coach:

> I stopped to watch them as they went higher and higher. After a while they had the bar set at five feet nine inches and none of them could jump over it. They were just about ready to call it a day when I asked if I might try it.
>
> I had a pair of overalls on, a hickory shirt, and a pair of gymnasium shoes I had picked up in the gym that belonged to someone [else]. I looked like anything but a high jumper. The track athletes snickered a bit as the bar was set up for me. I

cleared the bar on my first try, and, laughing at the astonished group of athletes, went on down to the lower field for the game. A student named Harry Archenbald, who had seen me take the jump with so little effort, reported the incident to Coach Warner. Next day he sent for me.

Warner recounted his first meeting with Jim Thorpe as follows:

> I immediately sent for Jim so that I could see who this mystery athlete was. When Jim arrived in my office an hour later, he asked, "You wanted to see me, Coach? Have I done anything wrong?"
>
> I then told him, "Son, you've only broken the school record in the high jump. That's all."
>
> Jim responded with a sigh of relief at my statement. He quickly noted to me, "Pop, I didn't think that very high. I think I can do better in a track suit."
>
> Putting my arm around his shoulder, I told Jim that we'd make sure he got a track uniform, because beginning that afternoon he would be on the Carlisle track team.

It is not possible to know how much, if any, of this story is true. What is true is that Jim was not a total newcomer to organized athletics when he came into contact with Pop Warner. Jim had competed for years in his father's informal track meets and had probably earned some pocket change playing prairie baseball back in Oklahoma. He had played some football informally at Haskell. There is evidence that he had been recruited to Carlisle as a promising athlete and that he had played in the Carlisle scrub football league before he made the famous high jump that got Warner's attention. But no matter what his path, Jim Thorpe suited up in 1907 and began working out with another new member of the team, Louis Tewanima.

Warner enjoyed telling the story of how he discovered Tewanima, who also was called Tewani and Tewanimi. Warner claimed that he was standing by the practice field one afternoon when he noticed a group of students watching from the sidelines. He described them as "a wild-looking bunch" with "huge earrings and furtive eyes." "Their leader," a thin, short individual with a round face; high, carved cheek-bones; and deep-set eyes, "sidled up" to Warner and let the coach know that he wanted to suit up.

"What for?" Warner said. "You're not big enough to do anything."

"Me run fast good," the student answered. "All Hopis run fast good."

Warner probably chuckled to himself, but he agreed to let the diminutive Hopi and his companions suit up for track practice. As was his style, Warner probably did not tell his new athletic recruits what to do but watched carefully as they took off running around the track. At first, Warner was not impressed. They were not very fast. Anyone could beat them. Fifteen minutes later, Warner took another look. The "wild-looking bunch" was still making its way around the track with the same stride—no faster, no slower. Half an hour later, Warner looked again. Tewanima and his Hopi friends were still running at the same pace. Warner was not a great track coach, but he did know great long-distance running when he saw it. As he later explained, "I learned afterward that the favorite Hopi amusement is running twenty miles or so on an afternoon, kicking a ball before them."

Warner was not the first white man to notice the powerful running skills of the Hopi. U.S. Army officers stationed near the Hopi lands in northern Arizona realized that their horses were no match for Native American runners. The white soldiers regularly hired Hopi runners to deliver important messages on foot. These Hopi messengers covered seventy-two miles in thirty-six hours for a dollar.

No two members of the 1907 Carlisle track team contrasted as sharply as Thorpe and Tewanima. Physically, Thorpe was a muscular twenty-year-old who stood close to six feet tall, while Tewanima was a thin, short 110-pound thirty-year-old. Upon Tewanima's arrival at Carlisle on January 26, 1907, the doctor had commented on his poor physical condition, noting Tewanima's "round shoulders, prominent clavicle," and "emaciated look."

Culturally, the contrast was just as great. Jim Thorpe was a man of mixed Irish or English, French, Potawatomi, Kickapoo, and Sac and Fox blood. He had grown up speaking English with a bootlegging father near one of the roughest whiskey towns on the frontier. Tewanima was a full-blooded Hopi who grew up speaking his native tongue, had a family of his own, and lived a traditional Hopi lifestyle. In many ways, Louis Tewanima was the true Native American hero that Jim Thorpe was later made out to have been.

Tewanima was born in about 1877 and raised in the village of Shongopavi, one of the oldest continually inhabited settlements in North America. Located on Second Mesa, an outcropping of the high-cliffed upland known as Black Mesa, in what is today northern Arizona, Shongopavi and its environs had been home to the Hopi for at least eight hundred years before Tewanima's birth. As an infant, Tewanima was bound on a board cradle and cared for by his mother, his aunts, and the other women of his maternal clan, the Sand Clan. As he grew older, he probably acted like other Hopi boys who chased prairie dogs, hauled firewood and water, and helped their fathers raise corn, beans, and melons in patches of sandy soil found along the base of the mesa some ten miles or more from their homes.

When winter came, Tewanima watched men from his village hunt jackrabbits with their boomerang-shaped rabbit sticks. Like other children of the time, he broke off greasewood branches and chased after rabbits on his own, zigging and zagging through the rocks and yucca until he became quick and strong enough to catch his prey. Tewanima later recalled that he and his friends enjoyed running barefoot from Second Mesa to Winslow, Arizona, a 120-mile round trip, just to watch the trains go by. When he was ten years old, Tewanima became a member of the Antelope Society, and he remained a member of that traditional Hopi society for the rest of his life.

Perhaps the greatest contrast between Thorpe and Tewanima was the path they followed to Carlisle. While Thorpe's parents supported the white educational system and sent their son away to several boarding schools, Tewanima was sentenced to serve time at Carlisle because of his opposition to white education.

The Hopi had long fought to maintain their traditional way of life. In 1680, they took part in the Pueblo Revolt and drove the Spanish from their lands. When the U.S. government built the Moqui (Hopi) Indian Training School, many of the members of the tribe refused to enroll their children in defiance of the white authorities. Tewanima was one of these "hostiles." He never attended white school and did not want to send his children to white schools either.

In 1894, the U.S. authorities arrested nineteen Hopi hostiles and sentenced them to hard labor at Alcatraz. By 1906, Hopi opposition to white authority had become such a problem that the Indian commissioner Leupp traveled to Arizona to meet in person with the tribal leaders. "No one who does not know these Indians can have any conception of their crass ignorance and superstition," Leupp said of the Hopi who met Leupp's threats with defiance. According to Leupp, the leader of the "hostiles" told him "that his people did not wish anything to do with the whites; that their fathers had warned them not to let their children go to school and learn white ways; [and] that he intended to follow the advice of the fathers rather than Washington."

With the support of President Roosevelt, Leupp took action to end the bitter factional dispute among the Hopi and to squash Hopi opposition to white schooling. Leupp dispatched troops from Fort Wingate who arrested the two main Hopi leaders and banished them permanently from the reservation. The U.S. soldiers took seventy-two "hostiles" into custody and sentenced them to ninety days of roadwork. Seventeen Hopi were imprisoned at hard labor at Fort Huachuca. Leupp ordered Tewanima and eleven other "hostiles" to serve five years away from the reservation in the Indian boarding school of their choice. The Hopi chose to attend the U.S. Indian School at Carlisle. Thirty years after Pratt brought the first class of "hostile" students to Carlisle as hostages to ensure good behavior, Tewanima and the other Hopi were incarcerated at Carlisle because of their refusal to accept white culture.

Warner later explained to reporters that Tewanima and the other Hopi "came to Carlisle virtually as prisoners of war. For some years the elders of their tribe had been stubbornly refusing to accept the white man's education and religion and the government, finally out of patience with their mulishness, picked up the sons of the leaders and shipped them East for a civilizing process."

Government dignitaries and curiosity seekers crowded onto the Carlisle grounds on April 26, 1907, to witness the effects of that "civilizing process" in the annual Arbor Day celebration.

To demonstrate their transformation, Tewanima and the other Hopi lined up in front of the newly planted Arbor Day tree in their crisp military uniforms and close-cropped hair. Miss Anna Goyituey, the teacher assigned to the Hopi, led her students in two verses of "America the Beautiful," a performance that greatly impressed the visitors. Then, to the thrill of the Carlisle staff, the Hopi began to sing the Carlisle fight song.

Words to the song were written by the man who would lead Tewan-ima and his teammate Jim Thorpe to the highest levels of athletic competition in the white world: the head of the Carlisle athletic program, Pop Warner.

9

A Perfect Football Machine

Working out with the 1907 Carlisle track team, Jim Thorpe found himself competing with top athletes. For the first time, he discovered that he needed more than natural ability to win. He needed training, and he needed discipline.

Pop Warner provided the discipline with his blunt coaching style. "You goddamn bonehead!" Warner yelled at his athletes as he paced impatiently, jabbing the air with his Turkish Trophy cigarette. Sometimes Warner motivated his athletes with a slap or a kick. Still, Warner did not believe in pushing his athletes too far. He knew that peer pressure worked best as a motivator for his Indian athletes, and he often relied on other Indian athletes to mentor promising young stars. One such mentor was Albert Exendine. Twenty-three years old in the spring of 1907, three years older than Thorpe, Exendine was the son of a Cherokee father and a full-blooded Delaware mother. Born in Bartlesville, Oklahoma, he had attended the Mautame Mission School, a Presbyterian mission school near the town of Anadarko, Oklahoma.

Exendine and a friend applied to Carlisle after seeing an advertisement for the school in Anadarko. Once accepted, Exendine needed six months to convince his father to let him go. In the end, his father relented, and Exendine and his friend set out for Carlisle on Christmas Day 1899. Exendine's friend contracted tuberculosis in Pennsylvania, returned to Oklahoma, and passed away. Ex, as he was called, thrived at Carlisle. He joined the Invincible Debating Society, acted as a clown and a gravedigger in a performance of *Hamlet*, and became a respected student leader. In 1901, he earned a spot as a tackle on the Carlisle varsity football squad and won a national reputation as one of the toughest players in the game. "I didn't know what football was until I went to Carlisle," an eighty-three-year-old Ex later told reporters. "But I was a mean son-of-a-gun. Those were the days of push, drag and slug football. I would get the ball and just stand there pumping my knees while other fellows pushed me into the line."

Ex also was one of Carlisle's best track performers, and he held many track and field records at Carlisle. In the spring of 1907 Warner hired him to work as an assistant coach and to pay special attention to Jim Thorpe.

Thorpe looked up to Ex, as much as he had looked up to Chauncey Archiquette at Haskell. Thorpe and Ex both came from Oklahoma. They shared the same sense of humor. They wrestled with one another and poked fun at Carlisle. While Thorpe worked at the tailoring shop, Exendine worked in the bakery. He later observed, "I always stayed close to the food."

He also stayed close to Thorpe. By his own example, Ex sparked Thorpe's enthusiasm for the training that top-level competition demanded. Thorpe was strong in the long jump and the high jump, and in middistance running events. He won the high jump and the high hurdles at the Carlisle School games and won second in the high hurdles and high jump against Bucknell. Warner could see potential in the quiet, tough youth.

Thorpe stayed at Carlisle through the summer of 1907. As one of Pop Warner's athletic boys, he was not forced to go on an "outing." Instead, he continued to work out with Ex, Tewanima, and the other athletes and looked forward to the football season.

In the fall, Frank Newman, a Carlisle teacher who had coached Thorpe's intramural football squad, took a bold step: he recommended that Thorpe try out for the varsity football team. Most athletes had to get Pop Warner's permission before they suited up for tryouts, but Newman was so impressed with Thorpe's ability that he was willing to surprise the cantankerous Warner.

Thorpe not only survived his first football practice, he also scored two touchdowns running the ball during tackling practice and earned a coveted spot on the Carlisle varsity as a substitute halfback. Then the real work began.

"What in the damn hell you think you're doin'?" Warner yelled at Thorpe, Ex, and the other Carlisle athletes. "Play football!" When he could hold himself back no longer, the burly, thirty-seven-year-old Warner demonstrated a proper blocking or tackling technique himself, knocking the Indian boys flat.

Thorpe drilled on the new play introduced after the rule changes in 1906, the long forward pass. Warner was one of the coaches who had opposed it, but once the rule was changed, he was one of the first coaches to harness the scoring power of the air attack. "Nobody knew how to throw it. But Pop came up with a theory," Exendine explained, "he decided to throw a spiral." Warner concentrated his efforts on thirty- to fifty-yard passes that could make game-winning scores.

Thorpe and the other backs spent hours practicing their spirals. They gradually learned how to roll the ball off their fingertips, resulting in increased distance and accuracy. Exendine moved from the tackle to the end. Again and again, he ran downfield to grab the wobbling spirals tossed by his teammates, becoming one of the first ends who actually specialized in receiving passes on the dead run. More than any other team, the Carlisle Indians transformed the pass from a lumbering toss to a soaring, long-distance scoring weapon. "How the Indians did take to it!" Warner later exclaimed. "Light on their feet as professional dancers, and every one amazingly skillful with his hands, the redskins pirouetted in and out until the receiver was well down the field, and then they shot the ball like a bullet."

"With the exception of the unbeaten Pitt team of 1916," Warner later said of the 1907 Carlisle football team, Jim Thorpe's first team, "it was about as perfect a football machine as I ever sent on the field. . . . The boys clicked into shape early in the season, and the very first game convinced me that a big year was ahead."

With a pool of only about 250 male students who were old enough to play football, Warner's Carlisle squads had only a few substitutes, and there was no platoon system at the time. "As a consequence, almost every boy could play several positions, and thought nothing of being switched around."

Jim Thorpe and his teammates bantered among themselves, joked about their ethnic background, and gave one another nicknames, exhibiting the self-deprecating sense of humor that Warner had noted in his previous Carlisle squads. A player with big ears was dubbed "Mule"; one with a protruding jaw was "Hippo." "Chicken" was the name given to a player with a prominent chest, who often opened up his locker door to find a "frightened pullet." "Skunk" was the nickname of a player who did not bathe enough. One player who looked like a bulldog was named "Dog." When Warner first came to Carlisle, he mistook this nickname for the Indian boy's real name. After the player made a good tackle, Warner yelled, "Good work, Dog," which cracked up the rest of the Indian players. On the Carlisle team, Thorpe and his teammates could relax enough to make fun of themselves while taking great pride in the fact that they were all Indians playing on an all-Indian team.

"They [the Carlisle athletes] did not manifest a school spirit, but they did have a racial spirit," Pop observed. "They seemed to recognize the fact that it was upon the athletic field that the Indians had an even chance against their white brothers, and they wanted to show that, given an even chance, they were the equal of their paleface brothers."

Carlisle began the season by trouncing Lebanon Valley 40–0. The following week, Thorpe, sitting on the bench, watched quarterback Frank Mt. Pleasant connect with Exendine for a game-winning touchdown pass against Penn State. According to press coverage of the game, Penn State "was simply outclassed."

On October 12, 1907, Thorpe and the rest of the team traveled to Buffalo, New York, to play Syracuse. Eight thousand fans packed Olympic Park, many of them Native Americans from tribes in the region, who cheered on Mt. Pleasant, a Tuscarora from upstate New York. Ford Park, one of the Syracuse players, recalled a particularly crafty strategy employed by Warner during the Syracuse game: "The Carlisle ends wore white helmets, the halfbacks red ones, and they had half footballs sewn on their shirts. When one of those high passes descended, they all took off and I would have my hands full keeping track of them. I broke up some of the passes by pushing the eligible receiver. There was no interference then." Such confusing decorations on players' jerseys were soon after ruled illegal.

It was a rough game. Carlisle's fullback, Pete Hauser, scored all the points for Carlisle and hit a would-be Syracuse tackle so hard that he knocked him unconscious. Syracuse punished the Indian halfback, Albert Payne, so badly that Warner had to replace him with his untried halfback, Jim Thorpe. In his first big-time football appearance, Thorpe did not make any breakaway runs or score any points. He later admitted that he hardly knew the signals. But he played a good, solid game in Carlisle's 14–6 victory over the Orangemen.

On October 19, 1907, the Indians welcomed Bucknell to the Carlisle field. Warner knew that Bucknell was not a great team and that playing on the small field at Carlisle would not generate much revenue. But he had other goals in mind, publicity goals. Before the Bucknell game, Warner and the Carlisle team invited the press to a Photographers' Day celebration, and posed for photos in front of cameramen from along the East Coast.

The shutterbugs alongside Indian Field watched Carlisle score against Bucknell within five minutes after the opening kickoff. Thorpe played most of the game at halfback. Late in the second half, he caught a kickoff and started downfield. For the first time in his career, he showed the slicing, bone-jarring form that had so impressed Warner on the practice field. Jim passed tangle-footed defenders, shook off tacklers, and thrilled the Carlisle home crowd as he made his way to the Bucknell goal line. Just as he appeared to be headed into the end zone, a Bucknell defender tripped him up. Thorpe hit the ground and fumbled. His teammate Theodore Owl scooped up the loose ball and carried it into the end zone for a touchdown. In covering the 15-to-0 Indian victory, the Carlisle school newspaper noted Jim's performance in print for the first time: "Thorpe did most of the work carrying the ball and proved to be an excellent ground gainer."

More than twenty thousand fans packed Philadelphia's Franklin Field on October 26, 1907 to watch Carlisle play against their biggest rival, the University of Pennsylvania. It was the largest attendance at any Philadelphia sporting event that year, and Carlisle did not disappoint the enormous crowd. "The entire Indian team played magnificent ball," the *New York Times* reported. "All of the Indians tackled like fiends, Penn being unable to gain through their line, around the ends or run back on punts. . . . Penn was defeated after the first five minutes of play. The Indians just swept them off their feet."

After Carlisle's starting halfback, Payne, hurt his knee in the first period, Thorpe went into the game. The first time he got the ball, he failed to follow his blockers and was thrown for a loss. The second time he got the ball, he sprinted around end and ran seventy-five yards for a touchdown. Thorpe's run was set up in part by the Carlisle passing game. The Indians passed from a punt formation as the ineligible receivers ran downfield, knocking over the defensive backs. The *Philadelphia North American* was amazed at how far the Indians could hurl the football, describing one pass as "a lordly throw, a hurl that went farther than many a kick."

"I'd see the ball sailing in my direction and at the same time came the thundering of what appeared to be a tribe of Indians racing at full tilt in my direction," said the Penn player Bill Hollenback about the game. "When this gang hits you, they just simply wiped you out and you lost all other interest in the football contest."

The reporter for the *Philadelphia Press* was equally impressed. "With racial savagery and ferocity, the Carlisle Indian eleven grabbed Penn's football scalp and dragged their victim up and down Franklin Field, not relinquishing their grip until the seventy minutes of the time allotted to the process was up and the figures 26 to 6 told the tale."

"Poor Pennsylvania," Warner later joked, "finally reached a point where the players ran around in circles, emitting wild yawps."

Pop Warner led Jim Thorpe and his teammates into New York City's Polo Grounds the next week to play in front of nearly thirty thousand fans, who gathered in a drenching rain to see the lordly Princeton Tigers play the Indians. An estimated ten thousand fans on the east side of the field broke through a wood-and-wire fence and took up positions behind a restraining rope, carefully monitored by a group of Pinkerton men in plain clothes. Most of the spectators in the grandstand sat without cover in the bucketing rain. Reporters took note of the "bright-colored gowns, and furs . . . and great feathered and beribboned hats that must have been hopelessly damaged."

Equally drenched were some of the greatest names in football, including Walter Camp, the head of football affairs at Yale, and the former Princeton stars "Doggy" Trenchard and "Beef" Wheeler. Despite the downpour, one reporter judged the tremendous throng to be "the best behaved crowd that ever gathered at a sporting event." Scalpers along Eighth Avenue got as much as $7 for a seat, but according to the press, "Betting was at a discount owing to the absence of Indians' money."

Immediately after Jim and the rest of the Carlisle team took to the field, the Princeton boosters started to cheer. The cheer ended with "Poor Mr. Indian."

Unfortunately for Carlisle, and for Thorpe, who started his first game at halfback, the cheer proved to be accurate. As the *New York Times* reported, Carlisle "fell from the high estate to which it had attained in the game with Pennsylvania and played a headless game, which failed to do justice to its real strength." A reporter for the *New York Journal* noted that the field was a "veritable quagmire" that "deprived Carlisle of their strongest asset, those long, brilliant, surely executed forward passes." Halfway through the game, a group described by reporters as "a delegation of Indian squaws and braves from the Hippodrome" made their way into the grandstand to the delight and the cheers of the Princeton supporters. Their presence adding nothing to the scoreboard and the Indians lost 16–0.

On November 9, 1907, in front of yet another record-setting crowd, estimated at thirty thousand, at Harvard Stadium in Cambridge, Massachusetts, Jim Thorpe and the Carlisle team bounced back from their Princeton defeat to face the perennial football powerhouse. Frank Mt. Pleasant was the star of the first half. He launched a long pass to Pete Hauser for one touchdown. Later, Mt. Pleasant ran the ball eighty-five yards to the Harvard five-yard line,in the words of the *New York Times* reporter, "casting the men off like flies."

In the second half, with Carlisle in firm command of the lead, play turned ugly. The Harvard right guard, Waldo Pierce, planted a stiff uppercut to Exendine's jaw and was thrown out of the game. Pierce would later travel to Paris to mingle with Ernest Hemingway, Gertrude Stein, and James Joyce and earn a reputation as one of the best American painters of the Lost Generation. But his artistic ability could not stop the Indians' football machine. After ten defeats, Carlisle finally beat Harvard.

"Speedy Indians Crush Harvard," reported the *New York Times*. "Harvard was scalped by the Indians this afternoon in the fastest game seen in the Stadium this fall, Carlisle quitting the field victors, 23 to 15."

The "Gypsies of the Gridiron," as the Carlisle team was known, set out on a road trip to play the University of Minnesota in Minneapolis in what the *New York Times* called be "the most spectacular game of football ever played in Minnesota." Thorpe started in the 12–10 Carlisle victory but was replaced by Payne. Even so, Exendine later commented, "Jim gave a good account of himself."

A week later, at Chicago's Marshall Field, twenty-eight thousand fans watched the Indians take on the undefeated Big Ten champions, the University of Chicago, coached by the legendary Amos Alonzo Stagg. In the clear, crisp fall air, thousands packed the stands and hundreds crowded onto standing-room-only platforms constructed at either end of the field. Along the sidelines, fans peeked through wire netting, the only thing separating them from the players.

Stagg had seen the Carlisle passing attack and was prepared for it. "They just kept knocking me down and knocking me down," Carlisle's great receiver Exendine later explained. "In those days you didn't have to wait until the receiver touched the ball to hit him. First the end would hit me, then the linebacker, then the halfback. They were doing the same thing to our other end." This was perhaps the first systematic pass defense ever devised.

Exendine and the Indians were doing the same thing to Chicago, particularly to Chicago's star, Wallie Steffen. William Gardner and Exendine did an excellent job of stifling Steffen every time he tried to run back a kick. In fact, they managed to disrupt his much-vaunted kicking game to such an extent that Steffen managed to make only one field goal. On the other hand, Carlisle's fullback, Pete Hauser, kicked three field goals and did most of the running, carrying the ball two-thirds of the time.

The Carlisle team could score field goals, but they desperately wanted a touchdown. With the ball down near the sidelines, Exendine came up with a plan. He told Hauser, "Hold that ball as long as you can, then throw it to me down by the goal line." At the snap, Ex took off running, out of bounds. When the defenders saw Ex step out of bounds, they stopped covering him and rushed Hauser, who had the ball. Ex dashed back behind the Chicago bench, then ran back onto the field about fifty yards downfield from the line of scrimmage. Hauser, who had managed to duck several would-be tacklers, launched a long pass. With no one covering him, Ex caught the fifty-yard bomb and ran thirty yards into the end zone for a touchdown.

Stagg was furious. He argued with the officials that an ineligible receiver had caught the pass. But the referee did not change the call; the touchdown stood. Warner had followed the letter, if not the spirit, of the rules. It was not until the following year that going out of bounds and coming back in bounds was declared illegal. "Glenn [Pop Warner] was never very active on the rules committee," Stagg later observed with classic understatement, "but we'd make a rule and Glenn would think up a way to get around it within our rules and then we'd have to meet the challenge. He kept us on our toes, I can tell you." Forty-eight years later, Carlisle's 18–4 victory over his Chicago team still annoyed Stagg. In speaking with a reporter about the game, Stagg noted, "That was the game where an ineligible man caught one of the touchdown passes." Warner later claimed, "Few things have ever given me greater satisfaction than that Chicago victory."

Perhaps the most courageous performance was by William Gardner. According to Warner, "Gardner, a star end, had his leg wrenched and his jaw broken . . . and [yet he] played on to the finish without telling me a word about it, afraid I would send in a substitute."

Walter Camp chose Exendine for his 1907 All-American second team, just as he had in 1906. Jim Thorpe did not receive any national honors. He was frustrated that he had not played much and that he had not played his best. Even thirty-five years later, when asked by a reporter about the 1907 season, Thorpe began to pace the floor and admitted, "I didn't like it much on the bench." But to the students at Carlisle, Jim Thorpe was a hero all the same. As the Carlisle student Sarah Mansur, a Sac and Fox, wrote to her family back in Oklahoma, "We are very proud of our only football boy from home, James Thorpe."

10

Spreading the Wealth

In addition to national press attention, Carlisle received considerable cash for the magnificent showing of its 1907 football team.
Carlisle's share of the gate receipts for the Princeton game alone
was $9,253, the largest amount Carlisle had ever earned in a single
chunk. The Chicago game was even more lucrative. "I remember that
Carlisle's share of the gate was $17,000," Warner remarked years later,
"an almost incredible sum in those days." The total earnings for the
year were equally incredible, more than $50,000. Carlisle's football
squad was one of the top-drawing attractions in the world of American
sports.

While he was the superintendent at Carlisle, Richard Henry Pratt
had kept tight control over the school's discipline and athletic operations as managed by Warner. William A. Mercer, Pratt's successor as
the Carlisle superintendent, was a much more hands-off administrator.
Unable to raise outside funds as Pratt had, Mercer had to rely on
Warner to make up for budgetary shortfalls. Warner, who had operated under Pratt's system of off-the-books financing, took almost a
free hand in managing the sports money that flooded into Carlisle
from ticket sales and game guarantees.

Under Mercer, Warner strengthened the Carlisle Indian School
Athletic Association, a business entity legally separate from the U.S.
Indian School. Warner served as the president of this association and

was one of three members of the Executive Committee, along with the school superintendent and Warner's financial clerk, William H. Miller. Student athletes served as nominal advisers to the association but had no control over its operations, scheduling, or financing.

As an employee of the association and not the school itself, Warner was not subject to the regulations governing federal employees. With no constraints on his operations, he maintained total control over collecting, investing, and spending money generated by Carlisle sports and was free to build an athletic empire. "Every cent spent on track and athletic field and training house and equipment came from [football] gate receipts," Warner later claimed. "Not only were the receipts from football adequate to support all athletics but these receipts paid my salary and built several permanent buildings on the grounds." Indeed, football funds from Warner's association built a new hospital for the school, the printing offices, new cottages for staff and visitors, and a greenhouse. He paid a local minister to hold weekly services in the Carlisle chapel.

Warner, who had worked his way through college in part by selling his watercolors, used athletic association funds to build a new art studio on campus, the Leupp Art Studio, named in honor of Francis E. Leupp, the commissioner of Indian Affairs. Leupp believed that there was value in promoting and preserving certain aspects of Indian culture and society. He supported training in silverwork, weaving, painting, and other traditional Indian handicrafts, though always with an eye to the bottom line. In one instance, he recommended that Navajo silversmiths at Carlisle focus on making "the sort of things which command a market in white communities—butter knives and napkin rings, salt cellars and trays" instead of just producing "jewelry and gee-gaws." Warner believed so strongly in the value of Indian art that he began collecting it for himself, filling his homes in Springville and Carlisle with beaded moccasins, basketry, and hunting spears.

Warner was influential in hiring Angel de Cora, America's leading Indian artist, to teach at the Leupp Art Studio. Joining de Cora at the Leupp Art Studio was a talented draftsman, illustrator, and running back, William "Lone Star" Dietz, whom she later married. The son of a German engineer and a Sioux mother, Dietz was working his way though Friends University in Kansas by playing professional baseball and football when he was hired by Warner, first as an art instructor, later as a football player, and finally as a coach. Dietz and Warner painted together sometimes and touched up the scenery on the Carlisle stage.

Warner purchased newspapers and magazines for the library and literary societies, subsidized a course of lectures over the school year, and even used the athletic funds to take students to the circus. Warner made his funds available to the superintendent as "an emergency fund to use whenever circumstances made it advisable to expend moneys which were not authorized by the Indian office in Washington but which were for the good of the school."

"Those were the days before big stadiums and large crowds," Warner later recalled, "and I have often thought that if the Carlisle Indians could have continued their successful gridiron career [they] . . . could have taken in receipts more than large enough to maintain the school without government help."

Since Carlisle was a federally funded institution that provided free tuition, room, and board to all its students, Warner did not have to worry about scholarship money once his athletes were admitted to school. The loose academic structure at the U.S. Indian School provided Warner with tremendous leeway in attracting and enrolling "students" to play sports. If any athlete wished to pursue his education at Conway Hall or Dickinson College in Carlisle, Warner paid for their tutoring. Although many of Warner's athletes were older than other students "studying" at the government-funded secondary school, they were younger than many of the "students" who played athletics for Harvard, the University of Chicago, the University of Pennsylvania, and other big-time colleges.

Warner separated Jim Thorpe and his "athletic boys," as he called them, from the rest of the Carlisle student body. They lived in a separate dormitory, renovated at a cost of $13,000 to include a new leisure room complete with a pool table, and a kitchen in which special meals were prepared for them, a diet far superior to that enjoyed by the other Carlisle students. Thorpe and Warner's other athletes received special attention from the school medical staff.

In addition to providing them with superior housing, food, and even medical attention, Warner provided the athletic boys with material rewards. He made generous "loans" and "expense" payments to his athletes that amounted to a total of $9,233 for the 1907 and 1908 seasons. Tewanima received $350 in loans. Thorpe received $500. Warner presented each of his athletic boys with a $25 suit of clothes and a $25 overcoat from Mose Blumenthal's clothing store in downtown Carlisle. Star players were given a charge account at Blumenthal's for a higher dollar amount. The store became a comfortable hangout where athletes and local sports boosters could swap stories amid the Carlisle pennants and sports paraphernalia and even share a discreet beverage or two in the back room. Athletic boys did not always have to go downtown for a drink. Carlisle employees sometimes made beer deliveries to the campus. On rare occasions, Warner himself invited his athletes to his home for a glass of beer.

For the inevitable times when his athletes were less discreet in their drinking or visited Bessie's sporting house in too blatant a manner, Warner paid Carlisle police officers and a local detective to bring his athletes back to campus and keep things quiet. If an athlete ran into problems with the Carlisle administration and wound up under lock and key in the school guardhouse, a common punishment, Warner sent one of his men to the superintendent with a written request for his release.

In addition to taking care of his athletes and his institution, Warner took care of himself. He built a new two-story home with $3,400 from the athletic association's funds and paid his utility bill with athletic money. With athletic money, he bought railway bonds at a local "bucket shop" and invested in the Springfield Canning Company, which supplied the food for the Carlisle training table. He also paid himself a generous salary. While the school superintendent earned only $2,650 a year, Warner pocketed a handsome $4,000 per year as the Carlisle coach and the athletic director. He became active in the Carlisle community as a Shriner and eventually became a third-degree Mason.

Warner understood that the future of Carlisle athletics depended on publicity as well as performance. He visited the offices of the local newspaper, the *Carlisle Herald*, so regularly that he wound up hiring the sports writer Arthur Martin as his secretary. In addition to Martin, Warner relied on the public relations skills of Hugh Miller, who often added the title "Colonel" to his name in recognition of his dubious service in the Spanish-American War. "Colonel" Miller maintained his "office" in a booth at the Chocolate Shop in downtown Carlisle. From a small single booth, he operated a news syndicate that distributed flashy stories and photos about Carlisle's colorful Indian athletes that at one point reached more than 150 newspapers across the country. Warner often met with coaches from nearby colleges at the Chocolate Shop, working out plays with salt and pepper shakers before visiting his broker to follow the market. According to one Carlisle resident of the time, "Unlike today, the stock investors were not looked upon very highly and Pop was forever sneaking in there without Mrs. Warner's knowledge."

The Carlisle superintendent, Mercer, resigned in December 1907. The reason Mercer gave for his resignation was ill health, but biology may not have been the only reason for his discomfort. Just before Mercer retired, federal investigators conducted an audit of Carlisle's finances and uncovered much questionable bookkeeping. Investigators found Frank Hudson, Warner's great kicker who had taken a job as the school clerk, guilty of embezzling $1,416 from the Carlisle accounts. Hudson and Mercer left Carlisle at about the same time.

The thirty-three-year-old Moses Friedman succeeded Mercer as the superintendent of Carlisle in April 1908. Born in Cincinnati in 1874 to a Jewish immigrant father from Germany and a mother from a well-connected southern family, Friedman graduated from the Teaching School of the University of Cincinnati in 1899 and taught in the Cincinnati school system for two years before joining the Indian Service. He taught at the Phoenix Indian School and in the Philippines before being appointed the assistant superintendent of the Haskell Institute in Lawrence, Kansas, when he was only twenty-four. With a young wife, Mary Butler, from a prominent Kentucky family, he had a reputation as a talented and ambitious administrator, a rising star in the federal educational establishment. Carlisle was his big opportunity.

Friedman focused much of his attention on pleasing Washington. He designed handy pocket-sized calendars for each student and organized elaborate six-day commencement exercises, which included military drills and home construction demonstrations. One year, the commencement featured performances of "The Captain from Plymouth," a musical comedy staring the Indian student Montreville Yuda as Miles Standish. Friedman realized that discipline among the students was seriously degenerating, but instead of enforcing the rules himself, he relied on Warner to discipline unruly students.

Friedman also allowed Warner to expand his sports program to help boost Carlisle's profile within the Indian Service. As the football coach, the athletic director, the disciplinarian, and the financial manager of the athletic association, which funded art studios, libraries, and campus landscaping, Warner was the highest-paid executive at the institution and the most powerful man on the Carlisle campus. His ability to recruit, train, and compensate athletes, manage finances, generate publicity, and develop game-winning training and performance strategies were all elements of what became known as "the Warner system."

Not everyone approved of the system. "Carlisle's Athletic Policy Criticized by Dr. Montezuma," ran a headline in the *Chicago Sunday Tribune* sports section on November 24, 1907, on the same page as coverage of the Carlisle–University of Chicago football game. "In the 1907 team there probably were not more than one-third of the members who were in actual attendance at the school as students," wrote the author. "As conducted this year the school [Carlisle] might just as well have farmed out its football work to anybody who would take the job."

Dr. Carlos Montezuma had been a physician at the U.S. Indian School at Carlisle in the last years of Richard Henry Pratt's tenure and had traveled with Warner and the Carlisle football team on their 1900 trip to California. A fervent supporter of Pratt, Montezuma felt that the school had taken a turn for the worse after Pratt's departure. Montezuma pinned most of the blame on Pop Warner for the corruption of the Carlisle athletics program and wrote, "The mistake in this football matter is due to the present management having lost, or, more correctly speaking, never having had, its bearings in the matter of properly conducting the Carlisle school."

Though he was blunt in his criticism of Warner, Montezuma refrained from the most serious accusations of misconduct that had come to his attention. Prior to submitting his article to the *Chicago Tribune*, Montezuma received a letter from W. G. Thompson, a former disciplinarian at Carlisle and the school's first football coach. In his letter to Montezuma, Thompson alleged that the corruption of Carlisle athletics began with Warner's arrival in 1899. He claimed that Warner allowed his athletes to stay out late, cut classes, drink, and otherwise flaunt school rules. Thompson leveled even more serious charges at Warner. "In 1900," Thompson wrote, "every player was paid something at the end of the season. This, of course, was in violation of the ethics of college sport and made the players professionals." Thompson maintained that Warner went so far as to keep a "schedule of prices" for his players, listing different levels of payment for touchdowns, blocked kicks, and other key plays.

Superintendent Peairs of the Haskell Institute joined in the critical chorus and accused Warner of paying wages, paying for touchdowns, allowing athletes to skip school, and recruiting ineligible players. Peairs wrote, "Three or four years ago we had a little taste of professional foot ball . . . and it has taken several years to get athletics on a good healthy basis. In fact it is going to be almost impossible to get entirely rid of that spirit in athletics, unless the larger schools will pull together. Boys who have any ambition in athletics and show any ability will of course be restless in a school where there is a determined effort to keep athletics on the right basis, as long as they know that there are schools where they are in demand as semi-professionals." A Haskell student-athlete, Jess Rowlodge, claimed that he was recruited by Warner to play for Carlisle but turned him down, saying, "No I come to go to school. I didn't come to play football."

Warner denied the charges vociferously. In the first issue of *The Indian Craftsman: A Magazine Not Only About Indians But Mainly By Indians*, Warner defended his actions as Carlisle's athletic supervisor in an article titled "Athletes at the Carlisle Indian School,"

> The success of the Indians has been due to the rough, hardy outdoor life that the players have been inured to since the time they were born. In addition to this purely physical explanation, there is a psychological one; the Indians know that people regard them as an inferior race, unable to compete successfully in any line of endeavor with the white men, and as a result they are imbued with a fighting spirit, when pitted against their white brethren, that carries them a long way toward victory.

Warner further maintained that "athletics at the school are financed by the receipts from the football games, the surplus being sufficient to

equip and maintain the other branches of sport. . . . This financial
success has not been due primarily to large gate receipts (since many
colleges whose athletic associations have to call for subscriptions
receive a larger income from athletics that does Carlisle) but to
economic business management."

Despite Montezuma's criticism and other rumors of improprieties
at the Indian School, the "Warner system" flourished, and Jim Thorpe
flourished along with it. He earned grades of "excellent" for his work
in history, civics, grammar, and literature, and a "good" for his vocational work as a "house and carriage painter." At twenty-one, he was
older than many of his classmates but still younger than many of his
fellow athletes. He was so well respected that one teacher turned the
class over to him to teach for a day. His classmates later praised Jim as
"a fine teacher." By the time the 1908 track season started, Thorpe's
tremendous natural talent was beginning to be recognized for the first
time, and he was beginning to feel a certain loyalty to Pop Warner,
Carlisle, and his fellow athletes.

Warner had a strong track team. Frank Mt. Pleasant was running
well, and Louis Tewanima, Pop's Hopi distance runner, was coming
into his own, even though his uniform bagged around him as he ran
his endless, smoothly paced laps. But Thorpe was Warner's best
prospect.

Albert Exendine, Carlisle's greatest track star, continued to work
closely with Thorpe. Ex understood that Thorpe had the talent but
not the attitude he needed to be a champion. Thorpe was only willing
to push himself under certain circumstances. At other times, he was
satisfied to just make do. "He wanted to win, but that was enough,"
Exendine recalled. "In races he sometimes took the last hurdle far in
front and then just strolled across the finish line."

Thorpe rarely seemed to take things seriously, though his fierce
temper occasionally flashed through. He was his own man, thankful
for the advice and guidance of Warner, Exendine, and his coaches, but
his own man nonetheless. He lived, and played, on his own terms. He
did not like practicing but, when challenged, he could draw on a vast
reservoir of athletic power. He enjoyed beating the competition, not
the clock.

Thorpe was the highest point scorer in the Carlisle victory over the
Syracuse track team on May 14, winning the 120-yard hurdles and the

220-yard hurdles, and tying Ex in the running high jump. Grover E. Long, one of his teammates, recalled watching Thorpe win one of the hurdle events: "After he cleared the final hurdle, he looked back over his shoulder with a teasing grin on his face as if to say, 'Come on boys, if you want to make a race of it.'" In a meet against Dickinson and Swarthmore on May 23 at Carlisle, Thorpe set a new school record in the shotput and broke the Carlisle record in the 220-yard hurdles, which he won in twenty-six seconds. He also won the high jump, the long jump, and the high hurdles. Louis Tewani, as he was identified in the Carlisle paper, won the 2-mile, helping give Carlisle an overall victory in the meet.

On May 30, 1908, at the State Intercollegiate meet in Harrisburg, Thorpe won the high jump and finished second in the low hurdles, the high hurdles, and the shot put. At the end of the 1908 track season, Thorpe joined the Carlisle baseball team, also coached by Warner. By the time Thorpe hit the field, the Carlisle team was already at the end of its twenty-seven-game schedule, which had included a series of games against a professional team from Hagerstown. The games were not on the formal season schedule, but they no doubt brought much appreciated income to Warner. Thorpe, the right-handed track star, helped out the squad by pitching a 1–0 shutout against Albright. Thorpe enjoyed playing baseball. Unlike track and field, there was money in the game, a chance to play for the pros. Several of his teammates played "summer ball" for semiprofessional teams in the region. Warner proudly distributed a letter to the press from J. Frank Ridenour with the Hagerstown, Maryland, baseball team, which had paid three of Warner's athletes to play summer ball.

"I feel that it would be remiss in me if [I] did not tell you that never in the history of baseball in Hagerstown were three men connected with the team whose services were so uniformly satisfactory as were those three boys—Balenti, Garlow and Newashe—the past season," Ridenour wrote to Warner, naming three of his most promising athletes. Warner distributed a similar letter from a summer ball team in Hershey, praising the play of three other Carlisle athletes.

While Thorpe heard about opportunities to play summer ball, he also no doubt heard that Warner was grooming athletes for a big track meet overseas, something called the Olympics. Thorpe competed in the high jump at the 1908 Eastern Olympic trials but did not make the team. Perhaps he did not give it his best effort. Or maybe the twenty-one-year-old Thorpe was just plain homesick. And tired of working for Warner. "Jim was a natural athlete," observed Henry Roberts, who had met Thorpe at Carlisle and played with him on the Carlisle football squad. "He made everything look easy. He couldn't see no sense in hard training. Pop used to get after him." For whatever reason, Thorpe applied to the school administration for leave to return to Oklahoma for the summer of 1908 and got Warner's reluctant okay. As Thorpe headed west, Moses Friedman sent a bulletin to the rest of the Indian Service: "I beg leave to inform you that the following pupil should not be enrolled at any Indian School—on leave from the Carlisle School: James Thorpe."

I I

The Olympic Idea

In 1908, the Olympics were a colorful sporting sideshow, an odd mixture of athleticism and nationalism that generated as much controversy as competition. The force behind the modern Olympic games was an equally odd mixture of a man, Pierre, Baron de Coubertin. Born on January 1, 1863, Coubertin was a French aristocrat who fixed upon education as his life's work. Stung by France's defeat in the Franco-Prussian War of 1870–1871, he studied the physical education techniques developed by more victorious nations to determine how sports could help strengthen the French national character and improve the performance of the French military.

The Olympic games of the ancient Greeks captured Coubertin's imagination more than any other training regimen. With records dating from 776 B.C. to A.D. 217, the Olympic games were a favorite fixation of the classically trained nineteenth-century elite.

Coubertin first proposed his romantic notion of an international athletic competition at the 1892 banquet of the Union of French Athletic Sports Clubs, an organization he had founded. Always an enthusiast, Coubertin was undeterred when his fellow sportsmen either ignored or ridiculed his Olympic idea. In 1894, he hosted a meeting of the International Congress of Amateurs. Although none of the seventy-nine delegates besides Dimítrios Vikélas of Greece and Professor William M. Sloane of Princeton appeared to have any interest in the games, Coubertin recalled that "a unanimous vote in favour of revival was rendered at the end of the Congress chiefly to please me." With this tepid endorsement, Coubertin established the International Olympic Committee and began planning the first games.

Coubertin envisioned the Olympic games as a medium for international conciliation, with the expressed hope that "the more the higher classes of different nations get to know one another, the less likelihood is there of their fighting." He took as his slogan *"Ludus pro Patria,"* Latin for "Games for the Fatherland."

In designing the games for the "higher classes," Coubertin decided to restrict competition to amateurs. He mistakenly believed that the athletes in ancient Greece participated in the games purely for the honor of victory, uninfluenced by the substantial rewards that scholars today believe they received. Onto this misunderstood classical ideal the baron grafted the concept of amateurism as defined by the British aristocracy, who invented the ideal of the amateur athlete primarily to bar the lower classes from their athletic events, in keeping with the rigid class segregation of Victorian England.

The British Amateur Rowing Association was one of the first sporting groups to restrict its activities to amateur competitors. The association passed a law declaring that no person was as amateur "who is or ever has been by trade or employment for wages a mechanic, artisan, or labourer or engaged in any menial duty." The rules for the Henley Regatta, a crew competition, drafted in 1878, included similar class restrictions and stated that "No person shall be considered an amateur oarsman or sculler . . . who is or has been by trade or employment for wages, a mechanic, artisan or laborer." As defined by another influential sporting group, the London-based Amateur Athletic Club, an amateur was "a gentleman." The club maintained that "the only way to keep . . . sport pure from the element of corruption" was to restrict competition to amateurs, since "the average workman has no idea of sport for its own sake." The basis of the British amateur ideal, which Coubertin adopted as the basic premise of his Olympic games, was that athletes who had to earn money for a living were corrupt. And sporting organizations that paid their athletes also were corrupt. Coubertin embraced this dubious ideal, and thus defined the Olympic games as a contest for wealthy sportsmen.

Even though he accepted the amateur ideal, Coubertin was troubled by its ramifications. Who exactly was an amateur? Did the amateur regulations include coaches? If only amateurs could compete in the Olympics, would they be allowed to receive money to cover their expenses? "Oh, what a stupid old business Olympic amateurism is," Coubertin said in an interview toward the end of his life. "It is respect in sport which interests me, and not respect from the ridiculous English concept which only allows millionaires to dedicate themselves to sport. That sort of amateurism is not what I wanted. It was the international federations who insisted on imposing it."

In 1893 Coubertin traveled to the United States to promote his Olympic idea at the World's Columbian Exposition in Chicago. He then visited with his staunch supporter Professor William Sloane, who specialized in French history. Sloane was intrigued by Coubertin's Olympic idea. He appreciated Coubertin's concept of holding the games every four years, as the Greeks had done, and of using the games as a forum for international competition in the fine arts, literature, and architecture as well as sports. But even Sloane understood early on that the question of amateurism would become "the most knotty, elusive and exasperating of all questions connected with sports."

Sloane arranged a dinner party for the French athletic promoter at the University Club in New York City, to which he invited the most powerful men in American sports. On November 27, 1893, Coubertin introduced the gathered sportsmen to his idea of starting the modern Olympics. The Americans were largely uninterested. The man who seemed to be most antagonistic to Coubertin was the leading American promoter of amateur sports, James Edward Sullivan.

Born in New York City on November 16, 1860, to working-class parents from County Kerry, Ireland, Sullivan was a runner and a boxer who joined New York City's Pastime Athletic Club in 1877. Sullivan enjoyed some success as an athlete. He won the Canadian half-mile championship in 1884 and the all-round championship of his club, which was one of the strongest sporting organizations in the United States.

In Sullivan's world of the late 1800s, American athletics was much simpler than it is today. Baseball was the only professional sport. Colleges and sports clubs sponsored most of the other athletic contests.

Colleges first formally adopted the amateur ideal at the Conference on Intercollegiate Athletics at Brown University in 1898. The conference adopted a report that said, "It is obvious that no student should be paid for his athletics. The practice of assisting young men through college in order that they may strengthen the athletic teams is degrading to amateur sport."

Taking a tip from their English counterparts, the most exclusive New York clubs formed the National Association of Amateur Athletes of America (N4A) in 1879. The N4A also restricted its sanctioned competitions to amateurs, defined as "any person who has never competed in an open competition for public or admission money, or with professionals for a prize . . . nor has at any period of his life taught or assisted in the pursuit of athletic exercises as a means of livelihood." Almost immediately, the New York athletic clubs began bending the amateur rules by allowing gifted athletes to compete no matter what their background, by recruiting athletes with material considerations, and by rewarding victorious athletes with valuable prizes.

James Sullivan realized that while he could not make a living by competing in sports, he could make quite a nice living writing about them. He went to work for Frank Leslie's publishing house in 1878. Two years later he founded the first track-and-field publication, *Athletic News*, then began working for the *New York Sporting News*. The rising sports journalist realized that the big money was in the control of the games themselves. Sullivan ignored the worlds of professional baseball and college athletics and focused instead on gaining control of the athletic clubs. In 1886, he helped to engineer the collapse of the N4A and, in 1888, he assisted in the creation of the organization that replaced the N4A, the Amateur Athletic Union (AAU).

Serving at various times as a board member, the president, the secretary, and the secretary-treasurer of the organization over the next quarter century, Sullivan used the AAU to gain control over American track and field, basketball, and lacrosse. He did this by enforcing a "sanction" system against athletes whom he deemed to be professionals. All athletes who competed in AAU-sponsored events had to register as amateurs with the AAU, and only athletes who were considered to be amateurs by the AAU could compete in AAU-sponsored events. As the AAU and only the AAU came to organize the major track-and-field events in the country, the AAU and only the AAU came to control who would compete in those events.

William B. "Father Bill" Curtis, one of the founders of the New York Athletic Club and a powerful sports publisher, was realistic about the amateur rule as it evolved under Sullivan. He admitted that the amateur-professional distinction was unfair to working-class athletes, but he rationalized it in the following way: "The practical point is that under existing laws there has grown up a system of clubs and associations whose best interests, pecuniary and social, would partially or wholly lose their value were the amateur fence to be taken down or even materially lowered."

In the clubby world of late-nineteenth-century athletics, Sullivan came to know the most powerful man in American sports, Albert Goodwill Spalding. In 1876, Al Spalding was one of professional baseball's greatest pitchers, leading the league with forty-six pitching victories for the Chicago White Stockings (who later became the Cubs). Spalding's skills in the boardroom were even greater than his skills on the field. He took control of the White Stockings and helped develop the National League of American Professional Baseball clubs, now known simply as the National League. Under Spalding's guidance, the National League brought modern management techniques to baseball. Spalding and the league introduced the use of player contracts and formalized the game scheduling and team-franchising processes to maximize league revenues.

In 1876, Spalding founded the sports equipment manufacturing company that still bears his name. In 1892, he expanded his empire still further with the creation of the American Sports Publishing Company, a publisher of rulebooks and guidebooks written by the leading names in American sports. The man Spalding chose to lead his sports publishing empire was James Sullivan.

Even in sports such as football, which was controlled by the colleges, and baseball, which was controlled by the professional leagues, Sullivan and the Spalding company made money by producing "official" rulebooks and equipment. In addition to overseeing publication of the "official" sports guidebooks, Sullivan handled Spalding's advertising budget, a position that gave him considerable influence over media coverage of the sporting world. Reporters and editors were reluctant to question Sullivan's actions lest they lose Spalding advertising dollars.

Sullivan worked hard to expand Spalding's vertical integration of the sporting goods business. He championed the development of youth athletic programs and joined the board of directors of several quasi-governmental sporting organizations, including the New York Public Recreation Committee and the New York Board of Education. Sullivan was in part responsible for creating the first playground and the first public bath in New York City. By the time he was introduced to Coubertin and the concept of the Olympics, Sullivan was accurately described as America's "first sports czar."

Though Sullivan did not trust Coubertin or his Olympics, the Irish New Yorker agreed to chair a committee to consider the Olympic idea. Also serving on the committee were A. G. Spalding; his brother J. Walter Spalding; and Caspar Whitney, one of the most influential sports journalists of the era. Whitney, who developed the All-American football team concept along with Walter Camp, was perhaps the most outspoken and ardent advocate of the amateur ideal. In 1894, he declared professional sports dead in America. The next year, he ridiculed the idea of "paying him [the working-class athlete] for time he may lose from his trade."

"The laboring class are all right in their way," Whitney wrote in his 1894 book *A Sporting Pilgrimage*. "Let them go their way in peace, and have their athletics in whatever manner best suits their inclination. . . . Let us have our sport among the more refined elements." The well-respected Whitney described working-class athletes as "vermin" and the "great unwashed."

While Sullivan and Whitney debated the pros and cons of Coubertin's Olympic idea, Sloane, the Princeton professor, became America's biggest Olympic booster. With minimal support from the American sports establishment, Sloane led a team of athletes mostly from Princeton and the Boston Athletic Association to the First Olympiad, held in Athens in 1896. Competing with entrants from thirteen other countries, the American collegiate athletes performed exceptionally well. James B. Connolly, who dropped out of Harvard in order to compete in the games and paid his own way, became the first modern Olympian victor when he won the first event of the games, the triple jump. Connolly later placed second in the high jump and third in the long jump, as the Americans dominated the competition.

The success of the 1896 games convinced Sullivan that there was merit in the Olympic idea. He tried to create an international track and field organization that would seize power over the Olympic games from Coubertin. When he failed in this effort, he traveled to Paris for the 1900 games as assistant American director of the games, along with Caspar Whitney, who was a member of the American Olympic Committee. Held as part of the International Exposition celebration, the Second Olympiad was so poorly organized that some of the participants and even the judges never realized that they were competing or judging in the Olympics. Whitney later described the Paris games committee as "an organization of incompetents" and wrote, "What this [French Olympic] committee does not know about sports would fill volumes."

After the Paris debacle, Sullivan became more determined than ever to take control of the Olympics. In November 1900, Coubertin announced that the 1904 Olympic games would be held in either New York or Chicago. Sullivan publicly attacked the French aristocrat as a fake and announced to the press that the baron "no longer [has] any power to name the place at which Olympian Games or international events of any character shall be held."

Sullivan then declared that the Pan-American Exposition, scheduled to be held in Buffalo in 1901, would host the Olympic games under AAU auspices, an assertion the International Olympic Committee immediately denied. Coubertin was understandably disturbed by Sullivan's actions. The games at that exposition were not Olympics, but they did attract some of America's greatest sports talent, including Pop Warner, whose Carlisle Indian baseball squad played under Sullivan's direction with equipment furnished by Sullivan's employer, Spalding.

Warner did not really believe in the amateur ideal. He believed that coaches and athletes should be compensated for good performance. Still, he respected Sullivan's power. Warner got to know Sullivan as he developed Carlisle's track and field team, and he took an interest in the Olympic games. He saw possibilities in the Olympics. Warner understood that international headlines could do nothing but raise the profile of his Carlisle athletic program.

Through intense lobbying and complex arm-twisting, Sullivan managed to wrest control of the 1904 Olympics away from

Coubertin and the International Olympic Committee, at least in part. Though Coubertin had persuaded President Theodore Roosevelt to support Chicago as the city for the 1904 Olympics, under Sullivan's influence, the games were eventually held in St. Louis as part of the Louisiana Purchase Exposition, celebrating the one-hundredth anniversary of the purchase. Though he was not a member of the IOC, Sullivan took the title "Chief of the Department of Physical Culture Section of the Louisiana Purchase Exposition." Sullivan directed the Olympics and authored an unofficial history of the event, *Spalding's Official Athletic Almanac for 1905 (Special Olympic Number)*. Coubertin had, in effect, ceded control of the games to Sullivan and the AAU.

Held over a period of four and a half months, the St. Louis games generated so little excitement and attracted so few European competitors that even Coubertin failed to attend. The Exposition featured exhibits based around the theme "man and his works," designed to display human evolution from the barbarism of primitive races to the ultimate refinement of the Anglo-Saxons. The noted Indian leader Geronimo and Jim Thorpe's future wife, Iva Miller, a young girl from Oklahoma, were on display as part of the "anthropological" exhibits. Iva recited poetry and sold postcards autographed by Geronimo, who tipped the girl with part of the proceeds. Some indigenous people left the exhibits to participate in sporting events such as mud fighting and pole climbing. On the midway known as the Pike, visitors could gawk at Zuni and Moki (Hopi) Indians who were advertised as having "never been shown before."

Sullivan tried to schedule some sort of sporting event every day for several months during the Exposition and insisted upon calling all the events Olympic. For example, Sullivan called the first event, which was actually the 1904 Missouri state high school track championships, the Olympic Interscholastic Meet.

Two Zulu tribesmen from South Africa, part of the Boer War exhibit, ran in the marathon, which turned out to be the most controversial event of the games. Fred Lorz, the first man to cross the finish line, later admitted that he had not run the whole distance. American Thomas Hicks won the twenty-six-mile-long race, but only after being helped along with doses of brandy and strychnine offered by sympathetic boosters.

Even though the St. Louis games were not a great success, Coubertin congratulated Sullivan for his efforts on behalf of the Olympic movement and presented him with the Olympic Medal, the highest nonsporting distinction awarded by the International Olympic Committee.

Sullivan was a patriot who viewed the games as vital to expanding American interests across the globe. The 1908 games were originally scheduled to take place in Rome, but after the eruption of Mount Vesuvius stretched the resources of the Italian government to the breaking point, the location of the games was switched to London, England. Before the games, Sullivan tried unsuccessfully to pressure Congress into appropriating $100,000 for the American team, arguing in the press that "the Nation should provide the sinews of war where the issue at stake is National and not individual." Even without this monetary support, the czar of American sports marshaled his forces to achieve victory at the 1908 Olympic games.

Although Thorpe did not make the team, two of his teammates did qualify for the 1908 games, Frank Mt. Pleasant and Louis Tewanima. Warner described the Tuscarora Mt. Pleasant as his "first track find," "a tall, slender boy, weighing only one hundred and thirty pounds" with "the speed of a frightened deer. . . . Baseball, football, sprinting, hurdling and jumping were as natural to him as breathing."

England, as the host country, supplied all the officials for the games. Almost immediately, problems arose. British officials disqualified the American John Carpenter in the 400-meter final for blocking the path of a British runner. Mt. Pleasant, who was suffering with a strained ligament, managed to finish sixth in the broad jump with a leap of 22 feet, 4 ½ inches, and sixth in the triple jump with a 45-foot, 10-inch effort. After the games, Mt. Pleasant defeated the Olympic champion long jumper at a meet in Paris.

The most anticipated event of the games was Tewanima's event, the marathon. Officials marked out the race so it would begin underneath the windows of Windsor Castle and end in front of the royal box at the newly constructed Olympic stadium. Thus, the 26-mile, 385-yard length of the race, the length that would become the standard for all future marathons, was set not according to ancient Greek tradition, but simply for the viewing convenience of King Edward VII, Queen Alexandra, and other members of the British royal family.

Tewanima took his position at the starting line on the lawn of Windsor Castle. He stood alongside fifty-four other marathon runners, including the controversial Canadian Indian runner Tom Longboat. Before the Olympics, Sullivan had protested the participation of "The Bronze Mercury," as Longboat was called, claiming that he had run for prize money in Boston and was therefore a professional. Canada, however, still classified Longboat as an amateur. Since the country of nationality was the only authority empowered to determine amateur status, and since the Canadians refused to disqualify Longboat, he was allowed to run.

The Hopi Tewanima and the Onondaga Longboat started together. The hot, humid conditions soon forced Longboat to drop out of the race. Tewanima was among the leaders until the last five miles of the race, then he began to fall back, feeling the pains of sore feet, bad knees, and lingering seasickness. As the runners neared the stadium, Dorando Pietri took the lead. The Italian candymaker was well ahead of Tewanima's American teammate, John Hayes, but just before entering the Olympic stadium, the Italian fell. After a supporter administered a syringe filled with strychnine or digitalis, Pietri staggered into the stadium to the cheers of sixty-eight thousand fans.

According to a reporter, Pietri was "dazed, bewildered, hardly conscious, in red shorts and white vest, his hair white with dust." Exhausted and confused, the marathon leader turned the wrong way on the track. Pietri began running away from the finish line until British officials stopped him and obligingly pointed him in the right direction. Pietri ran a few steps and collapsed. British officials helped Pietri to his feet. Pietri collapsed twice more, and twice more officials stood him up as he struggled onward. An American Olympic official, Gustavus Kirby, described the scene from the sidelines as "a horrible, sickening sight of an exhausted, done-up, almost dying man with the courage and desperation of his race stamped on his ashen features."

Finally, the Italian marathoner collapsed again, just thirty feet from the finish line as the American John Hayes entered the stadium. Hayes ran toward the finish line. Pietri lay still on the dirt track. Faced with the American success in the most prominent contest of the games, the British clerk of course, J. M. Andrews, grabbed Pietri "and carried, pushed, and pulled" him over the finish line. The English officials declared the Italian the winner. "No Roman of prime ever has borne himself better," Arthur Conan Doyle wrote in praise of Pietri. "The great breed is not yet extinct."

Sullivan was furious. The British officials were obviously showing favoritism, helping an Italian beat an American in front of the anti-American crowd. After Sullivan protested, the Italian was disqualified and Hayes was declared the winner with a time of 2:54:04. Hayes's teammate Louis Tewanima finished ninth in the 1908 Olympic marathon with a time of 3:09:15, an outstanding accomplishment considering that the Hopi had been running in the white world for less than a year, was not a U.S. citizen and was technically a prisoner of war.

Back home in the United States, President Roosevelt greeted Tewanima, Mt. Pleasant, and the rest of the U.S. Olympic team at his home, Sagamore Hill. After shaking hands all around, the president led the athletes into his drawing room, pointed out the animal heads hanging on the wall, and enthused, "These are the trophies I have won."

Noticing Tewanima looking inquisitively around the room, Roosevelt nodded toward the Hopi Olympian and observed, "There is one of the originals. He is a fine Indian."

Tewanima and other athletes had indeed done a fine job in London. But Sullivan was so angered by what he viewed as the injustice of the English officials that he persuaded the Amateur Athletic Union to appoint a commission to form a new International Olympic Committee and to draw up the statutes of future games. According to Coubertin, "Nobody listened to him." Moreover, Sullivan's win-at-all-costs attitude bothered many in the Olympic establishment, including Coubertin, who believed that "the importance of the Olympiads lies not so much in winning as in taking part."

The *New York Times* editorialized, "As a means of promoting international friendship, it [the 1908 Olympics] has been a deplorable failure." British commentators condemned American training methods as "ungentlemanly" but admitted that "the way to win in sport is to make it a business." By the fall 1908, Pop Warner was ready to get on with the business of football.

12

Starting Halfback

Jim Thorpe probably did not hear much about the 1908 Olympics back in Oklahoma. At that time, there was no radio and only limited newspaper coverage in rural areas of international events. As he later told his friends, Thorpe spent most of the summer of 1908 "fishing."

One of his favorite fishing buddies was his half brother Frank, who lived on a farm near the small settlement of Bellmont, just west of the original Thorpe homestead. Struggling to support his Shawnee wife and four children on thirty acres of cotton and corn, Frank Thorpe was described as a drinking man with "a hard name" who could not "stand temptation very well." With Prohibition approved by Oklahoma voters in 1907, the wild whiskey town of Keokuk Falls had gone dry. Still, growing up the sons of a bootlegger, the Thorpe boys probably were able to find something to slake their thirst.

In addition to visiting Frank, Jim Thorpe spent time with his half sister Mary. Injured in childhood, she could speak only in a hoarse whisper and often was treated as a deaf-mute. Mary was a big, strong woman who had by this time left two abusive husbands and raised a son. She was not afraid of punching a Shawnee policeman who dared to criticize her childrearing techniques or of joining pickup football games. Mary was known as the toughest woman in the Sac and Fox nation.

Jim also had time to spend with his full siblings. Jim's older brother George was married, working a farm, and scratching a meager living from the sandy, reddish soil. Jim's thirteen-year-old sister Adaline was about to attend the Chilocco school in northern Oklahoma. His nine-year-old brother Edward boarded at the Sac and Fox school where Jim had gone. Edward would later attend Haskell, where Jim also had gone. Edward Thorpe thought so much of his brother Jim that he actually began calling himself Jim Thorpe. Just like his brother, Edward Thorpe eventually ran away from Haskell, back to his home in Oklahoma.

Jim Thorpe relished the freedom he found in Oklahoma. He enjoyed the countryside and the company of his relatives. It seemed there were Thorpes everywhere, and they all had a kind word for the athletic young man who was making a name for himself at Carlisle.

In August 1908, Thorpe headed back to Carlisle with his friend Bill Newashe, a Sac and Fox youth who had played football at Haskell and who hoped to make the Carlisle team. At Carlisle, Thorpe moved back into the athletic quarters. Unlike Bill Newashe, he did not have to prove himself. He was sure he was going to start at halfback for Pop Warner.

Warner was ready for the beginning of the season. He had earned such a reputation as a successful coach that he launched a new business venture, offering coaches and players "a complete and comprehensive correspondence course" in football. A sophisticated marketer, Warner managed to secure a mailing list from a New York company that provided him with the address of every American high school and college.

Published in book form in 1912 under the title *A Course in Football for Players and Coaches*, the course provided instruction in everything from "How Players Should Be Outfitted" to "How to Make and Use Tackling Apparatus and Charging Sleds" to "How to Play Quarterback." A micromanager and a skilled craftsman, Warner had long tinkered with football equipment. At one point, his assistant Arthur Martin ran into him at the industrial shop. When Martin asked Warner what he was doing, Warner said that he was making extra-long cleats for his players for rainy conditions and explained, "The boys can't run in muddy weather because the cleats get all muddied up and they slip."

In 1903, Warner had sold several of his equipment designs to A. G.

Spalding, including one of the earliest designs for protective headgear and lightweight "hair pads" for hips and knees. "Anyone can easily make them," Warner mentioned in his book, "but such pads can be secured of A. G. Spalding and Bros." Warner also recommended the Spalding ankle brace, since it "almost wholly prevents side sprains of the ankle." Warner had such a close relationship with Spalding that the company advertised in the Carlisle Indian School publications and included photos of the Carlisle team in its "official" intercollegiate football guide.

Warner believed in no more than three hours of practice a day, a half hour of limbering up and a half-hour lecture in the morning followed by a hard physical workout for two hours in the afternoon. He was careful not to work Thorpe and the others too hard. He knew from his experience at Cornell that it was more difficult to revive an exhausted athlete than to inspire an underpracticed one. On Sundays, Warner led his players on walks of two or three miles into the country. It was a trick he had picked up from his coach Marshall Newell at Cornell. It gave his players time to think, it kept them loose, and it was good for morale. It was all part of the "Warner system."

Warner knew that Thorpe was going to be a key player for the 1908 Carlisle team. Thorpe had tremendous natural ability and seemed to be much more enthusiastic, determined, and self-disciplined after spending a summer back in Oklahoma. "I never had to do much coaching with Jim," Warner commented. "Like all Indians his powers of observation were remarkably keen, developed as they were through generations. The younger players always watched the older ones and they were quick to catch on. I guess the Carlisle Indians provided me with the easiest coaching job I ever had."

According to Warner, a halfback had to be "a fast, strong runner . . . clever in dodging the opposing tacklers, skilled in warding them off by use of the stiff-arm." "Above all," Warner observed, "they [halfbacks] should be fearless." For Thorpe, who had broken wild horses and regularly faced off against a heavy-fisted father, there was little to fear on the football gridiron. "I never saw him snarl and mostly he just laughed, talked to the other team and enjoyed himself," Warner said. "But even at that you couldn't keep him on the bench. He had a natural change of pace that just floated him past the defense. His reactions were so fast that sometimes you couldn't follow him with the eye.

Punishment didn't mean a thing to him. He was fearless and he hit so hard that the other fellow got all the bruises."

"Dad could take the pain and inflict it," Jack Thorpe remembered. "He had the ability to control his own fury."

Kicking came as naturally to Thorpe as running. With a quick two-step approach, he could consistently punt a football sixty yards and had the speed to cover his own punts. Years after his playing days, Thorpe told his son Bill Thorpe his punting secret. "Dad told me, it is the position and the drop of the ball," Bill Thorpe recalled years later. "You drop the ball just so to get the right spiral and the right rhythm. It's a lot like a golf swing."

As usual, Warner scheduled several conditioning games before the heavy competition of the 1908 season. The season opened at the Carlisle field on September 19, when the Indians faced off against Conway Hall, the prep school for Dickinson College in Carlisle. Al Payne started at halfback for Carlisle, but after he had the wind knocked out of him, Thorpe came into the game. Thorpe ran for five touchdowns of fifty yards or more and lofted a thirty-yard touchdown pass to Pete Hauser. That was all in the first half. Pop benched his star for the second half of the game. The following week, the Indians defeated Lebanon Valley College just as decisively.

The Indians ran into difficulties in their third matchup of the season. Facing off against Villanova College on September 26 with Thorpe on the bench, the game was a scoreless tie late in the second half. The crowd of Indian cadets, band members in their red and gold uniforms, and the Carlisle women in their large, fashionable hats began screaming, "We want Jim! We want Jim!"

Finally, Pop tapped Thorpe on the shoulder and sent him into the game. "What followed was the single most dramatic play I have ever seen in sports," recalled one eyewitness. "Jim took the very first handoff and blasted into the line with the loudest crash I have ever heard. When he was able to continue into their backfield, I couldn't believe my eyes! He didn't use one block on his way to the goal line seventy yards away while all the time he kept hollering, 'Out of my way! Get out of my way!'" After the touchdown, Warner pulled Thorpe out. The game was Carlisle's, and Warner did not want to risk an injury to his star so early in the season.

The significant games of the season began on October 3, when

Warner and the Carlisle Indians traveled to Wilkes-Barre, Pennsylvania, for their first away game, against the Nittany Lions of Penn State. The game showed Warner the strengths and weaknesses of his 1908 team. At the time, coaches were not allowed to coach the players on the field from the sidelines, and quarterbacks called their own plays. The Carlisle quarterback, Mike Balenti, was good at execution but did not have the game sense of Mt. Pleasant, the quarterback of the previous year. Fumbles and bad ball handling crippled the Carlisle attack. Penn State blocked a punt and ran it in for a touchdown.

Unable to score a touchdown, Warner told his players to focus on the kicking game. "Thorpe drops back, the little quarterback (Balenti) kneels on the ground, the Indian forwards dovetail themselves into a tight line of defense," wrote a journalist describing the Carlisle Indian field-goal-kicking operation. "The ball is shot back hard to the little quarter [back], quickly placed on the ground and bing! The cunning toe of Thorpe sends it spinning between the goal posts and four points go up on the scoreboard." The strategy worked as Jim Thorpe kicked three field goals and Carlisle won the game 12–5.

The next week, October 10, 1908, the Indians traveled for a game at Syracuse. Fresh from a victory over Yale, the Orangemen were looking forward to a thumping win over the Indians. Warner had been at work the previous week, telling the press that his team was beat up, demoralized, out of shape, and almost certain to lose. At practice before the game, Warner continued the charade, leading his players with bandaged fingers and heads through a listless practice.

Once the game began, the Indians proved that they were not hurting. Speed was the key to their performance in the 12–0 victory over the Orangemen. The win was highlighted by the speed of Thorpe and the other backs, the speed of the pass receivers, the speed of the defense, and the speed of ends and backs who seemed to get downfield way before any punted ball. "Indians on Warpath, Scalp Syracuse Braves," the *New York Tribune* reported. "The real star of the game, however, was Thorpe. The lanky Indian proved himself a great punter. His kicks were high and accurate, allowing his ends plenty of time to get down the field. Invariably when the ball descended there were one or two redmen within reaching distance, and on several occasions an Indian recovered the ball."

With the cancellation of their game against Susquehanna University,

Warner spent a week drilling the team on timing plays for the next contest, one that was sure to be brutal. On October 24, the Carlisle Indians traveled to Philadelphia to play the University of Pennsylvania, their fiercest rival.

As he had before the Syracuse game, Warner tried to gain a pregame advantage by describing to the press the beat-up condition of his team. Philadelphia football fans, eager to avenge the 26–6 loss of the previous year, would have none of it. One writer observed, "We place about as much stock in the ambulance clang that comes from Carlisle as we would in the story of a woman telling how old she is."

At the kickoff, a roaring capacity crowd of twenty-six thousand at Philadelphia's Franklin Field witnessed a bruising defensive battle. Penn's squad was loaded with talent, including two first-team All-Americans, Bill Hollenback at quarterback and H. W. Scarlett at end. The Penn players penetrated the backfield so quickly that Thorpe could not take advantage of his speed or open-field running ability. "Bill Hollenback of Penn, no one was in a class with him as a tackler," Thorpe later explained. "I could sidestep a lot of others or fake them into making foolish dives. But not Bill. When he came at me, I knew it was just a question of how hard he'd hit me. When he did hit me, it was like being struck by a battering ram. If Bill didn't pulverize or half-paralyze the man he hit in a head-on tackle, the man had a shaky feeling for the rest of the game. I know. I was among Bill's victims."

The Quakers scored first on a touchdown, but their ball handling was sloppy, resulting in eight Penn fumbles. The Indians fumbled only once and were able to move the ball, although it looked as though the hard-hitting Penn squad would hang on to its one-touchdown lead. In the second half, Thorpe began a run from scrimmage on the Quaker forty-yard line, sliced through an opening, and threw himself over the goal line for a touchdown. Thorpe converted the extra point to end the scoring for the game in a 6-all tie. It was to be Penn's only tie in an otherwise undefeated season and the only touchdown scored against Penn in 1908. Thorpe later described the contest as "the toughest game in my twenty-two years of college and professional football." It was tough on the fans as well. Some of the Carlisle girls who had come to the game cheered so much that they lost their voices.

On October 31, 1908, the Indians traveled to Annapolis for a game against Navy. Thorpe was suffering from a painfully sprained ankle.

He could play, but he could not kick. Luckily for the Carlisle team, there were other strong legs available. Mike Balenti took over the field-goal-kicking duties. Although he had never tried to kick a field goal in a game, he kicked four field goals that day, two from more than forty-five yards, to give the Indians a 16–6 victory over the Midshipmen. "I asked him afterwards how he did it," Warner recalled, "and he answered gravely that he had 'watched' Thorpe and Mt. Pleasant."

The next week, the Indians traveled to Cambridge, Massachusetts, to face a physically and numerically superior Harvard Crimson squad that was perhaps the best in the nation. Early in the game, Harvard scooped up an onside kick for a touchdown. The press reported that "Carlisle played some rattling good football." Thorpe and his teammates attacked the Crimson defense with hard line smashes, end runs, and long passes. The Indians brought the ball down to the Harvard two-yard line at one point but could not score a touchdown. Thorpe attempted eight field goals in that game but failed to score. The only time he sent the ball through the uprights was on a fifty-five-yard kickoff for no score. "Harvard Crushes Carlisle's Line," the headline in the *New York Times* accurately reported after the game, which Harvard won 17–0. "Crafty Indians Outplayed in Everything Except Handling Punts."

November 4, 1908, found the Indians in Pittsburgh for a game against the University of Western Pennsylvania. Playing conditions were terrible. The field was soaking wet, which slowed the Indian attack and dampened their morale. Warner, never able to sit on the bench, slogged back and forth across the muddy sidelines, his overshoes taped to his pant legs to keep out the muck. At the time, it was illegal for coaches to coach from the sidelines, and the Western Pennsylvania coach complained to the referee that Warner was giving secret signals to his players with the tape on his boots. Warner did not use the tape for secret signals, but he did indeed have a system of signals for coaching from the sidelines.

Neither Carlisle nor Western Pennsylvania could score until Thorpe burst through right tackle on a run from scrimmage and took the ball into the end zone. Warner's team won, but it was an exhausted bunch of players who boarded the train a few days later for a western swing of four games in fifteen days.

In Minneapolis on November 21, the Indians played poorly and lost 11–6 against the University of Minnesota. The team traveled south by rail to St. Louis and revived, thrashing the University of St. Louis 17–0 on November 26. In covering the Carlisle victory, the *St. Louis Globe Democrat* paid tribute to Jim Thorpe's outstanding performance. "It is said that an Indian neither forgets nor forgives an injury. Mr. Thorpe is a Sac and Fox. No Sac and Fox can either forget or forgive St. Louis. It was St. Louis that made the headmen of the Sac and Fox nation drunk and induced them in this condition to sign away the tribal lands. Mr. Thorpe humiliated us nicely, which was just as it should have been. It was coming to us."

Carlisle next defeated the University of Nebraska 31–6. The Nebraska papers praised the performance of the "Aborigines" and their "wonderful interference that sometimes bowled over as many as five or six Cornhuskers." In the devastating victory over Nebraska, Thorpe displayed the tremendous leg drive and running ability later described by a fellow Carlisle student, Vic "Choc" Kelley Sr. ("Choc" was short for Choctaw). "Often you'd see him knock out would-be tacklers simply by running right over the top of them. He didn't try to overpower you if he didn't have to, for Jim was a snaky ball carrier in a broken field. He gave you the leg and then took it away. . . . When you're talking about Big Jim's football ability you can't exaggerate. He was just the greatest, that's all."

At Denver, the team played the University of Denver, the Rocky Mountains Conference champion team, in the snow on a hard, frozen field. Jim fumbled and was shaken so badly after one play that his teammates had to call a time-out. Hauser kicked the two field goals that gave Carlisle the victory, 8–4.

Despite their two losses, the 1908 Carlisle football team had a lot to be proud of. In particular, Thorpe was proud to be named to Walter Camp's third-team All-American squad, largely for his kicking ability. Warner's athletic association collected about $26,000 from ticket sales, a lot less than it had in 1907. Still, Warner distributed $1,283 in loans and payments to his football players. Perhaps in response to the decrease in revenue, or perhaps due to pressure from reformers and critics of the Carlisle program, Warner stopped rewarding his athletes with loans or outright payments after the 1908 season. This did not sit well with Thorpe.

Perhaps it was the income squeeze. Or perhaps it was because his growing fame as an athlete made it all too easy for him to accept toasts from sports fans in downtown Carlisle and at local taverns on the road for postgame celebrations. Or perhaps it was the strict and aloof leadership of the Carlisle superintendent Friedman, who canceled the popular receptions attended by male and female students and required every student to carry a calendar card marked with required events. For whatever reason, Jim's classroom performance deteriorated after the 1908 football season. The story "Co-Fa-Che-Qui" by James Thorpe did appear in the *Carlisle Arrow*, the school newspaper, in the fall of 1908, but in February 1909, Thorpe left campus without permission along with fellow student Sampson Burd. Again in March, the two students left campus without permission. In a letter to the Sac and Fox Indian agent in Oklahoma, a concerned school superintendent Moses Friedman described Thorpe as "far from being a desirable student."

Thorpe continued to be a desirable athlete. He played basketball in the winter and was the captain of the 1909 Carlisle track team. Thorpe's natural ability carried him to victory after victory. He won gold medals in the high jump; the shot put; and two hurdle events, the 50 and the 220 yards, at the Georgetown University Athletic Association meet. He took silver in the 100-yard hurdles and gold in the shot put and long jump at the Johns Hopkins University meet.

Warner claimed that he did not fully appreciate the amazing athletic talent of Jim Thorpe until the Carlisle-Syracuse dual meet in May 1909. Thorpe won first place in the 120-yard hurdles, the 220-yard hurdles, the 16-pound shot and the running long jump, and won one second and two third places as well. He broke the Carlisle school records in the 220-yard hurdles and led Carlisle to a commanding victory.

"In the spring I tried him out in hurdling and jumping, and almost at once he became the star of the team," Warner later explained of the 1909 track season. "There seemed nothing he could not do, and whenever we needed points to win a meet, I would wait until Jim finished on the track and then throw him in the weight events. The 100-yard dash, the 120-yard and the 220-yard hurdles, the broad jump and high jump were his specialties, but he could also throw the hammer and put the shot with the best."

Thorpe's teammate Louis Tewanima performed just as well in a tough series of indoor and outdoor events. "A skinny little chap, never weighing more than 110 pounds, Tewanima proceeded to clean up everything that America had to offer in ten- and fifteen-mile races," Warner later recalled.

On Monday night, January 25, 1909, Tewanima entered a ten-mile indoor race presented by New York's Pastime Athletic Club at Madison Square Garden and billed as "the biggest ten-mile running race ever held indoors." According to Warner, "After looking at the track, which was ten laps to the mile, he [Tewanima] turned to me and said: 'Me afraid get mixed up go round and round. You tell me front man and I get him.' "

Tewanima started the race with fifty-six others including the favorite, Jimmy Lee of Boston. Four thousand excited fans cheered the runners for the first five miles as Tewanima held tight with the leaders, running his race in a succession of sprints from fifty to one hundred yards long.

"Along about the middle of the race I began to catch his eye and point out some runner who led him," Warner recalled, "and one by one he picked them up." In the last few miles, the race came down to a contest between Tewanima and Lee. "In the third lap of the ninth mile, Tewa closed on Lee and for a few strides passed him," the press reported. "Lee sprinted into the lead again at once, and the Indian hung on at his heels. As they finished the ninth mile, Tewanima again moved to the front and shook off Lee's efforts to sprint past him. Again and again in the final mile Lee tried to regain the lead, but Tewanima held. . . . When the warning at the beginning of the last half mile was given, Tewanima started a sprint that completely finished Lee, the Indian winning in commanding style in 54:27.4–5." The record-setting win sent the New York crowd into a frenzy and cata- pulted Tewanima's name into the headlines across the country. The *New York Herald* described the victory of "the tawny little aborigine" as "one of the pluckiest exhibitions seen in an athletic contest in this vicinity in years."

"It came close to proving a costly trip, however," Warner later recalled of the New York journey, "for I put Tewanima and two other Hopi runners in a hotel room and forgot to tell them about the gas. As a consequence, they blew it out. But for an open window there would have been three dead Indians. As it was, they were unconscious when I found them the next morning, and it was some time before we could bring them back to normal."

On another trip, Tewanima's teammates convinced the Hopi athletes that they had to pay every time they rode the hotel elevator to their rooms. At the end of the meet, Coach Warner was getting into the elevator when he noticed Tewanima and some other Hopi starting for the stairs. "Hey, there," he called, "what's the idea of walking?"

One of the Hopi turned to Warner and said, "No more money."

Tewanima became more sophisticated as he and Warner traveled to races across the country in the winter and spring of 1909. On February 6, Tewanima ran in a five-mile race in Boston. On the thirteenth, he ran in a fifteen-mile race in St. Louis. On the twentieth, he won a twenty-mile race in New Orleans in the time of 2 hours and 10 minutes, and a day after his return to the East Coast he won a ten-mile run in Trenton. Tewanima, who was one of the hardest workers Warner had ever seen, continued to dominate American distance running over the next two years. In April 1910 he won a five-mile race in Buffalo, a five-mile race in Pittsburgh, and set a new world's indoor record for the ten-mile, in New York City. On May 6, 1911, Tewanima won the *Evening Mail* Modified Marathon in New York City. "Tewanima's running was the most remarkable I have ever seen for a street race," said James E. Sullivan, whose organization, the AAU, hosted the event, "and when I say this I don't exaggerate in the least."

"The little Hopi is the greatest amateur runner in this country and probably in the world for distances of from twelve to twenty miles," Warner told the press. "Every one who knows him admires his gameness and the modest and unassuming way in which he takes his victories. He is the easiest athlete to train that I ever handled, because he has no bad habits, follows instructions, and never shirks practice."

Thorpe enjoyed track, but he was much more interested in playing baseball. After the last Carlisle track meet, he joined fellow football player Joe Libby on the Carlisle baseball team for the tail end of their twenty-seven-game schedule and pitched a 1–0 shutout against Millersville State before the end of the season.

As Thorpe and Tewanima made headlines and dominated the 1909 track season, Warner had a difficult time controlling his increasingly independent and unruly players. The Carlisle school newspaper reported on March 26, 1909 that Warner gave a stern talking to the track and baseball athletes, telling them that they were not wanted on the team if they did not live up to the rules. On April 30, the paper reported that a member of the baseball team and three members of the track team were dropped from athletics for breaking training rules. In his annual report, released in June 1909, Superintendent Friedman commented obliquely on the situation and wrote, "It has been impressed upon the students that . . . the various sports must be conducted in a thoroughly amateur way and absolutely free from everything savoring of professionalism."

Thorpe enjoyed winning for Carlisle, but he was no fool. He knew that the only game that paid was baseball. He knew all about Charles Albert Bender, the Carlisle student who had played for Warner and who was now one of the stars of the Philadelphia Athletics in the American League. Every summer Thorpe watched other athletes from Carlisle head out to play semiprofessional ball for pay. Mike Balenti, the 1908 quarterback, played baseball for the St. Paul Apostles in the American Association. Bill Newashe went to Atlantic City to play for a hotel team for room, board, and tips.

"He [Jim] had his mind set on a professional career," Warner later admitted. "Many a time he moaned to me, 'What's the use of bothering with all this [track] stuff? There's nothing in it.'

"Once as we were returning home from a meet he came through the train smoking a big cigar," Warner recalled. " 'Shucks, Pop, I'm through with track. It's me for baseball.' Pulling him down beside me, I pointed out the duty he owed to his school and to his race, and after a while he heaved a deep sigh and groaned, 'Oh, all right then, but I'd rather play baseball.' "

College athletes playing summer ball was such a common practice that many managers actively recruited college and prep school athletes for their teams. W. S. Wilkinson Sr., the secretary-treasurer of the newly formed Rocky Mount Railroaders, a ball club in the Eastern Carolina League, sent a telegram to his acquaintance Barney Dreyfuss, the president of the Pittsburgh Pirates, asking Dreyfuss to help him recruit players. Somehow the word from Rocky Mount got to Carlisle, and Joe Libby and Jesse Youngdeer signed to play. Thorpe went along with them. Libby later told Jim Thorpe's son Jack Thorpe that Warner was the one who set the boys up with the team in North

Carolina. Written records of such an arrangement have yet to be found, but Warner was the contact person at Carlisle for all athletic activities. If a member of the Pittsburgh Pirates' organization was scouting for ballplayers at Carlisle, he most probably would have contacted Warner.

Warner could hardly blame Thorpe and the other Carlisle Indians for wanting to play baseball. After all, Warner himself was a frustrated baseball player. But Warner later claimed that he tried to discourage his star athlete. "Thorpe finished his five-year term in 1909 after a brilliant year in track and on the gridiron," Warner later recalled, "and all of the officials urged him to stay on and graduate, but he insisted that he must return to his home in Oklahoma. That is where we supposed he went."

Not everyone supposed that Thorpe returned to Oklahoma. He met with Superintendent Friedman and requested a leave so he could play summer ball. Friedman argued with Thorpe. He told Thorpe that he had been given leave the previous summer with the understanding that he would come back to Carlisle and complete his studies, which he had not done. Thorpe was adamant in his desire to leave. Reluctantly, Friedman gave his permission. Just a few days after competing in the Middle Atlantic Association track and field meet in Philadelphia, Thorpe left Carlisle.

"A couple of Carlisle ballplayers, named Joseph Libby and Jesse Youngdeer, were going to North Carolina that summer to play baseball," Thorpe later recalled. "I didn't enjoy farming, so I tagged along, just for the trip."

Thorpe's official school record stated that he was "granted a summer leave to play baseball in the South."

13

Rocky Mount Railroader

T horpe, Joe Libby, and Jesse Youngdeer stepped off the train at
Rocky Mount, North Carolina, and made their way to the
Cambridge Hotel, just a few blocks from the depot. They
met W. E. Fenner, the manager of the Rocky Mount Railroaders.
Libby and Youngdeer changed into their uniforms and walked the
half-dozen blocks or so to the Rocky Mount Railroaders' home field,
Railroaders Park, while Thorpe watched the practice from the wooden
bleachers.

Rocky Mount was not the big time. It was a team in a Class D
minor league, the Eastern Carolina League, a recently formed collection of clubs from Wilson, Goldsboro, Wilmington, and three other
bright-leaf tobacco towns situated along North Carolina's coastal
plain. Fenner was excited about having Libby and Youngdeer on the
team. The season had begun in May, about a month before their
arrival, but the Rocky Mount team had not been doing so well, and
the crowds at the ball park had been shrinking. The manager was
certain that the Indian athletes would spark the team's play and boost
game attendance, especially the speedy left fielder Youngdeer. Thorpe
reported this story of how he wound up on the field after traveling with
his Carlisle teammates to Rocky Mount:

> Libby and Youngdeer were fair outfielders and they caught on
> with the Rocky Mount team. I became short of money, the

manager offered me fifteen dollars a week to play third base; I took it. There were a lot of other college boys playing around there too. I played my first game at Raleigh. After a while, the manager asked me if I could pitch. I told him I would give it a whirl.

Youngdeer was playing left field and Libby was playing right field on June 15, 1909, when Fenner sent Thorpe in to play third base in the sixth inning against the Raleigh Red Birds. Jim struck out his first two times at bat as the Railroaders lost 5–1. The next day, Thorpe took the mound, pitching for the Railroaders against Raleigh. He did well, allowing only five hits while connecting for two of his own, including a "leg hit," a bunt down the third-base line in the Railroaders' 4–1 victory over the Red Birds. "Thorpe, the Carlisle Indian and All-American half back," reported the *Raleigh News Observer* of June 17, only slightly incorrectly (he had been a third-team All-American), "proved to be very effective in the box."

In the games that followed, Thorpe's blinding speed and bold playing style attracted the attention of fans and the press. One person who saw Thorpe play recalled that Thorpe "ran the bases with the speed and ferocity of a whirlwind." Thorpe enjoyed his growing celebrity and the adulation it brought, especially from local children. Whenever the Railroaders played a home game, a crowd of youngsters gathered at their hotel to escort them on the walk to the ball field. "Each boy sought the privilege of carrying the shoes or glove or bat for one of the ballplayers," recalled Thomas McMillan Sr., who was one of the boys. "Big Jim seemed to favor me as his shoe and glove caddy." Years later McMillan, whom Jim called "Sonny," could still picture the twenty-two-year-old Thorpe "so unmistakably Indian—the face a mahogany color compared with the white ballplayers, the high cheek bones and the alert, dark eyes. He stood about ten feet tall in my eyes. It was more strength and speed than just size. To me he was always a gentle-man, a very gentle person."

The pay was not much, just $15 to $25 per week. It was less in terms of money and other considerations that he had received from playing college football for Pop Warner, but it was more than Thorpe had earned doing farmwork on the Carlisle outing system for $8 a month. Still, the pay was so low that Thorpe still relied on his income from his Oklahoma lands. In a letter dated July 12, 1909, from Rocky Mount, Thorpe wrote to Indian agent W. C. Kohlenberg, "Will you please send my annuity and lease money here at Rocky Mount where I am staying for the summer? . . . If you have sent the money to Carlisle please recall it for I am not at school any more. Resp, James Thorpe."

Neither Thorpe nor his teammates Youngdeer and Libby gave a moment's thought to the fact that they were playing semiprofessional sports and might be jeopardizing their standing as amateurs. All of them played under their own names, which the major eastern Carolina newspapers printed in the box scores daily. It probably never occurred to the Indian athletes that playing ball was any different from any other summer job. It was just more fun and more lucrative. Years later, when Jim Thorpe's son, Jack , asked Joe Libby if he had realized that he was playing semipro ball, Libby answered, "You've got to understand, that in 1909, we were having a rough time speaking English. We didn't know what the law was. We didn't know we were playing semipro ball. We didn't even call it that. We called it summer ball."

The issue of amateurism was not a major concern in the rough-and-ready Eastern Carolina League. The big worry for the Railroaders manager was making sure that he had enough players on the field. On July 7, 1909, the *Raleigh News Observer* reported that several Rocky Mount players became "revolvers," meaning they left the team to play for another. "After scouring the earth for baseball material the local management have landed on three men who they have every reason to believe are of the topnotch variety and will materially strengthen the Railroaders." Other players frequently came and went during the season. By late August, Thorpe was the only Carlisle player left in the Rocky Mount lineup. Youngdeer and Libby had washed out soon after joining the squad.

Even when the Railroaders could field a team, they did not always finish the game. After the team fell behind the Wilson Tobacconists by nine runs, the Railroaders manager claimed that the balls were being doctored. He forced the umpire to throw away so many balls that play was suspended so that the Wilson manager could leave the field to buy new balls. Before the Wilson manger returned to the stadium with the new balls, the Railroaders had quit the game. The umpire's official report read, "Rocky Mount refused to play further on the grounds the balls had been doctored."

Worse than the ball-tampering accusations were charges that Thorpe's team was throwing games to keep the Wilson Tobacconists from winning the pennant. A sworn affidavit appeared in the press from a player who claimed that the Railroaders' manager told him that "Rocky Mount has promised to throw all of her games to Wilmington." Another affidavit claimed that one of the Rocky Mount players said that "they would give Fayetteville every game played with them." Still another affidavit claimed that "one of [the Rocky Mount players] wanted to bet five dollars" that Fayetteville would sweep an upcoming series of three games.

Despite all the controversy, Thorpe enjoyed playing semipro baseball. He was a streaky player known at different times as "the iron man of the league" and a "goof-off." During one game, the Railroaders catcher got so fed up with Jim's slack pitching that he walked out to the mound and told Jim to throw faster. Jim reared back and threw the ball so hard it knocked the catcher off his feet. The catcher returned to the mound in a fury and told Jim never to hurl the ball that hard again. During another game, the press reported that "Big Chief [Thorpe] had a smile on, and kept the fans laughing at his little witticisms."

What he enjoyed most was the freedom to do what he wanted when he was not playing or practicing, a freedom he had not enjoyed while at Indian boarding schools. With Phifer Fullenwider, whom Jim dubbed "Cutie," and other newfound baseball buddies, Thorpe ate well, drank well, and had a great time raising hell.

" 'Big Chief' On Rampage," read the headline in the *News Observer* on August 27, 1909. "Indian Pitcher Thorpe of Rocky Mount Arrested; Took Three Policemen to Put Him in Raleigh Lockup for Disorder on the Street." According to the press report, Thorpe's "rampage" began at one of the "near beer" places on Exchange Street in Raleigh, when he got into a disagreement with one of his teammates. The disagreement turned into a fight, and the police were called in to break things up. Thorpe's teammate escaped before the authorities arrived, but Thorpe was not as lucky. "In getting the belligerent Indian into the lockup," the newspaper reported, "[Thorpe] had to be dragged bodily down steps, putting up a vigorous resistance." Thorpe spent the night in jail, paid a fine the next morning, and rejoined his ball club. On another occasion, when four policemen tried to subdue Thorpe, he reportedly deposited one of the law enforcement officials "into a trash can."

As the season drew to a close, three of the six teams in the Eastern Carolina League claimed the pennant. T. M. Washington, the president of the league, submitted his resignation and told the press that his former league was a "laughingstock." Amid the furor over doctored balls, fixed games, and final standings, Thorpe had performed fairly well in forty-four games as a pitcher and as an infielder for Rocky Mount. He had won nine games, lost ten, and batted .253 for the season. More impressive than his throwing ability or his hitting was his speed. "He hit a grounder in the hole toward third base," recalled John Glancy, who played shortstop for the Fayetteville Highlanders. "I came up with the ball all right but my second baseman hollered over, 'Hold it—don't throw! He's already there.' That's how fast Thorpe was getting down to first base."

Joe Libby returned to Carlisle in the fall of 1909, but Thorpe did not. As the season drew to a close, there were rumors that big-league scouts were about to sign him, but nothing materialized. Broke and out of work, twenty-two-year-old Thorpe made his way back to Oklahoma, where his friends and relatives helped him get by. At his sister Mary's farm, Thorpe did chores in exchange for room and board and kept his eye out for athletic opportunities.

While Jim was enjoying his relatives' hospitality, Joe Libby played football for Pop Warner as captain of the 1909 team. Since Warner was a micromanager who wanted to know all he could about his players, it is almost impossible to believe that he did not hear about Libby's experiences with Thorpe playing baseball in the Eastern Carolina League.

The 1909 football season was a tough one for Captain Joe Libby and the rest of the Carlisle football squad. Sloppy play led to a decisive 29–6 defeat of the Indians by the University of Pennsylvania, the first Penn victory over Carlisle in four years. The Indians also lost to the University of Pittsburgh and to Brown. Despite their lackluster performance, the team traveled to Cincinnati, Ohio, for their last game of the season, a Thanksgiving Day matchup against St. Louis University. The game had a personal component. Bill Warner, Pop's brother, was coaching the St. Louis University football team. The Carlisle Indians played one of their best games of the season, gaining 417 yards on the ground and 161 in the air to defeat St. Louis 32–0. The Carlisle players may have been inspired in part by the knowledge that their former teammate Jim Thorpe was sitting in the grandstand, cheering them on.

Warner had invited Thorpe to the game, no doubt to convince him to return to Carlisle. While the team returned to Carlisle after the game, Warner took Jim Thorpe hunting in eastern Oklahoma. Both the coach and the summer baseball player were avid hunters. As they spent time together shooting dove, turkey, and deer, Warner and Thorpe talked about the future. Though there are no records of their discussion, Warner probably praised Thorpe's athletic ability and his unrealized potential as both a football player and a track star. Warner probably emphasized that Jim had the chance to generate a great deal of publicity for himself, publicity that would eventually pay off financially. It is impossible to believe that while the two were out hunting, Thorpe and Warner did not talk about Thorpe's experiences playing summer baseball in North Carolina.

When he left Oklahoma, Warner invited Thorpe to return to Carlisle. Thorpe did indeed travel back to Carlisle, accompanying some Sac and Fox students to the school, and he spent Christmas 1909 in Pennsylvania with his former school chums. After the holidays, Thorpe headed back home to Oklahoma but promised to return in the spring. Thorpe never made good on his promise, but instead headed to North Carolina in the spring of 1910 to play another season as a Rocky Mount Railroader. On March 15, 1910, the Carlisle school paper reported that three Carlisle students, including Bill Newashe, had left for Harrisburg to play baseball with the Harrisburg semipro team during the upcoming season.

This was too much for Warner. Frustrated from losing his promising athletes to small-time professional baseball, Warner convinced Superintendent Moses Friedman to drop baseball as a sport at Carlisle in 1910 "because of summer professionalism." Warner went so far as to send out a press release announcing that the dropping of the sport at Carlisle "marked one of the most advanced steps taken in the country and the wisdom of the move is now being recognized by the best colleges and universities." For baseball Warner substituted lacrosse at Carlisle, a sport that was popular with the Indian students and actually generated more income for the athletic association than baseball. Pop declared, "Athletics at Carlisle are here for the students, not the students here for athletics."

Friedman was eager for positive publicity to offset some unfortunate press concerning other matters at Carlisle. In 1909, James Wheelock, the student leader of the Carlisle band, complained to federal authorities about what he felt was unfair incarceration of some of his fellow band-members in the school guardhouse. The Indian Office in Washington conducted a full investigation of the matter, held that Friedman's actions were justified, and exonerated him.

Unfortunately, Friedman's problems did not end there. In February 1911, Charles F. Pierce, a government auditor, examined Carlisle's enrollment lists and discovered that the school's books carried the names of 186 phantom pupils who were not in attendance but for whom the school had received federal compensation in excess of $32,000.

Although Friedman avoided any serious censure, the investigations left an open wound on campus. The students had little affection for or trust in Friedman, and Friedman, an aloof administrator, had little understanding of the students at his school. Friedman did not even have the trust of his faculty, particularly John Whitwell, an Englishman who served as the principal at Carlisle and who clashed with Friedman on numerous occasions. Unbeknownst to Friedman, Whitwell kept a meticulous record of his interactions with the superintendent that he would later make public.

Carlisle was not the only school having trouble with summer base-ball, which had been under attack in the press for many years. The muckraker Henry Beach Needham wrote in *McClure's* magazine in 1905, "No question relating to the amateur standing of athletes engaged in intercollegiate sports has produced more rabid discussion, with opinion greatly divided, than the proposal (sic) of 'summer ball.'" The *New York Times* reported on January 5, 1908, that college author-ities were concerned that the evil of payment for college baseball might start "infecting the whole fabric of intercollegiate athletics." Echoing the class prejudice of Caspar Whitney and other supporters of amateurism, the *Times* quoted academics who harshly criticized student athletes "who need money so badly that they must sacrifice their amateur standing." Some college administrators took the opposite opinion and flagrantly encouraged athletes to play summer baseball. "I believe in it," said Mike Murphy, a well-known Yale trainer and Warner protégé. "I think it's all right. A man has a right to get his board and take twenty-five dollars a week to help him through college."

Some radical reformers believed that the amateur athletic clubs were as bad as professional baseball teams and leveled serious accusations against the Amateur Athletic Union (AAU) and its iron-fisted administrator, James Sullivan. In June 1910, James B. Connolly, the American who won the first gold medal in the modern Olympics, published a blistering attack on the AAU in *Metropolitan Magazine*. Connolly told his readers that "amateur" athletes were "at the mercy of a body of men who are exploiting them in the interests of one of the most grasping, hide-bound 'trusts' in the country."

Connolly noted that the AAU had used a number of schemes to compensate athletes without paying them. One of the favorite scams was to award winners gold watches. The athletes called these awards "stock" watches because the athletes could return them to stores, where the watches would be put back into the "stock" while the athlete would be reimbursed with cash.

In his widely circulated attack on Sullivan and the AAU, Connolly mentioned the case of Charles W. Paddock, a world champion sprinter. Paddock claimed that promoters gained control over "amateur" athletes by paying inexperienced contestants "extra expenses." After taking the expense money, the athletes were at the mercy of the AAU. If they were unwilling to compete at a certain event, the AAU threatened to expose them as professionals, thereby ending their career. It was blackmail designed to protect the power of "amateur" sports promoters.

Connolly also cited the case of Arthur Duffey, another sprinter, who had written an article alleging that he had been paid to perform in athletic events by the AAU. Sullivan refused to give Duffey a hearing and refused to investigate the accused AAU officials. Sullivan simply announced, "Duffey by his own confession, is a professional" and barred him from any future competitions.

This was typical Sullivan. No hearing, no press, no investigation. Any athlete who threatened the AAU system was crushed—quickly and ruthlessly. James Sullivan even banned his own nephew from the game of basketball after his nephew played in a game that was not approved by the AAU.

As AAU officials fought to defend amateurism for athletes, they were paying themselves quite handsomely. In 1910, the AAU paid James E. Sullivan the comfortable salary of $1,500. This was in addition to his salary as an advertising and editorial director for A. G. Spalding's company. Sullivan had no problem using his powerful position in the world of amateur sports to bolster the Spalding bottom line. As America's leading manufacturer of balls, shoes, and other athletic equipment, and as the publisher of rulebooks and the Spalding Athletic Library, Sullivan's company was in the uniquely profitable position of being able to protect itself from the competition. For example, when Johnnie Garrells, a University of Michigan athlete, set a world record in the discus at an intercollegiate meet, his record was rejected by Sullivan and the AAU. The reason? The discus used was not regulation. And who made the only regulation discus? Spalding.

At the time, a favorite joke among amateur athletes was about a sprinter who crossed the finish line in record time. The official asked him, "Do you wear Spalding shoes?"

"No," admitted the sprinter.

"Well," the official said, "you don't get any record."

Connolly ended his article with the observation, "Every young man who registers as an AAU athlete today is simply another advertising agent for the Athletic Goods Trust."

It was as if one man, James Sullivan, were the head of *Sports Illustrated*, Nike, ESPN, the NCAA, and the U.S. Olympic Committee. Sullivan's power in the American world of track and field was almost absolute, and he wielded that power without hesitation.

While muckrakers attacked the athletic trust, Thorpe returned to Rocky Mount to play for the 1910 season. He arrived on May 1, three weeks before the season opener but threw so hard in practice that he injured his arm. After recovering from his injury, he batted .236 in twenty-nine games. His fearless baserunning was more remarkable than his batsmanship. In the bottom of the ninth, in a scoreless game against Wilson, Jim took off from first base when his teammate bounced a single to right field. Jim rounded second, rounded third, and headed for home. When he was twenty-five feet from the plate, Jim let out a whoop and jumped into the air with his spikes first, ready to tag the catcher or home plate, whichever got in his way first. Thorpe spiked home plate and won the game. The league ended the season on July 23 because Fayetteville had such a commanding lead in the league that fans had stopped coming to the games.

On August 12, Jim was traded to the Fayetteville Highlanders, where he played in sixteen games and batted .250. According to one of his Fayetteville teammates, Pete Boyle, "Thorpe did not burn up the league either as a pitcher or a first baseman but he was a willing worker and was always valuable on account of his great speed. He could circle the bases like a deer, and his running always made a hit with the crowds. . . . During a benefit a running race was arranged between Thorpe and myself as one of the features. I kept up with him for about a few yards, but soon I was lost in the rear."

As he had the previous season, Thorpe earned about $60 a month, and he enjoyed spending time with his team. On a hunting trip, some-one clicked a photo of Thorpe in his Fayetteville uniform, happily posing with his ballplaying buddies. Charley Clancy, the team manager, liked the photo so much that he kept it on his office wall. Toward the end of the season, Thorpe was hit with a thrown ball while trying to steal second. Blood gushed from his head. The crowd gasped, but according to the press, "The big Indian sat down on the plate and laughed." Thorpe spent his last few games as a Highlander in a hospital bed.

After recovering from his injury, Thorpe returned to Oklahoma, where he once again traded chores for room and board at the farms of friends and relatives. In October 1910, he requested that the Sac and Fox agent, Kohlenberg, retrieve any funds he might have from Carlisle so he could purchase a horse and buggy for his farmwork. Displeased by the request, Superintendent Friedman responded, "It is customary at this school, when students desert, that all funds to their credit are held until they return or until the matter is given special consideration after their original term of enrolment has expired." Friedman refused to send Jim's money but did forward two checks that had been received but not deposited to his account. Jim eventually bought his horse and buggy.

On June 12, 1911, Thorpe wrote to Kohlenberg from Anadarko inquiring about any lease money the agent might have. Thorpe told Kohlenberg, "If the money is in your charge, I wish you would send it out here to me. I am playing baseball here with the Anadarko team."

If the Rocky Mountain Railroaders played Class D ball, Thorpe's team from Anadarko, Oklahoma, played Class F. The team did not belong to a formal league and did not even have a name. But according to the *Anadarko Tribune*, they did quite well. By the first week of June, the Anadarko team was undefeated, the paper noted, and pulled off few "boneheads," as poor plays were called. After Anadarko took two games from Marlow, the paper proudly reported, "Anadarko has a team that ranks alone among many of the league teams in this section—every man on it draws a salary."

By June 21, 1911, the team had won thirteen straight games, but the club's financial situation was a bit shaky. "Money talks in baseball as well as in any other line of business," the *Anadarko Tribune* admonished its tightfisted readers. "You can't support a league team unless you are willing to dig up a little coin of the realm." By the end of July the Anadarko Champions, as they were then called, were drawing more than a thousand spectators to games they played against league teams from Oklahoma City and Chicago. With a record of forty-five wins and only four losses, Anadarko fought "a battle royal for the amateur championship of the state" with a team from Chectoal, Oklahoma, a series that ended in a tie.

By the time of the championship series, Thorpe was no longer with the team. According to one version of the story, the Anadarko manager fired Thorpe for breaking training rules. "Okay," Thorpe told the manager, "you're going to spend a nickel to read about me sometime." Thorpe had a more practical explanation for his firing. In a letter to the Sac and Fox agent, W. C. Kohlenberg, dated July 25, 1911, Thorpe requested $35. "I am not playing ball here any more," Thorpe wrote from Anadarko. "The mgr. said I was too expensive and that he had a cheaper man to take my place. It has been two weeks since I stoped. I need $35.00 to clear up and get home on and would like to get ready to go back to Carlisle on the first of September."

14

Marvel of the Age

T he person who finally lured Thorpe back to Carlisle was his friend, coach, teammate, and fellow Oklahoman Albert Exendine. Ex, who grew up in Anadarko, claimed that he "bumped into Thorpe on the street" in Anadarko. Perhaps. More likely, Exendine was sent by Warner to find Thorpe.

Broke and unemployed in the early summer of 1911, Thorpe was pleased to see his old friend. Ex was surprised at Thorpe's appearance. The skinny twenty-two-year-old he had known two years before had grown "big as a mule," standing 5 feet 11 inches and weighing 185 pounds. Ex later claimed that he phoned Warner after meeting Thorpe and told the Carlisle coach that Thorpe was in great shape. "Pop was a man of action," Ex recalled, "and it wasn't long until they had a man down here and Jim on the way back to Pennsylvania."

Warner later claimed that he wrote Thorpe a letter letting him know that he would be welcomed back to Carlisle and that he might be able to qualify for the Olympic games of 1912. Superintendent Friedman opposed readmitting Thorpe to Carlisle but acquiesced to Warner. "Of course," Exendine recalled, "Warner sorely wanted Jim's return to the Indian backfield. Pop realized his fat salary checks would not continue if he had another season like 1910." With eight wins and six losses, the 1910 football season had been Warner's worst season since 1901, when the Indians had won only five and lost seven.

According to Thorpe, when he arrived back at Carlisle in September 1911, Warner asked him. "Where have you been?"

Thorpe answered, "Playing ball."

"I never made any secret about it," Thorpe later explained about his first days back at Carlisle. "I often told the boys, with the coaches listening, about things that happened while I was at Rocky Mount."

Thorpe wrote to the Sac and Fox agent, requesting $50 for clothing and incidentals. "I have decided to stay [at Carlisle] for two years longer," Thorpe wrote to the agent, Kohlenberg, on September 24, 1911. "I think we will have a winning team this fall."

When Thorpe loped onto the Carlisle practice field for the first time in more than two years, he saw many familiar and supportive faces. The team captain was one of Thorpe's old running buddies: Sampson "Sam" Burd had literally run away from Carlisle with Thorpe in 1909. Henry Roberts had played scrub football with Thorpe at Haskell. After leaving Haskell, Roberts was recruited by Warner to play for Carlisle and earned a salary of $75 per month for doing minor clerical work. At tackle was Bill Newashe, a Sac and Fox who had traveled with Thorpe from Oklahoma for the 1909 football season and who played semipro baseball in Harrisburg in the summer of 1910. Two years younger than Thorpe, the 185-pound Bill Newashe had nothing but respect for his fellow Oklahoman. "A lot of people think Jim was all out for himself. He wasn't. . . . At Carlisle he was strictly a team man. Not exactly a leader but [he] was always encouraging the players and was good for the morale of the team." Newashe told a reporter many years later, "I'm proud to be a Sac and Fox Indian—the same as Jim and [I'm] proud to be able to be good enough to be Jim Thorpe's teammate."

One of the most talented newcomers was eighteen-year-old Gustavus Welch. Born on December 23, 1892, and raised in the lumber and lake country of northern Wisconsin, Welch was the son of an Irish logger father and a Chippewa mother. After his father died in a logging accident and his mother and five of his siblings succumbed to tuberculosis, Welch was raised by his grandmother, Chemamanon, the wife of Kewanzee, the chief of the La Couriterielle band of Chippewa. Chemamanon, who lived to be well over a hundred years old, taught Welch the traditional Chippewa skills—how to paddle a birch-bark canoe, to harvest wild rice, to collect sugar maple sap, and to trap furs.

Gus Welch did not attend local Indian schools run by the white authorities, but he did want to go to Carlisle to play sports. In 1907, he trapped a wolf, sold its hide, and bought a ticket to Minneapolis to see Thorpe and Carlisle play the University of Minnesota.

Welch arrived in town well before the game. Though he knew only a smattering of English, he managed to locate the hotel where the Carlisle team was staying. Once there, he found two "athletic boys" who could speak Chippewa and persuaded them to introduce him to Pop Warner. Warner was impressed by Welch's size and attitude and invited him to come out to the stadium to work out with the team. After seeing Welch in action, Warner invited him to sit on the bench during the game and encouraged him to apply for admission to Carlisle.

Welch set out for Carlisle in September 1908 along with his twelve-year-old brother Jimmy Welch. It was their first time on a sleeper train. When Gus saw the passengers lying in their berths, he asked the conductor, "When do we sleep here?"

"Do you have a reservation?" the conductor inquired.

"No, no," Gus responded. "We're not from a reservation; we live with our grandmother."

Jimmy Welch did not like Carlisle. He refused to stop speaking Chippewa and soon headed back to Wisconsin. Gus Welch did not mind learning English. He became a star student at Carlisle, a debater, a popular storyteller, and a promising athlete who worked his way up through the Carlisle shop league until he came to the attention of Pop Warner.

When Warner told Welch to move into the special dormitory for the athletic boys, the Chippewa athlete thought he was kidding. Warner had to tell him again the next day. Welch was even more astounded when he was assigned to room with his hero, Jim Thorpe.

Warner could not have picked two better roommates. Two orphans of mixed American Indian–Irish blood, Thorpe and Welch practiced together, studied together, and occasionally partied together. Whereas Thorpe was reticent, Welch loved to talk. The levelheaded Welch did much to temper Thorpe's wilder enthusiasms, and Thorpe admired Welch's academic and social skills. As the months passed, the two football players forged a bond of friendship and admiration that would last a lifetime.

On the practice field, Warner worked Thorpe, Welch, and his other football players, occasionally belting back gulps of "cough medicine" provided by the team trainer. Once again, the rules of the game had been changed. The time of the games was finally standard-ized at four fifteen-minute quarters. Quarterbacks no longer had to throw the ball from five yards to the right or left of the center, doing away with the need to checkerboard the playing field. However, the new rules outlawed passes of more than 20 yards, forcing Warner to alter his aerial attack and develop a quick ground game. He drilled his players to perfect precisely timed running plays. "You goddamn bone-head," Warner often shouted, "you sonofabitch!" Any player who made an error or forgot an assignment got swatted on the rear end by each of his teammates, a punishment that the players enjoyed dish-ing out.

Warner understood that the key to his team was his quarterback, his field commander. "The quarter-back position is without question the most important upon the team," Warner wrote in his football primer. According to Warner, the quarterback had to be the "liveliest, coolest and headiest player among the candidates." For the quarterback job, Warner picked Gus Welch. Though he was small—five feet, nine inches tall, and 155 pounds—Welch was smart and quick, a leader who could get the Carlisle team to perform their best.

"The battle is not always to the strong," Warner maintained, "but to the active, the vigilant, and the brave."

According to Welch, "He [Warner] let us use our own initiative and the more I see of sports the more I realize that was the greatest thing about him."

During practice, Thorpe rarely worked hard on his own initiative. He simply did not see any reason to prove his outstanding natural ability on every practice play. According to the Warner system, however, play execution demanded working at full speed, something Thorpe was often unwilling to do. "Goddamn Indian!" Warner threatened Thorpe at one point. "You don't want to learn. You just want to pout."

According to Warner's secretary Arthur Martin, "He [Thorpe] wouldn't exert himself until he was behind, then work like hell. I recall that many times Pop booted him in the rear end. Or he would put Thorpe on the second team to get what he wanted. Thorpe would tear the Indian first line to rags, then turn and laugh. I saw it. Thorpe was a wonder."

Off the field, Warner enjoyed taking players for a ride in his automobile, a Chalmers-Detroit 30. He painted with his halfback William "Lone Star" Dietz. As he perfected his team, he kept up his public relations efforts. "He [Thorpe] practiced baseball and played amateur baseball since leaving Carlisle," the *New York World* declared on September 4, 1911, "refusing numerous offers to play on prominent league teams."

"This Indian the Athletic Marvel of the Age" blared a profile of Jim Thorpe that appeared in the *Philadelphia Inquirer* and dozens of other papers around the country. "The red blood of his fathers, who, years ago, buried the war hatchet and watched with dimmed eyes the plow point of civilization desecrating his hunting grounds, while his people slowly vanished from the face of the earth, still courses through the veins of the scattered remnants of the race and occasionally so asserts itself in the most warlike of the peaceful pursuits of the paleface that it compels the descendant of the conqueror of his fathers to take the count." The byline on the story read "Jim Nasium," the pseudonym of Warner's public relations man, Hugh Miller.

As was customary, the first games of Carlisle's football season were home games. In 1911 the lopsided scores of these games demonstrated Carlisle's strength: 53–0 against Lebanon Valley College, 32–0 against Muhlenberg College. "I took Thorpe head-on in one play and when I hit the ground I thought my shoulder was broken," remembered Muhlenberg player Walter Reisner, who had actually broken his collarbone. "It was the first time I was glad to be taken out of a game."

The 17–0 victory against local rival Dickinson College featured an eighty-five-yard touchdown run by Thorpe. In the 46–5 victory against Mount St. Mary's College, Thorpe scored touchdowns on runs of twenty-eight, twelve, and sixty-seven yards in the first half.

Gus Welch went down early to Washington, D.C., to scout the

Georgetown team. He did a good job. It took the Indians only seven minutes to move the ball across the Georgetown goal line. In the second period, Thorpe electrified the crowd with a forty-five-yard run. Two passes by the Indians brought the ball downfield again, and a short run by Stansil "Possum" Powell scored another touchdown. Thorpe booted the extra point, then set up another Powell touchdown with a ten-yard end run. Thorpe kicked another extra point. Later, Thorpe faked a kick and set up a touchdown with a good run. Though Thorpe did not score a touchdown, his kicking, running, and ferocious tackling were the keys to Carlisle's stunning 28–5 victory over Georgetown.

"For the Indians," the press reported, "Thorpe stood out head and shoulders over the rest of his teammates, the big fellow carrying the ball time and time again for consistent gains. He did the bulk of Carlisle's punting and showed himself a master of the 'stiff arm' when, toward the last of the game, he skirted left end for twenty yards, evading Hegarty, his first tackler, by toppling the Georgetown man like a tenpin to the ground."

According to another press account, "Not since Custer made his last stand against Sitting Bull at the Little Big Horn has a battle between redskins and palefaces been so ferociously fought as that which was waged on Georgetown field."

The next week, reporters and twelve thousand fans at Pittsburgh's Forbes Field were even more impressed by Thorpe's speed and kicking ability in the game against the University of Pittsburgh. "This person Thorpe was a host in himself," the *Pittsburgh Dispatch* reported. "Tall and sinewy, as quick as a flash and as powerful as a turbine engine, he appeared to be impervious to injury. Kicking from 50 to 70 yards every time his shoe crashed against the ball, he seemed possessed of super-human speed, for wherever the pigskin alighted, there he was, ready either to grab it or to down the Pitt player who secured it. At line-bucking and general all around work, this Sac and Fox shone resplendent and then some."

According to his son Jack Thorpe, "Dad would watch people and figure out their weaknesses. He could intimidate the hell out of anyone. His stiff-arm hit like a punch to the forehead. Some players said that Dad would literally run up their bodies. When they came out of the game, they had cleat marks up their legs and backs."

Twice Thorpe managed to run downfield and catch his own punts. One of these receptions was particularly phenomenal. According to the *Pittsburgh Dispatch*, "[Thorpe] kicked a beautiful long spiral almost to the midst of five Pitt players and got down the field in time to grab the pigskin, shake off three or four would-be tacklers and dart twenty yards across the line for a touchdown." Carlisle won the game 17–0.

The next week the Indians traveled to Easton, Pennsylvania, to play Lafayette College. Thorpe once again astounded both spectators and the opposition by scoring a touchdown, kicking the extra point, kicking a thirty-five-yard field goal, and setting up two other field goals in the 19–0 victory. In the middle of the last period, he was taken out with a severely twisted ankle. The injury worried Warner because the following week Carlisle was scheduled to play their top rival, the University of Pennsylvania.

On the Monday morning before the Penn game Warner met with his secretary, Arthur Martin; his coaching assistants; and his two scouts, Pop Craver and Deed Harris, as he did every Monday morning during the season. "They'd sit there starting about nine o'clock and I had to take notes on what they'd say," Martin recalled. "Warner would ask them about plays the teams had made and Warner would ask Craver, 'Now, how would you break that up?' Craver would tell him. . . . Pop would light up own of those nice stinking Turkish Trophies, and he'd not use another match till about the middle of the afternoon. Mrs. Warner would come in with a sandwich or something and it was time to break it up. The house was full of smoke."

At a packed Franklin Field, the Carlisle band was joined by a small group of Carlisle students. One of these students was Jim Thorpe's special guest Iva Miller, an Oklahoma girl who had caught the half-back's eye.

Thorpe tried to punt and run before the game, but he was in such pain that he had to sit on the sidelines for the entire contest. Luckily, the best offensive player for the University of Pennsylvania also was sidelined with an injury. Without Thorpe, the Indians relied on their speed and execution to overpower the Penn eleven. Welch masterminded the running game, mixing end runs and line bucks. "We didn't have any huddles," Welch said. "We used to call signals so fast the defense didn't have time to get lined up."

The right halfback William "Lone Star" Dietz scored first for the Indians with a twenty-yard end run touchdown, culminating a sixty-yard drive. Welch picked up a punt on his own five-yard line and ran it back ninety-five yards for a touchdown. It was the most spectacular play in Carlisle's spectacular 16–0 defeat of the University of Pennsylvania. Welch was particularly pleased with his performance, since Iva Miller had caught his eye as well.

The next week, November 11, 1911, Carlisle traveled to Cambridge, Massachusetts, to play the Harvard Crimson, one of the best teams in the country. Welch, Thorpe, and the other Carlisle players revered everything Harvard stood for. "Harvard was the Indian idea of perfection," Warner later explained. "Anything very good was always commented on as 'Harvard style.'"

Warner, on the other hand, disliked Harvard and their arrogant coach, Percy Haughton. For his part, Haughton considered Warner's style of play to be mere "whiff-whaff." Haughton was so confident of his team that he did not even attend the Carlisle game. He left his team in the hands of his assistant coaches, told them to start the second team, and traveled to scout the Yale team, which Harvard was scheduled to play the following week.

The Indians took the field in Harvard Stadium in front of 40,000 fans, more fans than attended the attendance-breaking World Series game one in 1911, when Carlisle graduate Albert Bender pitched against the New York Giants' Christy Mathewson in front of 38,281 fans. The recently expanded stadium was America's largest venue for college sports. At the time, it was the largest reinforced concrete building in the world. Harvard alumni and students were bemused by the small group of Carlisle fans cheering the school yell, "Minnewa Ka, Kah Wah We! Minnewa Ka, Kah Wah We! Minnewa Ka, Kah Wah We! Carlisle! Carlisle! Carlisle!"

On the field, the Carlisle players knew they would have a tough fight. They only had sixteen players on their bench. The mighty Harvard Crimson had fifty. Henry Roberts, who played end, recalled, "Their line was supposed to be impregnable."

Thorpe's right ankle was so painful that Warner had spent much of the week tending to the sprain with electricity, vibrating machines, massage, and liniment. Before the game, Warner carefully encased Thorpe's ankle in adhesive plaster. Despite the injury, Warner started

Thorpe at halfback. As Warner later wrote in his coaching guidebook, "Only in the most serious cases is it necessary for a player to stay out of an important game by reason of a sprained ankle."

Outsized and outmanned and knowing that Thorpe was injured, Warner did, however, change his game plan. "I switched the plan of attack," Warner later explained, "and used him [Thorpe] only as interference through the entire first half."

After taking the kickoff, the Indians cut through the Harvard line with straight line plunges behind Thorpe's blocking but failed to carry the ball over the goal line. On their next possession, Thorpe stepped back for a field goal and sent it through the uprights despite his injured foot. Harvard answered with a field goal. Thorpe kicked yet another field goal, this one from forty-three yards out. But Harvard pounced on an Indian fumble and scored a touchdown, leaving the score 9–6 at the half.

The Indians knew that the second half would be even tougher than the first. At Warner's suggestion, Welch upped the tempo of the offense, running crisscrosses, reverses, and end runs instead of straight line bucks, and letting Thorpe carry the ball. Alex Arcasa plunged through the line for a touchdown, and Thorpe booted a thirty-seven-yard field goal, his third on a sprained ankle, to give the Indians a 15–9 advantage. As Bill Newashe recalled, "He was a marked man all the time, but he had tremendous stamina and could take it."

The referee did not make things easier for Thorpe. He was wearing a red sweater and golf trousers that closely resembled a Harvard uniform. "I am sure that I dodged him at least a dozen times in my open field runs and once or twice I dodged him only to run into the arms of a Harvard player," Thorpe remembered. "I asked him to change his sweater several times, but he apparently forgot what I had said to him."

By the fourth quarter, the game had become a war of endurance. Unfortunately for the Indians, Harvard was able to bring nine fresh players into the lineup, the best players on their squad. "Pop made very few substitutions because we were the best he had," Henry Roberts said. "I played the whole game. I don't believe I was ever more tired in my life."

As his teammates weakened, Thorpe refused to crack. "As Jim saw the day going against us," Warner later said, "he forgot his wretched leg and sprained ankle, and called for the ball. 'And get out of my way,' he gritted. 'I mean to do some real running.'

"And how that Indian did run!

"Jim could go skidding through first and second defense, knock off a tackler, stop short, and turn past another, ward off still another, and escape the entire pack. If he was finally cornered, Jim could go further with a tackler hanging on him than any man I ever saw." According to Warner, the Harvard players later admitted that trying to stop Thorpe "was like trying to stop a freight train."

Despite the fact that he was playing with a bandaged ankle, Thorpe gained 173 yards in the second half of the game. Still, Carlisle could not manage to score a touchdown. According to Roberts, "They hoped to wear us down and tried desperately to score and almost did. Pop wanted to take Jim out because he was about through, but we wouldn't let him. Without Jim, we would have folded up. He was the spark that kept us going."

"Although every movement must have been agony," Warner said, "not once did he take time out."

Late in the fourth quarter, the Carlisle offense stalled on the Harvard forty-eight-yard line. The Indian quarterback Gus Welch knew that the Carlisle defense could not hold. Harvard was bound to score. A six-point lead was not good enough.

"On fourth down I called for a place kick," Welch later said. "Thorpe and the boys were hot. Thorpe said, 'Who in the hell ever heard of a place kick from here? Punt the damn ball.' I said a place kick would be as good as a punt and we had a good chance to score. I finally won out. Thorpe got back a couple of extra steps and kicked the ball a wallop. It started low—a Crimson guard touched the ball, deflecting it up, and it finally gained height and it went through the middle of the goal and about twenty yards beyond the goal."

With the score 18–9 and only a few minutes to go, Thorpe, Welch, and the Carlisle Indians managed to hold Harvard once again. Carlisle could not move the ball. Thorpe took the snap and stepped forward to punt, but the Harvard center blocked the kick, picked up the ball, and ran it in for a touchdown. It was too little too late. Carlisle took control of the ball. As time ran out, a limping Jim Thorpe was carried off the field by his teammates. Even the Harvard fans cheered. Tearful

Harvard players congratulated the twenty-four-year-old Oklahoman on his magnificent effort.

The final score was 18–15. The U.S. Indian School at Carlisle, a federally funded high school for Indians, had defeated Harvard University, the mightiest private institution of higher learning in North America.

The *Boston American* said of Thorpe's performance, "He has placed his name in the Hall of Fame, not only of Carlisle but also of the entire football world. It was indeed a pleasure to see a man not only live up to a great reputation but add to it through work beautifully accomplished."

"When I hear people say that Indians can't stand the gaff, I always think of that finish against Harvard," Warner declared. "Jim Thorpe, particularly, had the heart of a lion."

The Carlisle Indians earned more than honor for their upset victory over America's football powerhouse. Pop Warner collected $10,400 in ticket sales, the largest one-day profit for the Carlisle athletic program since 1907.

After such an emotionally draining victory, Warner was concerned that his Indians would slump the next week, against the Orangemen of Syracuse. Unfortunately, Warner's worries were well founded. In a torrential rain, on a field that was a soup of mud and water, Thorpe and the rest of the Carlisle Indians played a listless first half. An injured Gus Welch had not even suited up, but came into the game as quarterback for the second half. But even Welch's presence could not save the Indians from a 21–11 defeat.

"Syracuse trounced us to the queen's taste," Warner recalled. "Not only was the field a sea of mud, but the Indians, worn out by their series of grueling encounters, played far below their form."

Thorpe was bitterly disappointed after the Syracuse game. The next week, against a weak Johns Hopkins team, Thorpe scored two touchdowns on the first two possessions and led the Indians to a 29–6 victory. Despite that strong showing, Warner knew his team was tired, and he wondered how they would perform in the last game of the season, scheduled for November 30, 1911, against Brown University in Providence.

Warner's concern increased at midmorning on Thanksgiving Day as the Indians ran out onto Andrews Field. On a muddy, wet field, as the *Providence Daily Journal* reported, Carlisle fought "with an attack that was almost irresistible and a defense which was like reinforced concrete." Ten minutes into the first quarter, Thorpe swept around end from the Carlisle thirty-five-yard line and broke for the goal. A single Brown player stood between Thorpe and a touchdown. "The crowd awaited the outcome of the race with bated breath," the paper reported. "On dashed the flying redskins, and the Brown captain, tense as a steel spring, waited for the shock with every muscle quivering." At the last possible moment, the Brown player "left his feet with a panther like spring, his arms closed around Thorpe's legs like a trap, and the goal was saved." A few plays later, Thorpe kicked a field goal, which was now worth three points. On the next Carlisle drive, Welch ran sixty-two yards for a touchdown and Thorpe kicked the extra point, giving Carlisle a 9–0 lead at the end of the first half.

Despite a heavy snow that began falling at halftime, Thorpe kicked another field goal and wowed the crowd with an eighty-three-yard punt. Carlisle won the game 12–6.

On the train back to Carlisle, Welch, Newashe, Lone Star, and the other players voted Thorpe captain of the 1912 football team. Later, Walter Camp named Thorpe as a first-team All-American halfback. "He was born a football player," Warner said. "No college player I ever saw had the natural aptitude for football possessed by Jim Thorpe. I never knew a football player who could penetrate a line as Thorpe could, nor did I ever know of a player who could see holes through which to break as could the big Indian. As for speed, none ever carried a pigskin down the field with the dazzling speed of Thorpe. . . . He knew everything a football player could be taught and then he could execute the play better than the coach ever dreamed of."

At the end of the football season, Warner began to work on another challenge for the best natural athlete he had ever seen: the 1912 Olympic games in Sweden.

Hiram P. Thorpe,
Jim Thorpe's father
(1852–1904), one of
the toughest men in
the Oklahoma Territory

Charlotte Vieux,
Jim Thorpe's mother
(1863–1901), a devout
Catholic of mixed Indian
and French blood

Young Oklahoma farm
boys: Jim Thorpe (at left)
and his twin brother,
Charles

The student body on the campus of the Carlisle Indian Industrial School, Carlisle,
Pennsylvania, which enforced strict military-style discipline. Its campus today is the
site of the U.S. Army War College.

The Harvard-Carlisle football game as covered by Stephen Crane in the *Journal American*, November 1, 1896. The Carlisle Indian football team was immediately popular with the New York press, which graphically celebrated the Indians' physical prowess.

Jim Thorpe (at right) posing in his
Carlisle school uniform with two
unidentified fellow students, circa 1907

Charles Albert Bender, who played baseball
with coach Pop Warner at the Carlisle
Indian Industrial School before joining the
Philadelphia Athletics in 1903. A skilled
jeweler and a competitive marksman, Bender
was one of the Athletics' most dependable
pitchers for more than a decade.

Jim Thorpe punting around 1907. One of the earliest known photos of Thorpe playing football, this photo appeared in Pop Warner's book *A Course in Football for Players and Coaches.*

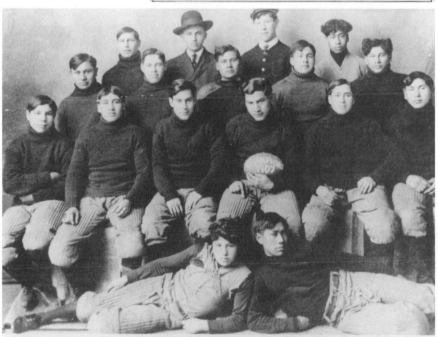

The 1907 Carlisle varsity football team, which Pop Warner characterized as "a perfect football machine." Jim Thorpe stands in the back row, second from right.

Louis Tewanima, in "before" photo (front row, second from left) and "after" photo (back row, first from left). These photos, which were taken at Carlisle in 1907, were distributed by Carlisle school administrators to newspapers in 1912 along with articles celebrating the civilizing influence of the Carlisle school experience.

Pop Warner posing in Indian regalia. A painter himself, Warner collected Indian art and funded classes in Indian art at Carlisle with proceeds from football game ticket sales. According to Warner's lifelong friend Dr. Ralph Waite, "His players called Pop 'The Old Man.' The Blackfeet Indians, who adopted him many, many years ago, had a more appropriate term. They called him 'The Charging Bear.'"

The 1908 Carlisle varsity track team with Pop Warner (back row, wearing tie), Louis Tewanima (front row, third from right), and Jim Thorpe (front row, legs folded)

Albert Exendine, one of Pop Warner's outstanding Carlisle athletes, was Jim Thorpe's track and field mentor.

One of the earliest images of Jim Thorpe in the New York press appeared in the *New York Herald* on January 26, 1909. The accompanying article detailed Louis Tewanima's performance at a Madison Square Garden track meet.

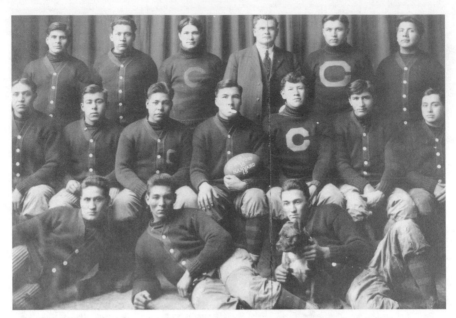

The 1911 Carlisle Indian varsity football team, posing with the game ball from their 18–15 victory over Harvard. Jim Thorpe sits third from right and Gus Welch reclines in front, holding the dog. Pop Warner stands in the back row.

James E. Sullivan (marked number 3), who controlled the Amateur Athletic Union, attending the Evening Mail Modified Marathon in New York City on May 6, 1911. Standing next to Sullivan is Barton S. Weeks (marked number 2), an AAU official who, along with Sullivan, forced Jim Thorpe to give up his Olympic medals.

Jim Thorpe (at left) running the 120-meter high hurdles around 1912

Thorpe in a three-point stance

Thorpe running, circa 1912

Thorpe throwing the javelin

From right to left, Jim Thorpe, Pop Warner, and Louis Tewanima pose before the 1912 Olympic games in Stockholm, Sweden.

Thorpe putting the shot at the 1912 Stockholm Olympics

Thorpe, with hat in hand, receiving the gold medal in the pentathlon from King
Gustav V of Sweden, on July 15, 1912. The king also presented Thorpe with a
trophy, a life-size bust of the king, visible on the dais.

From left to right, Pop Warner (in boater hat), Louis Tewanima (in boater hat), and
Jim Thorpe (with flower in his lapel) at their homecoming reception in Carlisle on
August 16, 1912

Jim Thorpe shaking hands with Moses Friedman, the superintendent of the
U.S. Indian School, after returning from the 1912 Olympics. Pop Warner
stands to the left of Thorpe and Louis Tewanima stands to his right.

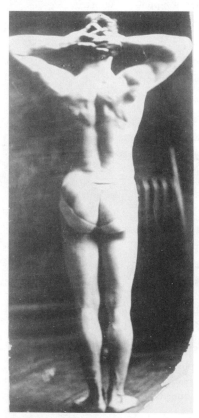

Jim Thorpe as photographed by scientific
investigators after his Olympic victories. These
investigators documented Thorpe's champion
physique by taking more than forty detailed
measurements of his body and a series of
revealing photographs.

Pop Warner looking on as Jim Thorpe hits a tackling dummy of Warner's design. In addition to the tackling dummy, Warner designed and constructed fiber pads, knee braces, wet-weather cleats, helmets, and other equipment for his football players.

The 1912 Carlisle varsity football team. Backfield from right to left: Jim Thorpe, Gus Welch, Stancil "Possum" Powell, and Alex Arcasa. Line from right to left: Roy Large, Joe Guyon, William Garlow, Joe Bergie, Elmer Busch, Pete Calac, and Charles Williams

Thorpe punting at the Carlisle–Toronto University game in Toronto on October 28, 1912

At center, Jim Thorpe on October 13, 1913, the day of his wedding to Iva Margaret Miller, seated in the wedding dress. Standing to the left of Thorpe is his best man, Gus Welch.

Jim Thorpe in his
New York Giants
uniform, 1913

Jim Thorpe and Tom Mix on the set of the 1932 motion picture
My Pal the King. After retiring from sports, Thorpe worked as an
actor, a laborer, and a lecturer and held a variety of other jobs.

15

The Greatest Athlete in the World

O n Christmas evening 1911, Carlisle students in their overcoats and red and gold scarves marched in formation along frozen paths to the gymnasium to receive their Christmas presents provided by the King's Daughters, a school social organization that raised money for the presents with an annual social. One by one, the students came up to get their gift from Santa Claus, who laughed loudly as he spread holiday cheer. Beneath a white beard and red jacket was twenty-four-year-old Jim Thorpe.

Thorpe the jolly Santa gloried in his celebrity status. He enjoyed the privilege of sharing a special dining hall with the other "athletic boys," where their own chef prepared a meat-rich diet. He liked visiting with the bakers who brought their pies and cakes out to the playing fields for the athletic boys to buy after practice. He looked forward to going off campus without his uniform and accepting the hospitality of the Carlisle community, even to the point of enjoying a toast or two or hanging around Halbert's Pool Hall. According to one Carlisle resident, "The people in town—a certain crowd—would get hold of them and start pouring liquor in them."

Reserved and moody by nature, gloomy at times, exuberant at others, Thorpe began to loosen up as the social restrictions on the Carlisle campus relaxed. With his chin raised high, Thorpe lectured the younger Carlisle students in his Oklahoma lilt on topics such as

"Athletics in General at Carlisle." The girls began to notice Carlisle's star athlete, and he began to notice the girls. "He [Thorpe] was my classmate; he sat right behind me," Fannie Kennerly remembered. "He used to put my hair in the inkwell and get it all mussed up. He was funny."

Kennerly also remembered that instead of going through the gate to the athletic field, Thorpe would jump over it. The show-off athlete was shy at social functions. Kennerly's sister, Bessie, spotted Thorpe at a dance, grabbed his arm, and said, "Jim, you're going to dance." Thorpe took to the dance floor and to Bessie's surprise was "just as graceful as could be." After that "you couldn't keep him off the dance floor."

The dance partner he liked best was Iva Margaret Miller. Iva, who was also known as Ivy, was six years younger than Thorpe, born on August 24, 1893, at Pryor Creek, Oklahoma, then Indian Territory. Her white father, Finas Miller, was a stage operator and hotelkeeper; her mother, Mattie Denton, perhaps had a trace of Cherokee blood. When Iva was five, both her parents passed away. The orphan girl was enrolled in the Chilocco Indian School in Oklahoma. She lived at the school until an aunt arranged for her transfer to Carlisle, bending the rules to accommodate a promising student with only a trace of Indian blood.

Iva did well at Carlisle. She was a nursing student who worked in the health clinic. She was the class elocutionist and graduated with an industrial certificate in plain sewing. In her graduation book, Iva fondly remembered the view from her Carlisle classroom, a view that displayed "a well-kept road winding through trees and cutting our beautiful campus, laid out in lawns, artistic flower beds, walks." On the wall of the classroom hung her class's blue and tan banner, embroidered with the slogan "Loyalty 1912." Beautiful, smart, outgoing, and lively, Iva was known as the "prettiest girl at Carlisle."

When she met Thorpe in 1911, the Indian athlete turned to her and said, "You're a cute thing." Iva did not know what to make of her admirer at first, but she grew to appreciate his admiration. She also appreciated the attention of Thorpe's roommate, the 1912 class president Gus Welch.

With the infusion of cash from the successful football season, Carlisle was growing. Superintendent Friedman hired new faculty, including a young poet named Marianne Moore, who began teaching at Carlisle in 1911. Moore taught a variety of subjects, including typing, stenography, bookkeeping, and English. "The commercial students, about thirty, were an ideal group," Moore later recalled. "Among which were James Thorpe, Gus Welch, and Iva Miller. . . . They were my salvation, open-minded, also intelligent."

Moore did not get to know the reserved Thorpe well but noted, "In the classroom he was a little laborious, but dependable; took time—head bent earnestly over the paper; wrote a fine, even clerical hand—every character legible; every terminal curving up—consistent and generous." Outside the classroom, Moore described him as "off-hand, modest, casual about everything in the way of fame or eminence achieved."

On one occasion, Thorpe and Gus Welch escorted the young poet to a circus in Carlisle. As they set out, the sky threatened rain. Thorpe noticed his teacher's heavy umbrella and graciously offered, "Miss Moore, may I carry your parasol?"

She answered, "Thank you James."

Comfortable with his school, surrounded by friends and admirers, Thorpe continued to perform well for his mentor and coach, Pop Warner. In the winter of 1912, Thorpe, Tewanima, and Welch, captain of the team, competed in several indoor track meets. In February, Thorpe broke the Carlisle high-jump record in Boston, with a leap of six feet, one-half inch. In Baltimore, Thorpe won the shot put and the high jump and placed second in the 100-yard hurdles, in which the winner set a new world's record.

The press reported that the Pittsburgh Athletic Club Indoor Meet on March 9, 1912, attracted a record crowd. "Interest, so far as individuals are concerned, centered in the marvelous Thorpe, of Carlisle, the greatest all-around college athlete in the world to-day." Before the games, Warner told the press that Thorpe would win every event he entered and bragged, "Jim is doing everything he tries better now than ever before in his career." Thorpe won four of the five events he entered, the 60-yard dash, the 60-yard hurdles, the twelve-pound shot put, and the running high jump. In the March 25 meet sponsored by the Middle Atlantic Association of the Amateur Athletic Union, Thorpe won four events and Gus Welch won the 300-yard dash.

As winter gave way to spring track, Thorpe continued his winning ways. At a triangular meet in Philadelphia in May, he won first in the shot put, high jump, and 220-yard hurdles, finished second in the long jump and 120-yard hurdles, and placed third in the 100-yard dash.

Tewanima upstaged Thorpe at the annual meet of the Pennsylvania Intercollegiate Athletic Association. Instead of traveling from Carlisle to Harrisburg by train, Tewanima ran the eighteen miles. Less than an hour and fifty minutes after setting out, "Little Tewanimi," as he was affectionately known, entered the stadium while the two-mile race was being run. As the crowd roared, the Hopi circled the field with the runners before pulling off the track, although many claimed years later that he won the event.

During the third week in April, Thorpe, Tewanima, and Welch attended the Carlisle commencement activities. The class president Welch enjoyed the lawn party, eating strawberry ice cream and playing croquet with the rest of the Carlisle students in the warm spring sun. Welch graduated with his class, and Tewanima received a certificate as a tailor. Thorpe received neither a diploma nor a certificate. He was the best-known Indian student in the country but never managed to earn a diploma or even a certificate of training from an Indian educational institution.

After the ceremony, Warner drove to his home in Springville, New York, bringing Tewanima and Thorpe with him. Tewanima, who had not competed much in the spring, was not in great shape. For several weeks, the Indian athletes lived with Warner and worked out at Dygert's Field in Springville, far from the prying eyes of scouts and reporters. It was Warner's way of focusing his athletes on the biggest athletic contest of their careers.

As he worked with his athletes in the winter and spring of 1912, Warner continued to generate headlines. "Savage Hopi Indians Are Transformed Into Model Students" announced a headline in February 1912 in a story that ran in various papers into the summer of 1912. The article featured striking "before and after" photos of Tewanima and the other Hopi who had been taken prisoner in 1906 and sent to Carlisle. The "before" picture showed Tewanima and his fellow Hopi with long hair and ragged clothes. The "after" picture showed them neatly shorn and wearing trim, military-style uniforms. The photos were similar to "before and after" postcards of "savage" Indians transformed into students that had been extremely popular with visitors when the school first opened more than thirty years before. "These 12 Hopi when they came here five years ago were crude specimens of a low order of civilization," the copy read. "Where before they were sun worshippers and the snake dance was one of their principal ceremonies, they have all joined Christian congregations."

According to Warner, "Both Thorpe and Tewanima were selected for the Olympic team without trials, a rare honor but well deserved. Tewanima had gone great guns that winter . . . and Thorpe loomed so far above other candidates that any tests would have been absurd."

Actually, Thorpe did appear at New York City's Celtic Park on May 18, 1912, in a special tryout for a newly introduced Olympic event, the pentathlon. Baron Coubertin, the founder of the modern Olympic movement, instituted the pentathlon in response to critics of the games who claimed that the participants were too specialized. Coubertin believed that the pentathlon competition, which included five events, would test all-around ability rather than a particular skill.

According to the *New York Times* coverage of the tryout, "Jimmy Thorpe, the wonderful Carlisle athlete, proved to be in a class by himself."

Abel Kiviat saw Jim Thorpe for the first time at the pentathlon try-outs.

> The first event I saw him in was the shotput. He did everything wrong; his stance, his footwork, his follow-through. It was all backwards. Warner never taught him a thing. He probably just handed him the shot, and said, "Here, throw this." But Thorpe beat every shotputter in the trials. That is when I knew he was a marvel. He was beating all these guys—and they were doing it right.

When the Olympic decathlon tryouts were cancelled, Warner quickly scheduled a dual track meet between Carlisle and Lafayette College in Easton, Pennsylvania, a meet that quickly became a Thorpe legend.

Harold Anson Bruce, the Lafayette coach, had heavily promoted the meet and was waiting anxiously for the arrival of the Carlisle team at the Central Railroad station in Lafayette.

According to Grantland Rice, one of America's greatest sports writers,

"All were stunned when a party of two alighted at Easton—Warner and Thorpe.

"'What's this?' demanded Bruce. 'We expected the Carlisle track team.'

"'Here it is," replied Warner, casually pointing to Jim."

According to another version of the story, Bruce asked Thorpe, "You mean there are just two of you?"

"No, just me," Thorpe supposedly answered. "He's the manager."

In reality, seven Carlisle Indians took the field against the thirty-odd athletes from Lafayette. Thorpe won six firsts, Welch took the quarter and half miles, and Tewanima won the mile and the two-mile as Carlisle easily defeated their opponents. "He just picked things up and did it," Lafayette's coach Bruce recalled years later. "After it was all over, Thorpe couldn't tell you how he did it. Everything came natural."

James Sullivan not only attended the pentathlon trial but also acted as referee. He wanted Warner's athletes to compete for the team but realized that Mike Murphy, the former Yale trainer and the coach of the U.S. Olympic team, had never worked with either Thorpe or Tewanima and would not know how to handle the Indian athletes. The best way to ensure that the Indians performed at their best in Stockholm was to make sure that Warner was there. Warner claimed that since the Indians were not U.S. citizens but officially wards of the government, "I was asked by the school's super-intendent, Moses Friedman, to accompany them on their trip to Stockholm for the 1912 Olympic Games."

Support for Sullivan's Olympic effort was far from universal. In January 1912, the *New York Times* reported that the Philadelphia YMCA had voted to secede from the AAU, because the Christian organization believed that sports should be conducted on "more democratic and less despotic lines." In June 1912, the educator H. F. Kallenberg complained about the position of the AAU as America's leading athletic association in the pages of the *American Physical Journal Review*. Kallenberg claimed that the AAU did "little or nothing in the way of promoting the educational view of athletics." In conclusion Kallenberg wrote, "For colleges . . . playgrounds, etc., to accept the Amateur Athletic Union as the national controlling body would mean the adoption of a viewpoint wholly out of sympathy with the general policy and objections of these organizations."

Despite opposition to the AAU, Sullivan and the American Olympic Committee managed to raise more than $100,000 to pay for the expenses of the American team. Still, Thorpe and the other athletes needed some extra cash to make the trip. "Unfortunately," Warner observed, "amateur athletics is not for the poor and friendless."

Thorpe wrote the following letter to the Indian agent at the Sac and Fox Agency on May 24, 1912:

> Dear Sir,
>
> Please send me $100.00 from my account or funds. Will need same this summer in taking trip to Sweden with Olympic Team. Very Respectfully, James Thorpe.

Horace Johnson, the Indian Agent, refused to send the funds, citing Thorpe's profligate spending of $300 over the past year. Johnson further commented on the whole notion of Olympic spending:

> I understand that the trip might be of considerable benefit to the young man, but I am strongly convinced that instead of being a benefit it will be a detriment. He has now reached the age, when, instead of gallivanting around the country, he should be at work on his allotment, or in some other location, where, instead of being a tax on his resources, he would be adding something thereto.

On June 12, 1912, the same day that the Indian agent expressed his disapproval of the Olympics, Thorpe and Tewanima participated in a promotional pre-Olympic meet in New York City. Thorpe defeated the champion Alma Richards in the high jump, clearing the bar at six feet, five inches. When Sullivan noticed that Tewanima was entered in the 3,500-meter run against two of the strongest American runners, he asked Warner, "Why do you run the boy in this event?" Warner told Sullivan that Tewanima needed the workout. In the final lap of the race, Tewanima sprinted into the lead and won by four yards.

On Friday, June 14, 1912, Warner, Tewanima, and Thorpe boarded the SS *Finland* of the Red Star Line and set out for Europe. They found themselves crossing the Atlantic as part of a remarkably diverse U.S. Olympic team. Among the 164 athletes were Duke Paoa Kahinu

Makoe Hulikohoa Kahanamoku, the twenty-two-year-old swimming
sensation who was descended from Hawaiian royalty; Howard Drew, a
black sprinter who held the world's record for the 100 meters; Pat
McDonald, a New York City traffic cop and shot putter; the U.S.
Army lieutenant George Smith Patton Jr., a horseman and marksman
ready for competition in the modern pentathlon; Andrew Sockalexis, a
Penobscot Indian marathoner from Maine; Avery Brundage, the scion
of a wealthy midwestern family who would participate with Thorpe in
the pentathlon; and Abel Kiviat, a Jewish miler who ran for the Irish-
American Athletic Club in New York City and who roomed with
Thorpe on the *Finland* for a few days.

The American team worked out hard on the ten-day Atlantic crossing. Coach Mike Murphy set up a special 100-yard cork track and a
canvas swimming pool in which swimmers could practice their strokes
restrained by a rope tied around their waists. Thorpe and the other
high jumpers leaped over ropes and worked out with weights set up in
the bow of the ship, as tennis players practiced their strokes in a hastily
built practice area. It was tough to stay in shape in the cramped space.
Tewanima felt seasick for much of the voyage and was unable to take
long practice runs. He stuck close to Warner on the ship. At one
point, a bystander overheard Warner tell his Hopi athlete, "Louis, go
out and win the marathon and you'll have a bankroll within a year big
enough to choke a horse."

"You betcher, Pop," Tewanima replied. "I'm going to try hard."

Thorpe's reserve and his well-known dislike of practice may have
been responsible in part for the rumors that circulated about his activities on board ship. "Thorpe did little training," Grantland Rice wrote.
He continued,

> Francis Albertanti, who covered the 1912 games for the old
> *Evening Mail*, told me that going over on the old Red Star liner
> *Finland* Thorpe would sit alone while the rest of the track
> squad pounded a stretch of cork laid down on one of the decks.
>
> "What are you doing, Jim," asked Albertanti one day,
> "thinking of your Uncle Sitting Bull?"
>
> "No . . . I'm practicing the broad [long] jump," replied
> Thorpe. "I've just jumped twenty-three feet, eight inches. I
> think that can win it."

Rice reported another story, passed on to him by John Hayes, the winner of the 1908 marathon, who also was part of the 1912 team:

> One hot morning out on the track Mike [Murphy] missed Thorpe for the third consecutive day. He blew his top and hunted him out. He found Thorpe asleep in a hammock behind the living quarters of the marathon team. Seated nearby and soaking up the Swedish sun was Warner.
>
> Pop eyed Mike benignly, then he said: "Mike, don't worry. All those two-for-a-nickel events you've got lined up for Thorpe won't bother him. He's in shape . . . what with football, lacrosse, baseball and track back at school, how could he be out of shape? This sleeping is the best training ever—for Jim."

The sprinter Ralph Craig recalled a much different Thorpe: "I can certainly remember running laps and doing calisthenics with Jim every day on the ship. In fact, Jim and I nearly overdid it on more than one occasion because we were always challenging one another in the sprints."

The *Finland* docked at Antwerp on June 24, and the Americans stretched out at the Beershot Athletic Club for three days before the four-day passage to Stockholm. Once in Stockholm, the team used the *Finland* as their quarters for the duration of the games. At the suggestion of runner John Hayes, Warner paid for Thorpe to work out at a private training ground outside of town.

When they weren't training, the athletes had time to do a little sightseeing. "At night we went girl-hunting," Abel Kiviat fondly remembered. "Great-looking women, the Swedes. Thorpe liked the girls, too. He didn't say much; he just looked them up and down. I remember they had these sidewalk cafés with hedges around them. More than once I saw Thorpe reach through the hedge, grab a beer when no one was looking, drink it and put the [empty] back."

Though the tennis matches had started in May, and the games included everything from shooting "running deer" to a competition in literature that was won, and judged, by Coubertin, the organizers of the Fifth Olympiad understood that track and field was the heart of the games. Thus the official opening ceremonies were held before the opening of the track and field events. On July 6, 1912, thirty thousand sports enthusiasts—Scandinavians, Russians, Brits, Americans—

dressed in their sunbonnets, corsets, and boaters, packed the gray brick and granite stands of the new Stockholm Olympic stadium.

Between two octagonal towers decorated with sculpted heroes from Norse mythology, 2,547 athletes from twenty-seven nations marched and took up their positions on the field. According to an ancient Swedish custom, the gathered crowd chanted a chorus recited by soldiers before joining battle. The Reverend Clemens Åfeldt, the royal pastor, read a prayer in Swedish, which was followed with a prayer in English from the Reverend R. S. de Courcy Laffan.

After speeches from the Swedish Olympic Committee and the Crown Prince of Sweden, the king declared the Olympic games open. All the spectators then joined a chorus of 4,400 voices in singing Martin Luther's hymn "Ein feste Burg ist unser Gott" ("A Mighty Fortress Is Our God"). The Olympians proceeded onto the cinder track of the horseshoe-shaped stadium and passed the royal box, where King Gustav V of Sweden, Crown Prince Gustav Adolph, and Grand Duke Dmitri of Russia doffed their hats to acknowledge each nation's athletes. According to James Sullivan, "Everything that went to make the inaugural was glorious."

Politics was not far from the surface. The Finns marched behind their own flag with the permission from the International Olympic Committee, although their nation was still under Russian domination. Irish athletes marched under the British flag, though they, too, were seeking independence from their colonial ties. Thorpe and Tewanima did not protest the fact that they were representing the United States, even though they were not American citizens but legally wards of the federal government.

The Fifth Olympiad in Stockholm ran so smoothly that it was dubbed the "Swedish Masterpiece." To avoid the alleged favoritism of the 1908 games, an international team of judges was selected to oversee the competition. These officials utilized electronic timing devices and loudspeakers for the first time in an Olympics, innovations that enhanced the spirit of the games.

The competition was as outstanding as the organization. From the beginning, the American team dominated, as it swept the first event, the 100-meter run. The real test for the Americans came the next day. On Sunday, July 7, at one thirty in the afternoon the pentathlon competition began, the first time the event was contested internationally.

Since the Europeans were supposed to dominate the competition, it was important for America's prestige to win the event, and America's hopes rested on the shoulders of Jim Thorpe.

Thorpe prepared himself for the first event of the pentathlon, the running long jump. He took a deep breath, his forty-one-inch chest filling his white cotton T-shirt emblazoned with the American shield. As he eyed the path leading up to the jumping pit, he felt good, as relaxed as if he were about to take off across the hills of Oklahoma with his favorite hunting dog.

Pop Warner was not relaxed as he stood on the grassy infield sucking on a Turkish Trophy cigarette. With his painter's eye, he noted the afternoon light, which warmed Thorpe's muscular figure. At just under six feet tall and 185 pounds, Thorpe did not have an overpowering build, but one that was perfectly proportioned, stretched taut with ropelike muscles. He held his head high, his chin up, his body coiled back on his heels, his toes turned up slightly. "Equilibrium with no strictures" was how the poet Marianne Moore described her student's appearance on the athletic field. "The epitome of concentration, wary, with an effect of plenty in reserve."

"In addition to having every physical asset, Thorpe had a rare spirit," Warner later told Grantland Rice. "Nothing bothered Jim. When he was 'right' the sheer joy of playing carried him through. When he wasn't, he showed it. For that reason I used to call him 'a lazy Indian' to his face. I'll admit, though, it didn't bother him. But when he was right, he was the best." This was the question that tormented Warner on that warm Swedish afternoon: would Jim Thorpe be "right"?

Thorpe exploded down the track, his back straight, his thin, powerful legs pounding a smooth stride. He hit his mark perfectly and launched into the air. His legs bent at the knees, his arms held straight over his head, Thorpe soared 23 feet, 2.7 inches and won the event.

"He could do anything but he didn't know how he did it," his roommate Abel Kiviat recalled. "He would watch you do it, then he'd do it. Give him the javelin, and he'd throw it farther than the regular javelin throwers on the team." In the pentathlon competition, Thorpe's javelin throw was only good enough for a second, but he ran the 200-meter dash in 22.9 seconds—beating two of his American teammates by a tenth of a second. Thorpe hurled the discus 116 feet and 8.4 inches, far enough to win the event over Avery Brundage. In the final event of the pentathlon, the 1,500-meter run, Ferdinand Bie, a Norwegian, and Brundage set the pace for the first lap. Midway through the second lap Thorpe made his move. He passed Brundage and Bie and held on to finish in 4 minutes, 44.8 seconds, winning the race and the pentathlon in a commanding fashion.

Sullivan was elated by Thorpe's performance. "It answers the charge that Americans specialize in athletics," Sullivan said. "It also answers the allegations that most of our runners are of foreign parentage, for Thorpe is a real American if ever there was one."

Tewanima was the other "real American" on the team. On July 8 at 4:15 P.M., he took his place on the starting line for the 10,000-meter run. For years, the Finns had dominated international long-distance running events. This race was expected to be no different. The favorite was Johan Pietori Kolehmainen, a twenty-two-year-old vegetarian bricklayer known as "Smiling Hannes," one of the "Flying Finns."

As the runners took off, the crowd picked the wiry, 110-pound, thirty-five-year-old Hopi as their favorite. They cheered as Tewanima held his own against Kolehmainen in the initial lap. Tewanima started to ease the pace, but Kolehmainen held firm. Tewanima was not at his best after the difficult sea voyage. Still, he pushed, fighting to overtake the Finn. His effort was not enough. By the sixth lap, Kolehmainen had dropped the field. The Hopi crossed the finish line forty-seven seconds after Kolehmainen's world-record time of 31:20.8. The Flying Finn went on to win gold in the individual cross-country race and the 5,000-meter run, defeating France's Jean Bouin by a tenth of a second in world-record time.

Tewanima had only won silver in the 10,000-meter run, but he had won the admiration of the world. His showing would not be surpassed by an American until the 1964 Olympics in Tokyo when Billy Mills, a Cherokee who had attended Haskell Institute, won Olympic gold.

Tewanima also competed in the 1912 Olympic marathon, along with eleven other Americans including Andrew Sockalexis, a Penobscot Indian from Maine. Conditions were so hot and humid on the afternoon of July 14 when the race was run that the Portuguese marathoner Francisco Lázaro collapsed at mile nineteen and later died, the first Olympic fatality. Tewanima finished sixteenth with a time of 2:52:41.4, well back of the winner, the South African Kennedy McArthur, and the American Andrew Sockalexis, who finished fourth.

As the Fifth Olympiad progressed, the American team continued to do extraordinarily well. In swimming, Duke Kahanamoku won the 100-yard freestyle. Pat McDonald won a crowd-pleasing upset victory in the shotput. Still, the athlete who impressed the American Olympic coach Mike Murphy the most was Jim Thorpe.

"Why, that guy was fantastic," Murphy said of Thorpe. "He would run a ten-second dash, broad [long] and high jump close to the world record, throw the discus out of the stadium, pick up two or three other firsts—and then complain because there wasn't enough action."

"My God, Thorpe," Murphy told Thorpe at one point during the games, "how many events do you want to enter?"

"All of 'em," Jim responded. "What's the fun in watching someone else?"

Although he enjoyed the action, Thorpe did not do particularly well in the individual events. On July 8, he tied for fourth in the open division high jump, and on July 12 he placed seventh in the long jump.

James Sullivan, with his walrus mustache and bowler hat, looked on approvingly from his seat in the Olympic grandstand as he puffed on a cigar. He was determined to defeat all his adversaries, particularly the British, and to defeat them soundly. As England did poorly in the games, the British press leveled broad criticism at Sullivan and his cronies for bending the rules of amateurism. The *New York Times'* London correspondent noted that the Olympic enthusiasts expressed a "wholehearted dislike of the particular crowd . . . which controls Olympic matters in America and of what are commonly called the political and Tammany methods which that crowd represents." During the games, International Olympic Committee officials heard a report about violations of the amateur rules, and formed a committee to study the issue, a committee that eventually recommended a tightening of the rules to cut down on creeping professionalism.

On the last three days of the Olympics, the eyes of the world focused on Jim Thorpe and the twenty-eight other athletes who competed in the ultimate test of overall athletic ability, the decathlon. The Swedes had devised the decathlon competition as a ten-event test of strength and overall athletic ability. The Swedish athlete Hugo

Wieslander probably had more experience in the decathlon than any of the other competitors, having won three decathlons prior to the 1912 Olympics. Wieslander was the Swedish favorite to win the event. On Saturday, July 13, 1912, the first day of the event, Jim and Warner entered the Olympic stadium in a pouring rain. Warner remembered only too well another rainy day, the day of the 1911 Carlisle Indian football game against Syracuse, the only Carlisle loss of the 1911 season. Jim competed best when he was enjoying himself, and it was difficult for him to enjoy himself in the rain.

Three events were scheduled for the first day of the decathlon: the 100-meter dash, the running long jump, and the shot put. Thorpe was slow in the dash, finishing second to one of his teammates with a time of 11.2 seconds. Warner knew Jim could do better. He usually ran the hundred in under ten seconds. Things looked even worse in the long jump. Thorpe was the only competitor to double-fault on the slippery takeoff board. A third fault would mean no score and, probably, no American victory. Before his third and last jump, Thorpe was perfectly calm. He started off with a high step, ran carefully down the track, hit his mark, and made a clean jump, 22 feet, 2.3 inches. It was only good enough for second place, but Thorpe was still in the game.

Knowing the psychological boost from warm clothes, Warner made Thorpe take off his wet uniform and put on a dry warmup suit for the last event of the day, the shot put. Again, Thorpe finished second. Although he had not won an event, his point total gave him a slight lead over the other competitors.

The next day, the sky cleared and the wind stopped. Warner watched Thorpe dominate the first of the day's events, as he won the high jump with a leap of 6 feet, 1.6 inches. In the 400-meter run, Thorpe finished 2.3 seconds behind his American teammate, clocking 52.2 seconds, and placed second in the discus. With his fluid style, his powerful step, and his uncanny physical grace, Thorpe powered through the day's final event, the 110-meter hurdles, winning it in a fast 15.6 seconds.

On the final day of the decathlon, the last day of the Fifth Olympiad, Jim finished third in the pole vault. According to Warner, he quit the pole vault competition after clearing 10 feet, 3 inches without missing a jump because "he was rather heavy and feared he might break the pole and seriously injure himself."

Thorpe placed fourth in the javelin before entering the final event of the decathlon, the culminating event of the Fifth Olympiad, the 1,500-meter run. Thorpe began strong and finished stronger, electrifying the stadium capacity crowd by demolishing the competition and his own pentathlon mark in the 1,500 with a winning time of 4 minutes, 40.1 seconds. "At no time during the competition was I worried or nervous," Thorpe later explained. "I had trained well and hard and had confidence in my ability. I felt that I would win."

Thorpe won the decathlon far ahead of the second-place finisher, Hugo Wieslander of Sweden. Thorpe's decathlon victory set a world record that would stand for sixteen years. His times and distances were strong enough to place him in the top ten decathlon finishers for the next forty-four years of Olympic competition. He was to be the only athlete in history to win both the pentathlon and the decathlon, as the pentathlon was dropped after the 1924 Olympics. Winning so decisively in such high-profile events, Thorpe's performance set a standard for Olympic greatness that has perhaps never been equaled.

"All through the meet," Warner recalled, "as Thorpe went from one strenuous event to another, never seeming to feel fatigue, the wonder and admiration of the onlooking athletes found expression in what came to be a stock phrase, 'Isn't he a horse!' " Thorpe's performance so dominated the Fifth Olympiad that it came to be known as "the Jim Thorpe Olympics." According to one writer, Thorpe made his stunning triumph seem "as easy as picking strawberries out of a dish."

At the awards ceremony held at five P.M. on the day of Thorpe's decathlon victory, Sweden's king, Gustav V, stood on a carpeted podium in a top hat and formal coat to present the medals and congratulate the athletes. The king was warm and personal in expressing his admiration for the victors. "I was the first man up," the American Roger Craig, the winner of the 100-meter dash, told author Robert Wheeler. "When I returned for the 200-meter the king said, 'What, you are back again?' "

Thorpe stood in a suit and tie, nervously fidgeting with his Panama hat as he waited his turn at the podium. According to the *New York Times*, "When James Thorpe, the Carlisle Indian and finest all-around athlete in the world, appeared to claim the prize for winning the Pentathlon, there was a great burst of cheers led by the King. The immense crowd cheered itself hoarse."

The king placed a laurel wreath atop Thorpe's head and awarded Thorpe his gold medal for the pentathlon. In addition, the king presented Thorpe with a life-size bronze bust of his own likeness. Thorpe was called again into the king's presence for the awarding of the day's last medal, the gold medal for the decathlon. The king led the crowd in raising an even greater second cheer for the Indian champion. For a second time, King Gustav bent down from his carpeted podium and placed a laurel wreath on Thorpe's thick black hair. Thorpe adjusted his strange headdress as newsreel cameramen and still photographers jostled on the edge of the cinder track to capture the image of the greatest American Olympian.

King Gustav presented Thorpe with his gold medal and yet another prize—a thirty-pound chalice in the form of a Viking ship, covered with gold and semiprecious stones. It was a tribute to Thorpe from Czar Nicholas II of Russia, the last ruler of the House of Romanov.

After making the presentation, King Gustav took Thorpe's hand and shook it warmly. In an emotional voice, the Swedish ruler told the Oklahoma Indian, "Sir, you are the greatest athlete in the world."

Thorpe mumbled a few words that even the sharp-eared newsmen could not catch. Later, Thorpe confessed to his best friend, Gus Welch, that he had simply told the monarch, "Thanks, King."

Decades later, looking back on a career spent at the highest level of athletic accomplishment, Thorpe observed, "That was the proudest moment of my life."

16

All-American

Immediately after the Olympic awards ceremony, Thorpe and the rest of the American team broke training. "Jim was one of the first to sample the delights of Swedish punch," Warner recalled, "and came back to the *Finland* that night more than a little cheered."

Grantland Rice heard the story of what happened later that evening from Dan Ferris, Sullivan's personal secretary. "When the tender finally poured Thorpe's party aboard, Jim proceeded to leap about the deck, jumping and kicking in cabin doors. I remember he kept yelling, 'I'm a horse! I'm a horse!' In the midst of all this confusion a delegate came to our ship to request Thorpe to visit the King. . . . We had to inform him that Thorpe wasn't aboard." Jack Thorpe heard that his father was drinking with some Swedish friends after the games when he received word that the king wished to see him. To the amazement and delight of his companions, Thorpe declined the invitation and told the messenger, "I'm with my friends."

However much Thorpe celebrated, he deserved it, as his triumph was trumpeted in the press across America and the world. "Jim Thorpe of Carlisle will go down in athletic history as the 'noblest redskin of them all,'" wrote W. J. MacBeth in the *New York American*. "It is doubtful that any human being ever [before] combined the manifold athletic proclivities of this young buck of the Sac and Fox tribe. By winning the pentathlon and decathlon in Stockholm, this aborigine proved to be the greatest individual star in the world." The press in North Carolina took particular pride in the fact that Thorpe had played semipro baseball in their state. On July 18, 1912, the *Charlotte Observer* ran a story that bragged of Thorpe as "the Big Chief" of the Carolina League and a "sensation at the bag." The article mentioned Thorpe's former manager Charles Clancy as well as Peter Boyle and others who had played summer ball with the Indian Olympic champion.

The British press reacted quite differently to the outstanding performance of Thorpe and the other Americans. Some British reporters complained that the Americans should not have allowed Negroes or Indians to compete on their team. The *Spectator* in London accused America of going too far in specialized athletic training. "For many months, sometimes even years, Americans subject themselves to a professional trainer who takes possession of their lives." English journalists claimed that America had "sacrificed its amateur status because of the money which was spent on it," a direct attack on Sullivan and the AAU.

Sullivan defended himself vigorously. "The work of our men in the two all-around competitions, the Decathlon and the Pentathlon, and the showing of James Thorpe, the winner of them, should forever remove from any doubting minds the impression that Americans specialized for one event. Thorpe's record has not been equaled and will not be equaled for many years. And Thorpe had a reputation in other lines of sport long before he began to attract attention in track and field athletics, for besides being a splendid baseball player, he is a star lacrosse player and has the honor of being selected by the leading authority of football in America, Mr. Walter Camp, as a member of the blue ribbon-though-mythical-team, the 'All-American Football Team.' "

In the pages of Caspar Whitney's *Outing* magazine, Sullivan lavished praise on Pop Warner and the Olympic coaching staff. "It is coaching, more than anything else that puts us in a class far above the other countries. . . . We owe a great debt to these coaches, amateur and professional alike, to whom can be traced to a great extent the American team's wonderful showing in the fifth of the modern Olympics."

Warner returned to Carlisle immediately after the games, carrying with him Thorpe's trophies and medals. Tewanima traveled home with

Warner, while Thorpe remained in Europe to compete with other members of the American team in a series of post-Olympic meets.

In Reims, France, Thorpe defeated the Olympic gold medalist Fred Kelly in the 110 meter high hurdles, with the world-class time of 15.6 seconds. Thorpe traveled to Paris with Abel Kiviat, who had won a silver medal in the 1,500-meter run. "He [Thorpe] was a hell of a nice gentleman, but he never had a nickel," Kiviat recalled. "When we'd buy a beer, he couldn't. He just didn't have anything." Thorpe did well in the other post-Olympic meets. "We were exhausted," Kiviat recalled. "Thorpe held up the best, and he was the one who was under the most strain. I only remember him losing one race, and that was in Paris. He was running the hurdles and a plane flew over the stadium. He had never seen a plane before. He looked up, his foot hit the next hurdle, and boom, down he went. It took our trainer an hour to pick the cinders out of his face. He didn't care. He kept saying, 'Did you see the plane?' He was a big kid in a lot of ways."

Kiviat and Thorpe were excited about the possibility of winning the prizes offered for a competition in Paris, twelve quarts of champagne for first place, six for second, and three for third. They later found out that under the newly tightened rules of amateurism, they would not be allowed to receive any prizes. According to Kiviat, "The American officials told us no [prizes] because that would make us professionals. But they did say we could help ourselves to the punch bowl after the competition and we did."

Not even the International Olympic Committee could keep the athletes from competing for prizes among themselves. When the American athletes discovered a chandelier high off the floor in their Paris hotel, they all put a dollar into a betting pool to see who would be the first athlete to touch it. According to Abel Kiviat, "Thorpe didn't have a buck but we gave him credit. There were about fourteen of us in the room. Everybody tried it. Alma Richards of Brigham Young, who won the [Olympic] high jump at six feet, four inches, tried, but he couldn't [reach the chandelier]. But Jim Thorpe did, and he was about four inches shorter than Richards." If the motivation was right, Thorpe could meet any physical challenge.

After Thorpe's return from Europe, he met up with Warner and Tewanima for a triumphant return to Carlisle. As the Olympians stepped off the twelve thirty P.M. train on Friday, August 16, 1912, they were greeted with banners emblazoned with slogans such as "Hail to Chief Thorpe" and "The Greatest Coach in the World." Thousands turned out at Dickinson College's Biddle Field as bands played and students cheered to welcome home the conquering heroes. Friedman had even sent an invitation to Thorpe's parents at the Sac and Fox Agency. The return telegram said simply, "Thorpe's parents dead."

From a temporary grandstand, Friedman addressed the jubilant crowd. He praised Louis Tewanima for his "advancement in civilization and as a man" since having come to Carlisle "virtually as a prisoner of war." Then Friedman turned to Thorpe. "By your achievement you have immeasurably helped your own race," he declared. "By your victory you have inspired your people to live a cleaner, healthier, more vigorous life." The superintendent then presented a congratulatory letter from President William Howard Taft that read in part, "Your victory will serve as an incentive to all to improve those qualities which characterize the best type of American citizen." After the words of some local dignitaries, Warner acknowledged the crowd and said, "I thank you for all you have done."

Thorpe stood up and declared, "All I can say is that you showed me a good time."

Finally, Tewanima addressed the crowd, saying simply, "I thank you."

After fireworks, a parade, and a dance at Carlisle, Warner, Thorpe, and Tewanima took a victory lap around the Northeast. In Philadelphia, they were invited to a Philadelphia Athletics versus Detroit Tigers baseball game and attended a banquet along with Ty Cobb and other sports celebrities. In New York City, they joined the rest of the U.S. Olympic medal winners for a theater party, banquet, and a victory parade down Fifth Avenue. Joined by groups of marching war veterans, Boy Scouts, and athletic clubs, each athlete sat in his own car, with his name marked on the front. Pat McDonald, the New York City traffic cop who had won a surprise victory in the shot put, greeted the cheering crowd, estimated at almost a million, with easy smiles and friendly waves.

Riding stiffly in another car, Thorpe had a different reaction to the enthusiastic fans. According to the *New York Times*, Thorpe sat in the car next to his trophies in embarrassed silence, chewing gum, his Panama hat pulled over his eyes. "True to his race's traditions, [he] seldom looked to right or left, and rarely . . . permitted himself to depart from his accustomed stoicism."

When the parade stopped at City Hall, Thorpe spotted James Sullivan in the grandstand and finally broke into a smile. He rushed up to the czar of amateur sports and pumped his hand. The New York City mayor, William J. Gaynor, praised the "victorious athletes," declaring, "You have shown that you possessed American stomachs, hearts, muscles and heads."

After their victory tour, the Olympic heroes returned to Carlisle, where they gave away souvenirs of their adventures to their friends and fellow students. Thorpe presented Gus Welch with his Panama hat and one of the track shoes he had worn to win the decathlon. Tewanima gave away most of his track medals, which some girls proudly turned into shoe buckles. A short time later, Tewanima returned to the Hopi reservation in Arizona. From that time on, Tewanima rarely left the land of his people. Despite the news reports from Carlisle that Tewanima had embraced Christianity and the white man's way of life, Tewanima turned his back on the white world. Like his ancestors before him, he tended his sheep and his fruit trees and participated in ritual celebrations. The Hopi Olympian lived according to the Hopi way until an accidental fall from Second Mesa ended his noble life in 1969.

Back at Carlisle, a board of medical experts made an anthropometric study of Thorpe, taking some forty-six measurements of his body and a series of photographs. Although he was a medical marvel and the most famous athlete in the world, Thorpe was broke. In an attempt to gather some cash, he wrote to the Indian agent Horace Johnson to get his funds transferred to Carlisle. Johnson agreed to transfer the amount, $295.23, but did so with some reservations about Thorpe's character, which he expressed in a letter to Superintendent Friedman: "I am told that he [Thorpe] visited the agency last year and that he is not a bad appearing fellow though somewhat inclined to indulge his appetite in intoxicating liquors. As to how that may be I do not know but if he does he comes by it honestly enough. I knew his father quite well over the years and he was quite notorious as a 'Booze Fighter.'"

Promoters inundated Thorpe with lucrative offers to play baseball or participate in other professional sports activities. Despite that fact that Gus Welch and others encouraged Thorpe to cash in immediately, he agreed to take part in one last track and field event sponsored by the AAU. Thorpe almost did not make the meet, as he fell sick and was hospitalized, perhaps due to excessive celebrating. He was released from the hospital on September 1. The next day, a rainy Labor Day in New York City's Celtic Park, Thorpe won the AAU All-Around Championship of 1912 competing in ten events, all in a single day. "Thorpe is the greatest athlete that ever lived," the former AAU all-around champion Martin Sheridan told the *New York American*. "He has me beaten fifty ways. Even when I was in my prime I could not do what he did today." The *New York Herald* called Thorpe's performance that day "one of the most remarkable feats in the annals of amateur athletics."

Sullivan and other AAU officials pushed Thorpe to compete in a series of track meets across the country, but he refused. "I have trained hard for this meet and now need a rest," Thorpe told the press, "which I will take immediately."

Thorpe did not rest for long. In a letter to his brother Frank dated September 17, 1912, Thorpe wrote, "Well, Bud, I'm right in the game again, playing football. We have our first game next Saturday. . . . Frank, I have the chance to make a bunch of dough after leaving this school. Just started going today. God but it's hard to go back again, but it is for my good, so I will make the best of things."

Instead of going professional or competing in amateur track, Thorpe decided to play one more year of football for Pop Warner's Carlisle Indians. A number of factors probably influenced his decision. He liked and trusted Warner, who no doubt pressured him to return to the gridiron. He was loyal to his teammates and took pride in the fact that they were all Indians. Most of all, he just plain liked football—the running, the kicking, and the hitting. Although he liked the money from baseball, football was Thorpe's favorite game.

What Thorpe did not like was practice. "Hell's bells," Warner later wrote of his star. "He was lazy, didn't like to practice, and he gave out his best effort only when he felt like it. And that was about 40 percent of the time. Football was just a good time to Jim."

Warner was pleased about the prospects for the 1912 season. Joe Guyon, a Chippewa, was a strong addition to the line, and Pete Calac also joined the squad. "Oh! He was my idol!" Calac later said of Thorpe. "Actually, he was the idol of every Indian boy. I had read about him in the papers when he was competing in the Olympics. All the students looked up to him." William "Lone Star" Dietz worked as an assistant coach, helping introduce new players to the crisscrosses, reverses, quick line bucks, and short passes that were key to the Carlisle offense.

Thorpe worked as hard as he could, but he was quiet and moody. He could play the responsible hero for only so long, before he had to let loose, relax, and sneak a beer or two with Welch near the outbuildings of the school farm or with some admirer at a Carlisle watering hole. According to his teacher Marianne Moore, "He was liked by all, rather than venerated or idolized. He was off-hand, modest, casual about everything in the way of fame or eminence achieved. This modesty, with top performance, was characteristic of him, and no back talk . . . I never saw him irascible, sour or primed for vengeance."

Warner relied on Welch to help motivate his star halfback. Welch was a dependable, smart player with a big heart. Warner enjoyed telling the story of finding Gus Welch rummaging around in the locker room one day, looking through the equipment. "What are you doing?" Warner asked his quarterback.

Welch told Warner that he was looking for worn-out equipment that the younger Carlisle students might use. "We want these kids to grow up big and strong and take the lesson of health with them when they go back home," Warner reported Welch as saying. "Now that we are no longer people of the chase, poor physical condition is the curse of the Indian. A game of some kind is our one chance against tuberculosis."

The Carlisle Indians started the season with blowouts against Albright College, 50–7, and Lebanon Valley, 45–0. In the third game of the season, Dickinson put up a good fight, at least for the first period. Then the Indian scoring machine got to work. Thorpe took the ball straight through the line for a twenty-nine-yard touchdown jaunt. On their next possession, Carlisle was forced to punt from their own end zone. Thorpe stood back to take the snap, which sailed over his head. He managed to recover the ball, but instead of touching it down for a safety, he ran out of his own end zone to the Dickinson end zone for a touchdown. Gus Welch returned a kickoff eighty-five yards for another touchdown, contributing to the final score of 34–0 for Carlisle.

Four days later, Carlisle romped over Villanova, 65–0. The Indians got an unwelcome surprise in Washington, Pennsylvania, when they faced off against Washington and Jefferson College. Washington and Jefferson held the Indians to a scoreless tie despite the fact that Thorpe made four interceptions. On the rail journey back to Carlisle, the team had a stopover in Pittsburgh. Thorpe was so disgusted with his subpar performance that he sneaked off to a bar with Gus Welch to boost his spirits.

Feeling better after a drink or two, Welch left the bar to join the rest of the Carlisle team at a hotel dining room. Warner asked Welch where Thorpe was. Welch told him that Thorpe was still drinking at the bar. Warner was furious. "I went down and brought him to the hotel where he [Thorpe] created excitement by his loud talking and boisterous attitude toward me," Warner later related in his memoirs. "A crowd gathered and as I saw Thorpe was making an exhibition of himself, I induced him to go inside the hotel and keep quiet. When train time came we got him through a side gate and on the train."

Warner added, "Old-timers will recall the exaggerated and unwarranted story that Thorpe and I had gotten drunk and that he and I had gone to the floor in a free-for-all scrap."

After the unfortunate incident, Warner forced his wayward athlete to apologize to the entire team.

"By golly," Thorpe said, "I'll never take another drink of beer!"

"Or anything else!" Warner shouted.

"Yep," Thorpe added, "or anything else."

On October 12, 1912, Carlisle traveled to Syracuse, New York, to play the Orangemen, the only team to defeat them during the previous season. The conditions in Syracuse were bad—muddy and rainy. Although Carlisle controlled the game, they could not dominate the scoreboard. At halftime, Warner blew up at Thorpe and his team-mates. "I lashed into them," Warner later recalled, "insisting that they must try some line plunging if they wanted to win the game.

"Where's your sense, Jim?" he told his star halfback. "Don't you see that speed isn't getting you anything on this slippery ground? For heaven's sake, use your weight.

"In the second half," Warner recalled, "the quarterback began feeding the ball to Thorpe for straight bucks and slants off tackle. . . . The big

Indian tore the Syracuse line into shreds on every play and we won the game handily (33–0)."

Dr. Joseph Alexander, who would go on to become a three-time All-American at Syracuse, was just a boy at the time and watched Thorpe play from a hill overlooking the football stadium. "He had terrific flexibility and his coordination was absolutely beautiful," Dr. Alexander recalled. "He was not powerful in the sense that he had so much strength; it was his coordination that made him strong. His movements were all easy, simple, and flexible, and most important of all, he never played football with any anxiety or fear or anything to hinder his mind from acting on a split second's notice."

For Thorpe and the other Carlisle players, life on the road between games was a time to relax and enjoy themselves. They often pulled pranks, particularly on the players who were new to the squad. One of the favorite jokes was to tell the new players, "Now when you go to bed tonight, put your shoes out in the hallway and a man will come along and shine them up and they will be all ready for you, in good appearance, tomorrow morning." When they woke up, the new players discovered their shoes mixed up and tied together in mismatched pairs.

Gus Welch later claimed that he motivated the large but sometimes lethargic guard Elmer Busch by biting him, punching him, and kicking him in pileups, and blaming it on the other team. After every attack, Busch complained bitterly to the officials and then tore up the opposition.

After their last game together, Welch asked Busch, "Well, Elmer, how did you enjoy your football? Did you get anything out of the game?"

Busch answered solemnly, "I tell you Gus. For the first year I enjoyed it, but the last two years I never saw so many dirty white men."

"At this every man on the squad almost dies laughing," Welch recalled, "so I tell Elmer the trick we played on him. He's quiet for a minute and then he grins. 'Well,' he says, 'You're a smart quarterback, Gus, but I guess I ought to go and apologize now to all those officials.'"

Before the game against the University of Pittsburgh, Warner made sure that Thorpe saw a press clipping in which a Pittsburgh official was quoted as saying, "Thorpe will never run through us . . . we've got him figured." The article was enough to get Thorpe fired up. Early in the game, he got the ball on a delayed pass, went through one side of the Pitt line, warded off some tacklers, sidestepped others, and stiff-armed the last Pittsburgh player on the field as he ran in for a touchdown. He later kicked a forty-four-yard field goal and wound up scoring thirty-two points in the Indians' 45–8 victory. Reporting on the game, the *New York Times* ran a headline, "Thorpe Nearly a Team."

Traffic was snarled for blocks around the Georgetown stadium when Carlisle played the Catholic university on October 26, 1912. Gus Welch often recounted the visit by Senator Boies Penrose of Pennsylvania to the Carlisle dressing room before the game. According to Welch, the senator, who was a big Carlisle fan, told the team how important it was to win the game. "The Carlisle School Appropriation Bill was before Congress and the senator said a victory would surely help the bill through Congress. And he said, 'Thorpe, if you go out there and play a great game we might make you a citizen of this great country. And Welch, if you go out there and call a smart game, you could become a citizen.' And then the senator turned to Big Bear [guard Elmer Busch] and said, 'Big Bear, you go out there and tear that Irish line to pieces and you might be granted citizenship.' Big Bear shook his head in the negative and Senator Penrose said, 'What, you don't want to become a citizen?' Big Bear shook his head and said, 'No, Senator. They tell me if I become a citizen, I will have to pay taxes.'"

Carlisle started off strong, scoring 34 points in the first half to beat Georgetown 34–20. Although his teammates Alex Arcasa and Possum Powell scored all the touchdowns, Thorpe's blocking, running, kicking, and tackling dazzled the assembled fans. "Thorpe is a wizard of the gridiron," wrote H. C. Byrd, reporting on the game from Washington. "His work stands out as conspicuously as if he were the only man on the field. His powers of endurance and ability to cope with various situations are so remarkable as to cause one to wonder at the status of the man."

After the game, Oklahoma congressman Charles Carter, the first congressman from the former Indian Territory, entertained the Carlisle team at his home. His daughter Julia graciously welcomed the Indians. Julia agreed to go out on a date with Carlisle player Joe Guyon and was equally impressed by Gus Welch, whom she later married.

The next week, the Carlisle Indians traveled to Toronto to play a team made up of Canada's best rugby players in a game that was organized to celebrate the hundredth anniversary of the War of 1812 and the Canadian Thanksgiving. They played the first half of the game by American rules, the second half by Canadian rules. The Canadian fans were much more interested in Thorpe than in the game. According to a Toronto newspaper, a Canadian cheerleader invited Thorpe to come to the sidelines so the Canadian fans could have a closer look at the world's greatest athlete. When Thorpe ambled over to the sidelines, "He stood stoically, like a statue, in front of the stand, accepted the cheers, bowed, and smiled, and then loped back to his position at left half." The Indians won the first official football game to be played in Canada 49–1.

The next week, Carlisle returned to the United States to play Lehigh. After the first kickoff the Lehigh quarterback led his team downfield, only to have his pass intercepted by Thorpe ten yards deep in the end zone. Thorpe took off up the field, broke through the defense, and headed for the goal line. He jogged down the field until he took a look behind and noticed the Lehigh quarterback, the fastest Lehigh player, catching up to him. Thorpe smiled, shifted into high gear, and blazed in for the touchdown, well ahead of the winded defender.

Even more remarkable than Thorpe and the other Indians' playing skills was their attitude. During halftime of the Lehigh game, the Indians did not head into the locker room but instead hung around the side of the field, talking and laughing. Some of the Lehigh players thought Thorpe and his teammates were being arrogant. They were not. They were just having fun.

During the second half, Thorpe and the others started playing mind games with Lehigh. As the Carlisle offense lined up over the ball, Thorpe yelled at his roommate Welch, the quarterback, "How about through left tackle this time?" The Lehigh players thought it was a trick until Thorpe smashed through left tackle, just as promised.

The Indians even maintained their sense of fun during a goal-line pileup. While the officials frantically separated the men to see if Carlisle had scored a touchdown, the Carlisle center, William Garlow, launched into an eloquent discourse that was recalled by a Lehigh player. "It's a distressing thing to have to break this news to you gentlemen, but I very much fear it is over," Garlow pontificated. "We should much prefer that this were happening to somebody else, but the facts are clear and you will very soon see that the little pellet is resting securely beyond the last white line. We regret it, I am sure you regret it, and I hope that nothing happening here will spoil what for us has been a very pleasant afternoon." The touchdown was good, and Carlisle defeated Lehigh 34–14.

Carlisle played its biggest game of the year at West Point, New York, against the U.S. Military Academy. It was a historic contest between two federally funded schools, one dedicated to training Indians in the ways of the white world, the other dedicated to training U.S. Army officers in the ways of war. It was November 9, 1912, just twenty-two years after the U.S. Army massacre of Lakota Sioux at Wounded Knee in the Dakota Territory marked the sad end to the Indian wars. "Warner had no trouble getting the boys keyed up for the game," recalled Gus Welch, who later served with distinction as an officer with the U.S. Army in France during World War I. "He reminded the boys that it was the fathers and grandfathers of these Army players who fought the Indians. That was enough!"

Warner understood the Indian attitude quite well. "When playing against college teams, it was not to them so much the Carlisle School against Pennsylvania or Harvard, as the case might be, but it was the Indian against the White Man," Warner later explained. "It was not that they felt any definite bitterness against the conquering white, or against the government for years of unfair treatment, but rather that they believed the armed contests between red men and white had never been waged on equal terms.

"If there was one team that the Indians liked to beat more than another," Warner recalled, "that team was Army."

Warner also was excited about facing off against Army. For Warner, the Army game, and every football game, was a war. According to Warner's football guidebook, "Each scrimmage represents a battle in which the opposing forces are lined up opposite each other, one side defending itself against the attack of the other. The lines represent the infantry, and the backs can be likened to cavalry, quick moving and able to charge the enemy at any spot, or rush to the support of any position attacked."

After watching a dress parade of cadets, the Carlisle Indians gathered in the locker room. Pete Calac remembered that Coach Warner was unusually excited before this game. "[Warner] stood at one end of the locker room facing the team who were standing on the benches, and he began to pace back and forth and then up and down the aisle between the men to give them individual instructions."

Warner was not a sermonizing coach. He spoke straight to his team. They were smaller than the opposition, averaging only 170 pounds. At just under six feet, Thorpe was the tallest player on the squad. To beat Army, the Indians would have to rely on speed and execution. A fumble, a missed block, a broken tackle could cost them the game.

With a cigarette burning between his fingers, Warner pointed to each player, making sure he knew his assignment. "Cotton Vetternack, a Chippewa weighing 137 pounds, played end," Joe Guyon recalled. "He was the best tackle on our team but lacked the blocking equipment. Consequently, the tackles and ends switched positions on offense. Thorpe and I were detailed to block Army Captain All-American Devore."

As the Indians ran out of the locker room, large dark clouds hung over the Hudson River Valley. According to the press, "It was a day for furs, or if one had no furs, to lie abed and think of starving Esquimaux in the Arctic regions." The west stands in the stadium were filled with slate-color-clad West Point cadets. Enlisted men in olive drab cheered from the south stands. The Army team, led by captain Leland S. Devore, an All-American tackle, thought the Indians in their crimson blankets on the sidelines looked small, intimidated, and easy to defeat.

At three o'clock in the afternoon, Army kicked off. At the line of scrimmage, quarterback Welch gave a signal, and the Indians shifted their offensive formation. Thorpe at left halfback moved up close to the line, flanking the defensive tackle. It was one of Warner's greatest tactical innovations, something he called the "wingback" formation, also known as the "single wing." Warner had used it for years and hoped that against Army it would give the Indians the blocking power of an eight-man line and a more versatile attack. The key to the wingback formation was the left halfback, who had to be able to run, block, or throw. With his thick neck and jutting jaw, barrel-chested Jim Thorpe was the perfect wingback player.

Army had never seen anything like the wingback. In the first play from scrimmage, Alex Arcasa went around end for fifteen yards. Then

Thorpe went around end for fifteen yards. Possum Powell broke through center for eight. Thorpe went off tackle for twenty. After getting hit hard by the Army defense, Thorpe lay motionless on the turf. Warner took a deep pull on his cigarette as the clock ticked off the time: thirty seconds; a minute; a minute and a half. The referee motioned to restart play but was interrupted by the Army captain. "Hell's bells, Mr. Referee," Devore said, loud enough so that Thorpe could hear him. "We don't stand on technicalities at West Point. Give him all the time he wants."

Thorpe got up and got angry. He played hard, sweeping around the ends, busting up the middle, crushing over tackle, and punting high spirals more than fifty yards. "Jim could really run and he was shifty," Pete Calac recalled. "He had a way of fading, that is, he would fade away from you and then when you went to tackle him, he would come by you with that hip of his. He could catch the tacklers alongside of the head somehow and just roll them over and away he would go! He ran with his knees high and if you tackled him head on, boy you were really asking for it! He could knock you out with those knees."

The murderous operation of Thorpe at wingback would change the game of football forever. Warner's formation became the prototype for the single wing, the double wing, and other modern offensive sets. The wingback formation was the greatest innovation of the Warner system.

Still, Army played hard behind the running of their halfback, Dwight David Eisenhower, who would later command the Allied forces in Europe in World War II and become the thirty-fourth American president. After a Carlisle player was thrown out of the game for slugging, the Indians were penalized twenty yards, half the distance to the goal line. Eisenhower and the other Army backs worked the ball downfield and scored a touchdown but missed the extra point. The Indians responded quickly with a touchdown and an extra point, giving them a 7–6 lead at the half.

In the second half, Carlisle took control of the game. The blocking of Guyon and Thorpe succeeded in taking Army's Devore out of the game. After one play, a frustrated Devore jumped on Guyon's back as he lay on the field. "He only weighed 240 pounds to my 180," Guyon later joked. "Of course another Indian bit the dust." Although Guyon continued to play, the Army captain was thrown out of the game.

Eisenhower did not make it through the game either. According to Gus Welch, Eisenhower broke his leg trying to tackle Thorpe on a run around left end. Other sources say that the Army halfback left the field with a badly twisted knee. Ike denied the stories, recalling that he and another Army player were going in for a tackle on Thorpe in the third quarter. Thorpe stopped short, and the two Army players collided. Eisenhower said, "Apparently, when we got up, we staggered a little bit and the Coach, Captain Ernest Graves, was signaling to call us out. The both of us ran to the sidelines and begged him to let us remain in the game but he said to take a rest and then return in the next quarter." Ike claimed that he was not put back in the third quarter, and by the fourth quarter, Carlisle was so far ahead that the coach told him to go to the showers.

"Thorpe's Indians Crush West Point. Brilliancy of Carlisle Redskins' Play Amazes Cadets and Spectators," reported the *New York Times*. "Jim Thorpe and his redoubtable band of Carlisle Indian gridiron stars invaded the plains this afternoon to match their prowess against the moleskin gladiators of Uncle Sam's Military Academy. . . . Standing out resplendent in a galaxy of Indian stars was Jim Thorpe, recently crowned the athletic marvel of the age. . . . [A]t times the game was almost forgotten while the spectators gazed on Thorpe, the individual, to wonder at his prowess. . . . He simply ran wild, while the Cadets tried in vain to stop his progress. It was like trying to catch a shadow. Thorpe went through the West Point line as if it was an open door; his defensive play was on par with his attack and his every move was that of a past master."

After the game, Leland Devore told reporters in the locker room, "That Indian is the greatest player I have ever stacked up against in my five years experience. . . . He is super-human, that is all. . . . There is nothing he can't do. He kicks superbly, worms his way through a field like a combination of grey-hound, jackrabbit, and eel. He is as cunning and strategic as a fox. He follows interference like the hangers-on follow an army."

In a ghostwritten article carrying his byline published in the *New York American* Devore called Carlisle's 27–6 margin of victory "the biggest ever run up on the Army team, and football at the academy is no new game." On the same page, in a ghostwritten article carrying the byline "Jim Thorpe," the Indian athlete was quoted as saying,

"We played today 100 percent better than we played in any other game."

Gus Welch recalled that Walter Camp accompanied the team on the trip back to New York City after the Army game. Camp, the father of American football who had initially recommended Warner for the Carlisle coaching position, spent the journey talking with the Carlisle players about their performance. "The boys had a lot of fun talking over the game with him," Welch remembered fondly. "Camp said we had a strong team and that Thorpe was a great runner, but he said, 'Your quarterback (I was the quarterback) calls his plays too fast, he doesn't study the defense.' Thorpe said, 'Mr. Camp, how can he study the defense when there isn't any defense?'

"Five times during the game we went into punt formation on fourth down and ran the ball instead of kicking—two of the plays resulted in touchdowns and the other three plays went for good gains. Mr. Camp said, 'At Yale we don't play that kind of ball—your quarterback should have used Thorpe's kicking ability.' Big Bear [Elmer Busch] spoke up and said, 'Mr. Camp, we didn't want Thorpe to punt but we wanted touchdowns.'"

Thorpe and his teammates suffered the all-too-predictable letdown the following week and lost to a weak University of Pennsylvania team 34–26. "It was a game I particularly hated to lose," Warner later recalled, "for Thorpe gave one of his greatest exhibitions that afternoon. Once he took the ball well back in Carlisle territory and raced eighty yards for a touchdown, as beautiful a piece of open-field running as I ever expect to see. Twice it seemed that they had pulled him down, but each time he shook them off." By the end of the first half, Thorpe had scored two touchdowns and kicked two extra points.

In a less generous mood, Warner mentioned elsewhere that Thorpe's attitude was in part responsible for the Penn victory. "Carelessness was another of Thorpe's great faults," Warner recalled. "There was a game with Pennsylvania that we lost in the last quarter, the Quakers completing a long forward pass for a touchdown. It seemed to me that Thorpe could have made the interception easily, and after the game I asked him about it. 'Sure, I could have batted it down easy. I didn't try because I never thought the receiver had any chance to reach the ball.'"

Later Warner commented that Thorpe "would ease up when he felt safe in doing so. Sometimes he found it wasn't as safe as he thought it was, and this made him a bit of an in-and-outer. I'll pick the all-outer over the in-and-outer any time."

The second-to-last game of the season was meant to be little more than a scrimmage against the Springfield YMCA team in Springfield, Massachusetts. Instead, it turned into a hard-fought game that the Indians barely managed to win 30–24. While watching Thorpe and the Carlisle Indians warm up for the game, reporters from the nearby city of Worcester, Massachusetts, picked up on a rumor: Thorpe was not an amateur at the time he won his Olympic medals. He was a professional athlete who had played ball in the South. There were newspaper clippings, photos, and even an eyewitness, Charles Clancy, who claimed to have coached Thorpe in North Carolina and was spending the winter in Southbridge, Massachusetts. Roy Johnson, a reporter at the *Worcester Telegram*, began reporting the story.

Thorpe's spirits dipped once again before the Thanksgiving Day game against Brown, the last game of the season. According to Grantland Rice, Thorpe took a drink before the game, Warner found out about it, and the two got into a heated argument. Adding to Warner's worries were the playing conditions: cold and snowy.

Warner recalled the game:

> The ground was covered with snow, an icy wind blew down the field, and the Indians played wretchedly all through the first half, being lucky to hold Brown scoreless. Talking to the team between halves, a bright idea came to me and I pointed out to the boys that it was Jim Thorpe's last game, and that they owed him a victory in return for the many he had won for them. Before I finished my little talk, I saw the young redskins tightening up, and every man took the field with a grim, determined face and set jaw. Brown must have thought a cyclone had blown up, for the Indians swept forward for touchdown after touchdown with resistless fury.

With Welch injured and out of the game, Arcasa played quarterback. It was old-fashioned straight-ahead-running football with a typical Warner twist, the "dead Indian" or "wing shift" play. After being tackled, the Carlisle running back got up woozily, pretending to be hurt. As the opposition looked at the "injured" running back, the rest of the Carlisle team lined up on one side of the ball and the injured back, now playing center, snapped the ball. The first time Carlisle tried the series play, it did not work. The second time, it resulted in a sixty-five-yard touchdown run.

Thorpe scored three touchdowns and kicked two field goals in the 32–0 Indian victory. Forced to punt, this time from behind his own goal line, Thorpe instead faked the kick and ran 110 yards for a touchdown. "I've seen the greatest football player ever," Michael Thompson, the referee who worked the game, later told Grantland Rice. "[Jim Thorpe] was a tornado."

In the last few minutes of play, Thorpe threw a twenty-yard pass to his end. On the next play, Thorpe smashed through the line for an eighteen-yard touchdown run, the last touchdown of his college career. "He is a man of whalebone whose anatomy is impervious to injury," the *New York Item* reported. "He is as near a perfect type as can be found anywhere."

Thorpe was the perfect type of athlete for Warner's wingback formation, the formation that brought college football into the modern era. Together, Thorpe and Warner transformed what had once been a game of brawn controlled by Ivy League sportsmen into a game of speed, strength, and grace that all Americans, even a team of Indians, could play and win.

Walter Camp did not rate the Carlisle Indians as the top football team of 1912, but their record was astonishing. In a fourteen-game season against tough opponents, they won twelve games, lost one, and tied one. They outscored their opponents 504–114. Jim Thorpe tallied an incredible 198 points to lead the nation in scoring. Camp did honor the team by naming Jim Thorpe as a first-team All-American for the second year in a row and naming Gus Welch and Joe Guyon as second-string All-Americans.

Perhaps the greatest tribute to Thorpe's ability on the football field came from his coach, Pop Warner. Though Warner did not approve of Thorpe's attitude, Warner appreciated his astounding athletic ability. "Thorpe, in physical equipment, stands without peer in football annals," Warner observed. "He could do a hundred yards in close to ten seconds, and this speed, backed by one hundred and eighty pounds of bone and muscle, made him almost unstoppable. In addition, he had a change of pace, a deceptive pivot; and his high knee-lift and powerful straight-arm worked havoc with tacklers. Even when they piled on him like wolves, I have seen Jim carry the pack for five and ten yards before being dragged down.

"He was both a long and sure passer, his big right hand cuddling the oval as though it were a baseball. And when it came to kicking, not only was he deadly on field goals as far back as the fifty-yard lines, but his punts averaged sixty yards. Moreover, his kicking, like his passing, was remarkable for its consistency and accuracy. He could come pretty close to calling his shots." In short, Warner described Thorpe as "the most marvelous all-around athlete that the world has ever seen."

According to the former Army halfback President Dwight D. Eisenhower, "[Thorpe] was able to do everything that anyone else could, but he could do it better."

17

The Swindle

In the late winter of 1912, Jim Thorpe returned home to Oklahoma to enjoy the holidays. He visited with his older sister Mary, his older brother Frank, and his other relatives, and checked up on his 160 acres of allotment land, which were leased out to a farmer. Thorpe requested a $125 advance on his lease payment from the Indian agent Horace Johnson. In a letter dated December 23, 1912, Johnson recommended to his superiors that Thorpe be given the money but included a harsh assessment of the world's greatest athlete. "I am personally acquainted with the applicant. He is 26 years of age and for the last several years has been a student in Carlisle Indian School, Carlisle, Pennsylvania. . . . To the best of my knowledge he has accumulated no property. He is not industrious. His reputation is not good. It is reported that he is addicted to the use of intoxicants."

By January 18, 1913, Thorpe was back at Carlisle, enjoying the adulation of the Carlisle community. Jim participated fully in the social events of the New Year and even won a cake for his two-step at the annual reception of the Mercer Society.

Thorpe kept in touch with the beautiful, intelligent, and hardworking Iva Miller. Iva, who had only a trace of Indian blood, had moved to California after graduating from Carlisle in the spring of 1912. Her relatives and others, including Pop Warner, counseled her against her relationship with Jim Thorpe, but Iva was strong willed. She turned down the advances of Gus Welch and from a distance carried on a secret romance with Jim Thorpe. They thought about the possibility of marriage. They both loved children and wanted to raise a family. Over time, Jim professed his love to Iva, and Iva grew to love Jim.

Thorpe realized that he could not marry Iva while still a student at Carlisle. He had fame. Now he needed money. While Pop Warner was one of the best-paid coaches in America, Jim Thorpe, the world's greatest athlete, had to survive on the income from his allotment lands in Oklahoma, which totaled some $250 per year. In late 1912 and early 1913, Thorpe entertained even more lucrative offers than those he had rejected before the football season. Professional baseball, which was going through a bit of an attendance slump, saw Thorpe as the "red hope" that could draw fans back to the game. The press reported that Pittsburgh offered Thorpe 7,000 "bones" a year to sign. Another club offered him $500 a month. Thorpe was flattered by the offers but turned them down. Pop Warner told him to stay away from professional baseball. So did James Sullivan, who hoped to lure Thorpe back to compete in AAU-sponsored track meets.

Thorpe was comfortable at Carlisle. Though life at the Indian boarding school was tough, it was the only life he had ever really known. He decided to maintain his amateur status a while longer. Thorpe was confident that he would somehow turn his victories into cash. He had faith in Warner and Sullivan, just as Iva had faith in Thorpe.

"Then when life was juicy fat for Jim Thorpe," Warner later recalled, "Fate decided to intervene."

"Thorpe with Professional Baseball Team Says Clancy" read the headline of the *Worcester Telegram* on January 22, 1913. The article claimed "that the great Jim Thorpe, the Sac and Fox Indian, world's amateur champion athlete, played professional baseball in the Carolina association for two years" in a statement made by Charles Clancy, "manager of the Winston-Salem team of the Carolina association." The article speculated, "Whether he will be stripped of his honors and the title of world champion is a question for the athletic authorities to decide."

The unbylined article, later attributed to the reporter Roy Johnson, had an unsavory tone, almost as if the author were trying to blemish Thorpe's character to make the "crime" of professionalism anathema to readers. The article quoted Clancy as saying, "There is a trace of Irish in Thorpe on his paternal side, so he told me. He is lighter complexioned than some of the Indians, showing the strain of Caucasian blood."

After questioning Thorpe's racial purity, Clancy attacked his athletic skill. "I signed him up at a pitcher but I thought he had a yellow streak at times. His weakness at bat was on a curve. He could hit speed all right, but the curve used to fool him." Clancy then attacked the Olympic hero's sobriety, describing Jim as sauntering "down the main street . . . with a gallon jug in his hand," stopping every few yards to "take a satisfying swig" and "let out a warwhoop." Clancy told a story about Thorpe jumping through the plate glass window of a saloon, then doing the same thing through a grocery store window when "the glass scalped him right on top of the head.

"That is a sample of the work cut out for me while Thorpe was on the team," Clancy was reported as saying. "It was no cinch."

The racist attack on Thorpe echoed the attacks on the heavyweight boxing champion Jack Johnson. Before his 1910 title bout against the white challenger Jim Jeffries, the *Chicago Daily Tribune* vilified the black athlete as "Sambo Remo Rastus Brown," and a "coward" who took up "fighting to gain money." When Johnson won the fight, race riots broke out in New York City, Atlanta, and several other cities.

The story snowballed into the most talked-about celebrity sports scandal in the nation. Was Thorpe a professional who lied about his status to compete in Stockholm? If he was a professional, would he return his medals and trophies and give up his records? Even more damaging to Thorpe were Clancy's accusations about his character. Was Jim Thorpe, the world's greatest athlete, actually nothing but a drunkard of mixed blood with a yellow streak? Unfortunately for Jim Thorpe, the world was ready to believe the worst. The unsigned article in the *Worcester Telegram* tarnished his reputation for the rest of his life.

The scandal spread quickly and posed a significant threat to Sullivan, Warner, and the U.S. Indian School. Sullivan had built his reputation, the reputation of the AAU, and the international reputation of American sports on the rule of strict amateurism. It was his gospel, his defense against the accusations of unfair competition from the British and other sports organizations. To have America's greatest amateur revealed as a professional was Sullivan's nightmare. Sullivan immediately denied the allegations. "I don't believe there is any truth in the charges of professionalism against Thorpe," Sullivan told the press. "I have every confidence in his amateur status."

Warner knew that Thorpe had played summer baseball. He had probably even arranged it. Warner also knew that if he admitted he had known about Thorpe's baseball career prior to the Olympic games, he would probably be banned from coaching amateur athletics. His career would be over. In addition, the scandal threatened to expose the financial details of the Carlisle Athletic Association, Warner's business empire that operated on the edge of legality. An investigation of the association would bring up questions that Warner did not want to answer, especially in public.

Warner acted immediately to protect himself and denied everything. In an interview published in the *New York Times* on January 25, 1913, just three days after the *Worcester Telegram* story appeared, Warner claimed, "All I know about the charges against Thorpe have been gleaned from the newspaper reports to the effect that a Mr. Clancy, Manager of a Southern ball team, has been quoted as saying that Thorpe played professional baseball with a Winston-Salem team under his management." Warner showed the *Times* reporter a newspaper clipping in which Clancy denied making the statement attributed to him in the *Worcester Telegram*. Warner further quoted a letter he had received from Clancy that stated in part, "As a matter of fact and record, Mr. Thorpe has never pitched a game of ball for the Winston-Salem team or played in any other position in that club or in the Carolina League, and I have never paid Thorpe any money any time for any purpose." At the end of the interview, Warner added, "I am further assured by Thorpe that there is nothing in the story."

James Sullivan supported Warner's story for the most part. In an article dated Saturday, January 25, in the *New York Tribune*, Sullivan told reporters that he had spoken with Warner and that Warner had been in contact with Clancy, who denied the story. According to Sullivan, Clancy told Warner that "Thorpe had been down at Winston-Salem hunting foxes and while there had practiced a little with his team" but "had not received any money or played professionally."

At the same time, Sullivan began to hedge his bets. He told the press that he had wired Warner for complete information about

Thorpe's athletic background and that representatives of the AAU had gone to North Carolina for further investigation. "If Thorpe is found guilty," Sullivan said, hedging his bet on Warner, "his trophies will have to be returned and his records erased from the books."

On the same day that Sullivan's interview appeared in the *New York Tribune*, the paper reported that the New England Association of the Amateur Athletic Union had filed charges against Thorpe, claiming that he had played professional baseball under his own name in North Carolina and could not be considered an amateur.

James Sullivan was suddenly vulnerable. He had squashed newspaper stories in the past, but formal charges against the AAU's most outstanding athlete were something else. Many members of the AAU were angry with Thorpe for returning to Carlisle in the fall of 1912 instead of touring as an AAU track star. Sullivan, who had known Warner for more than a decade, probably knew what Warner knew— that America's greatest amateur athlete had played summer baseball. Like Warner, Sullivan was a micromanager with an encyclopedic knowledge of the top athletes who belonged to the AAU. Sullivan had closely followed Thorpe's career for years. In praising Thorpe after his Olympic victory, Sullivan himself had acknowledged that Thorpe was "a great baseball player," even though Thorpe had pitched only a handful of games for Carlisle. The Thorpe scandal threatened Sullivan as much as Warner. It was a threat Sullivan could not tolerate.

Almost immediately, hard evidence of Thorpe's Carolina baseball career came to light. On January 26, the *New York Tribune* reported that "a study of the records of the Eastern Carolina League disclosed the fact that a Thorpe did play in that league in the summers of 1909 and 1910." Records showed that Clancy had not paid Thorpe to play for Winston-Salem but had paid him to play for Fayetteville.

In addition to the written record, there was ample verbal testimony from eyewitnesses. Several umpires recalled Thorpe as one of the most popular players in the league. Peter Boyle was quoted in the *New York Times* as saying he had played with Thorpe on the Fayetteville team in 1910. "His work was heady and his throwing a revelation," Boyle reported. "Thorpe was the swiftest man who ever played ball in this section."

On January 27, the *New York Tribune* reported that "Charles McDonald, a former sporting editor of the Raleigh paper, five members of the Eastern Carolina League, and Sherwood Upchurch, an umpire" all confirmed that Jim Thorpe had played summer ball in North Carolina. The paper went on to report that "when Thorpe won Olympic honors North Carolina papers printed his pictures, and he has been claimed by the 'fans' since. They never thought of possible disqualification."

Warner later told the press that the entire Thorpe scandal was nothing more than a professional baseball squeeze play. According to Warner, the story in the *Worcester Telegram* was not a case of good investigative reporting, but a scheme cooked up by an aggressive professional baseball scout to force Thorpe out of the amateur ranks and onto the professional baseball diamond. "I believe a certain scout in the employ of the Pirates had a good deal to do with this affair," Warner told a reporter from the *New York Tribune* in an article dated January 29, 1913. "It was planned to get a lot of advertising and to then get Thorpe to sign a contract."

Warner's observations might well have been accurate. In 1912, professional baseball was a tough, unregulated business. Oversight of gambling and other unscrupulous practices in baseball did not come until after the Black Sox gambling scandal of 1921, with the establishment of the office of the commissioner of baseball that served as a policing body for the sport.

One of the biggest stars in professional baseball, Christy Mathewson, agreed with Warner's assessment of the Thorpe scandal. In 1913, Mathewson knew baseball as well as or better than any man alive. He was one of the first college graduates to enter the game professionally, and he played for "Mugsy" McGraw's New York Giants from 1900 to 1916. The dominant pitcher of his era, Mathewson was one of the original inductees into the Baseball Hall of Fame, and his was one of the most trusted names in American sports.

With the ghostwriter John N. Wheeler, Mathewson wrote a series of syndicated newspaper columns about America's national pastime that were published in 1912 under the title "Pitching in a Pinch or Baseball from the Inside." At the time of the Thorpe scandal, Mathewson's byline still appeared on a column about baseball penned by the ghostwriter, Wheeler.

"A smart Pittsburgh scout is held responsible for the discovery that Thorpe played professional baseball," Mathewson and Wheeler wrote for the *New York American* on February 3, 1913. "He had two purposes in doing this. One was to induce Thorpe to join the professional ranks, which he had refused to do while his amateur status was intact, and the other was for the valuable advertising he would receive.

"Many persons who do not know baseball scouts may blame this man for his action, but it is all in the business. These scouts are hired to get ball players, and the competition is so keen that they resort to all methods. The discovery of a star means much money to the scout."

As the hard evidence continued to pour out of North Carolina, Warner conferred with Sullivan. They decided to end the scandal as quickly as possible. There would be no investigation, no trial, no public exposure of Sullivan's or Warner's sports empires. Thorpe would have to take the fall, and Warner would have to push him. Thorpe would take responsibility for the entire escapade and blame his ignorance of amateur rules, an ignorance that was probably true. Sullivan's and Warner's own knowledge of Thorpe's athletic career would be shielded.

Warner did not like having to sell out Jim Thorpe and did not appreciate Sullivan's amateur rule. Warner believed that athletes should be paid for their performance, and he did his best through the system that he had created at Carlisle to do just that. He also understood that if he admitted all that he knew about Thorpe's ballplaying, his own coaching career would be over.

At the same time, Warner had to think of Thorpe's future. What would be best for the twenty-six-year-old athlete? His days as an amateur were over. He had to become a professional athlete, and the only professional game was baseball, a game he had always wanted to play. Thorpe needed to start earning money if he was going to get married and raise a family. There was only one choice. Thorpe had to confess to playing summer ball, and Warner and Sullivan had to lie.

Warner explained the situation to Superintendent Moses Friedman, and Friedman agreed to follow his lead.

In later years, Warner told the following version of the heartbreaking discussion he had with his greatest star. Warner claimed that he confronted Thorpe with the evidence, and Thorpe acknowledged what he had done. "Yes, Pop," Thorpe said, according to Warner, "it's true. It was back in the summer of 1909, the year you thought I left school for home. I played with the Rocky Mount team down in the North Carolina League. I didn't see any harm in earning a little honest money, Pop. What was wrong with it?"

"I tried to explain to him the delicate distinction between amateurism and professionalism, but he could not grasp it. There were, he told me, many other athletic stars from other northern colleges who played on the same team under assumed names, while he was honest enough to use his own.

"I made the statement then, and I make it now, that it was a brutal business, for as Jim said to me, not angrily but pathetically, 'I don't understand, Pop. What's that two months of baseball got to do with all the jumping and running and field work I did in Stockholm? I never got paid for any of that, did I?'"

There was probably a good deal of truth in Warner's version of the story. What he had to tell Thorpe was a "brutal business." He told his star athlete that he had to make a complete confession, admitting that he played summer baseball and absolving Warner, Sullivan, and everyone at Carlisle of having any knowledge of his professional activities. Warner probably told Thorpe that if he confessed he would be treated kindly by the AAU. At the very least, Warner probably told Thorpe that he would be able to get him a great contract playing baseball.

Thorpe had no money, no lawyer, no financial adviser, or any other mentor besides Pop Warner, the man who had been his manager and coach for about six years, the man who was legally responsible for his well-being as a ward of the federal government. Thorpe was probably confused by the accusations. Yes, he had played summer ball in North Carolina, but he had made just as much or even more money playing football at Carlisle.

Thorpe discussed the situation with Gus Welch and his other friends. They were probably just as confused as Thorpe, though less trusting of Pop Warner. They knew that Thorpe was bullheaded and would have to make the final decision on his own. Thorpe was a proud individual who did not want to dishonor himself, his coach, his school, his race, or his teammates. Admitting his mistake seemed the honorable thing to do. Jim Thorpe never did care much about records, medals, or glory. The thrilling rush of victory was what mattered the most to him.

In the end, Thorpe decided to stick by his coach. Warner gave

Thorpe a carefully crafted letter of confession addressed to Sullivan. Thorpe copied the letter in his own hand and signed it.

Friedman spoke with the press and told them that Thorpe was the victim of circumstances and not morally guilty of any offense. As proof of his amateur intentions, Friedman claimed, incorrectly, that Thorpe had enough money to live on from his lease payments in Oklahoma. In addition, Friedman drafted a letter for Warner to take to Sullivan. In the letter to Sullivan, Friedman wrote, "I have just learned that Thorpe acknowledges having played with a Southern professional baseball team. It is with profound regret that this information is conveyed to you, and I hasten to assure your committee that the faculty of the school and the athletic director, Mr. Glenn Warner, were without any knowledge of this fact until today."

On Monday, January 27, 1913, just five days after the accusations first appeared in the *Worcester Telegram*, Warner took Thorpe's confession and Friedman's letter of explanation and traveled to New York City to meet with Sullivan. Sullivan had already prepared the press for Thorpe's carefully crafted admission of guilt. While Warner was meeting with Sullivan, the *New York Times* carried an article in which Sullivan blamed Thorpe and the Warner system for the entire scandal.

"Here we have an Indian youth taken from environments that to say the least for them are peculiar," Sullivan was quoted as saying, "put in an institution controlled by the United States Government and from reports emanating from these institutions from time to time we are prone to feel proud of the way we are bringing up the heretofore benighted red man. . . . It has been the custom to make pets of the crack Indian athletes, and because of their strange origin nothing back of their Government school careers has ever been delved into." Sullivan provided a weak defense of Thorpe's actions. "In the case of an Indian whose life is laid out in grooves altogether different from ours there is something to be said that can't be brought to bear on the case of the boy whose upbringing has been on the best and most approved lines."

"Many others were playing in the same league but they were careful and wise enough to play under assumed names," Warner told the press, knowing full well that Joe Libby and Jesse Youngdeer had played summer ball with Thorpe under their own names. "In a way, the boys at the Indian school were children mentally and did not understand the fine distinctions between amateurism and professional-ism."

No minutes were kept of the two-hour meeting between Sullivan and Warner, but what took place can be surmised. Sullivan told Warner that there would be no hearing, no trial, no investigation. In the face of the irrefutable evidence, Thorpe would be stripped of his medals and banished from the amateur ranks immediately. His trophies would be returned to the International Olympic Committee and his records expunged from the books. The AAU and Warner would both blame the incident on Thorpe's ignorance and lie about their own knowledge of Thorpe's background to protect themselves, the stature of the AAU, and the American Olympic movement. Warner probably suffered a tongue-lashing from Sullivan for being so careless as to overlook the obvious evidence of Thorpe's North Carolina baseball career.

"Olympic Hero to Be Stripped of His Honors" ran the front-page headline in the *New York Tribune* on Tuesday, January 28, 1913. Newspapers across the country reprinted Thorpe's confession in full. The letter, addressed to James E. Sullivan and dated January 26, 1913, is one of the saddest documents in the history of sports.

In the letter, Thorpe "confessed" that he had played baseball at Rocky Mount and Fayetteville in the summers of 1909 and 1910 under his own name and wrote:

> I did not play for the money there was in it because my property brings me in enough money to live on, but because I liked to play ball. I was not very wise to the ways of the world and did not realize that this was wrong, and it would make me a professional in track sports, although I learned from the other players that it would be better for me not to let any one know that I was playing, and for that reason I never told any one at the school about it until to-day.

Thorpe went on to explain that he had reapplied for admission to Carlisle in 1911 and had filled out and signed his application for registration with the AAU. He wrote that he had handed his application to Warner and had received his card allowing him to compete in AAU-sanctioned events. Thorpe wrote:

> I never realized until now what a big mistake I made by keeping
> it a secret about my ball playing and I am sorry I did so. I hope
> I would be partly excused because of the fact that I was simply
> an Indian schoolboy and did not know all about such things. In
> fact, I did not know that I was doing wrong because I was
> doing what I know several other college men had done, except
> that they did not use their own names.

Along with Thorpe's confession, the papers also reported on a meeting that had been held among Sullivan; Gustavus Kirby, the president of the AAU and the vice president of the American Olympic Committee; and Bartow S. Weeks, the chairman of the Legislation Committee of the AAU and the vice president of the American Olympic Committee. These three officials issued a statement saying that they had decided to send a public apology from the American Olympic Committee through the International Olympic Committee to all the nations of the world for having allowed Thorpe to compete. They also said that all Thorpe's prizes would be returned. The statement professed prior ignorance of Thorpe's professional play by the AAU. Although the statement described Glenn Warner as "a man whose reputation is of the highest and whose accuracy of statement has never been doubted," it criticized him indirectly by stating that "the American Olympic Committee and the Amateur Athletic Union feel that while Thorpe is deserving of the severest condemnation for concealing the fact that he had professionalized himself by receiving money for playing baseball, they also feel that those who knew of his professional acts are deserving of still greater censure for their silence." The whole operation was vintage Sullivan—injustice swift and sure intended to protect the athletic bureaucracy at the expense of an outstanding athlete. In Sullivan's steel grip, the AOC operated without a constitution or procedural rules. There was no investigation. No trial.

Warner and Thorpe returned to Carlisle, where they were deluged by well-wishers and reporters. On January 28, Thorpe released a press statement, probably dictated again by Warner, in which Thorpe said, "As every one around here knows, I have never really been a professional in spirit, although technically guilty. . . . This position in which I have been placed really forces me to become a professional in spirit, as I can't continue, of course, in amateur competition. I will likely play baseball, but I have by no means decided what team I will connect with." Some of Thorpe's supporters began taking up a collection to replace his trophies and medals with duplicates. Thorpe rejected the offer of help and asked that the money be turned over to charity.

In New York, the press reaction to Thorpe's confession was mixed. Though they praised Thorpe for his honesty, most of the New York papers avoided criticism of James Sullivan. For the New York reporters, Sullivan was above reproach—a New York icon, a public servant who had served on New York City's Board of Education and managed Spalding's American Sports Publishing Company.

In an editorial, the *New York Tribune* praised "the honorable efforts of the athletic authorities in this country to make amends" and bemoaned the impact of the Thorpe scandal on the international community. "It is bad enough to be always washing the dirty linen of summer baseball in this country without having it hanging on the clotheslines of Europe."

Outside of New York City, editors and sportswriters expressed stunned amazement at the injustice to Thorpe. "The Amateur Athletic Union should feel proud over its accomplishment in 'purifying' athletics by disgracing Thorpe and kicking up a muss that will be heralded the world over as a disgrace to this country," the *Philadelphia Times* editorialized sarcastically. "All aspiring athletes will do well to ponder this action of the American Athletic Union and not play croquet, ping-pong, tiddly winks, or button-button-who's-got-the-button for compensation. It puts them in the ranks of professionals and absolutely disqualifies them from being able to run, jump, hurdle, throw the discus, pole vault, or wrestle." The editorial continued, "If their move against Thorpe was not animated by sinister and personal motives . . . [the AAU] will have a busy time cleaning up the ranks of collegiate athletics in order to make all amateurs as thoroughly amateurish as the AAU insists Thorpe should have been in order to keep the honors he so clearly won."

An editorial in the *Buffalo Enquirer* was even more critical of Sullivan and the AAU: "AAU officials think nothing of taking money for their services as managers of athletic meets at the various world's expositions, still these men at the head of this AAU, who accept thousands of dollars, are so 'pure' that they cannot be approached. To talk of that bunch as 'money getters' would be *lese-majesté*, but the fact is becoming more evident every day that the people of this country refuse to accept the judgement of this clique as to the athletic standing of a man."

Some college administrators who resented Sullivan's sports czar system reacted to the Thorpe scandal by announcing that they would allow their students to play professional baseball in the summer and still compete for their college teams. Charles S. Miller, the director of athletics at the University of Pittsburgh, made such a declaration, adding for the benefit of reporters, "No, we are not controlled by the American Athletic Union. That is a different body. We conduct our own affairs." Miller pointed out that Brown, Penn State, and other colleges already allowed summer baseball.

Overseas, even among the anti-American British, the reaction was almost unanimously pro-Thorpe. "Great Britain thinks none the worse of the Indian for his baseball crime," ran a headline in the *London Daily News*. The president of the South London Harriers' Club suggested opening up the next Olympics to both amateur and professional athletes.

Reports from Stockholm quoted leading authorities in the field of sports expressing the opinion that "Thorpe is entitled to retain the prizes he won in the pentathlon and decathlon, as the question of his status has been raised too late." Indeed it had. According to the Official Report of the 1912 Olympics, Rule Number 13 of the General Rules for the Olympic Games, "Objections to the qualifications of a competitor must be made in writing . . . to the Swedish Olympic Committee . . . before the lapse of thirty days from the distribution of prizes." The complaint about Thorpe's eligibility had come almost six months after the distribution of prizes.

On January 31, 1913, the Swedish paper *Dagens Nyheter* reported, "There is no power in the world that can, according to the Olympic rules, deprive Thorpe of the prizes he won, and if they are really sent back to Sweden now . . . Thorpe will have given up the prizes of his own free will, perhaps upon a hint from the American Olympic Committee which, according to the rules, is responsible for each contestant being an amateur."

After Sullivan and the AAU ruled to disqualify Jim Thorpe from the Olympics, the case was forwarded to the U.S. Olympic Committee, which endorsed the AAU's decision. Because of the insistence of the

Americans, the International Olympic Committee had no choice but to ignore their own rules and reluctantly ratify the U.S. Olympic Committee's decision. The IOC acted on May 26, 1913, noting in its resolution that Thorpe was "an Indian of limited experience and education in the ways of other than his own people" and making special mention of "the firm and sporting attitude of the American IOC members." Thorpe's medals and his trophies were returned to European Olympic officials. The second-place finishers in the decathlon and the pentathlon, Hugo Wieslander of Sweden and Ferdinand Bie of Norway, respectively, were awarded his gold medals, an honor they dutifully accepted. Thorpe's trophies were crated up and housed at the IOC headquarters in Lausanne, Switzerland. Jim Thorpe became the first athlete in history to have his name stricken from the Olympic records for professionalism. Sullivan later commented, "Thorpe's case is at once one of the greatest tragedies and marvels of amateur athletics."

Years later, Jim Thorpe summed up the actions of Sullivan and the AAU most accurately when he observed, "Basically, they used me as a guinea pig to make up the rules."

18

A Man with No Principle

As soon as Thorpe's confession came out, Warner claimed that he "wired all of the major league ball clubs notifying them that the highest bidder would get Jim's services. He was set to sign with the Cincinnati Reds, when my old friend, John McGraw, the manager of the New York Giants, telephoned to tell me that if Jim was going to play professional baseball, he was in the market to sign him. When I told McGraw that Cincinnati had been the highest bidder so far, in characteristic McGraw style he offered to double the Reds' offer. On hearing this, I told McGraw he had a deal."

The last entry in Jim Thorpe's record as a Carlisle student reads "2-1-13 [February 1, 1913] discharged to play baseball." On that day, just one week after the Olympic scandal first broke in the press, Thorpe and Warner traveled to New York City to visit the offices of the New York Giants on Fifth Avenue. The word was out: Thorpe was going to sign with McGraw's ball club.

Professional baseball managers from around the country pounced on Thorpe's deal with the Giants. The Fayetteville club claimed they had Thorpe under contract, but their efforts to extort cash from the Giants failed, and Thorpe met with the New York ball club as a free agent, with Pop Warner as his business adviser.

Publicity photos show a straight-backed Thorpe in a well-pressed suit, seated stiffly at a wide desk, a pen in his hand poised over a document. At a reported $6,000 for his first year, plus a $500 signing bonus, the contract made Thorpe the highest-paid recruit in baseball and one of the highest-paid untested players ever signed to a professional baseball team. For his efforts as Thorpe's manager, Warner reportedly pocketed a healthy $2,500.

At the press conference after the signing, sports reporters understood the deal. According to the *New York Times*, "Everyone believes Thorpe has been corralled chiefly for publicity purposes." The *New York American* reported, "McGraw has now the best advertised athlete in the world." Reporters speculated that Thorpe would make a great drawing card for the Giants, maybe even pitching with the Giants' popular catcher John Tortes "Chief" Meyers, creating the first all-Indian pitcher-catcher combination in baseball. The sharp-tongued McGraw denied the rumors. "I hired Jim as a baseball prospect, pure and simple, and not as any advertising freak."

After signing, Thorpe stood in front of the battery of photographers and reporters, striking a quiet, dignified pose. "There is little about Thorpe to suggest the redman of the forest," wrote the *New York Times*. "He looked more like a big college student who had stepped out of a Broadway toggery shop." Wearing "a natty blue Norfolk suit" and carrying a purple fedora, Thorpe handled himself well. With Warner by his side, he told reporters, "It has been my ambition to become a big time ball player when my school days were over, and now I have a chance to have the ambition of my life realized."

The press corps saw Thorpe for what he was, a modest, plainspoken Oklahoma athlete who was going to make good money playing baseball. When one of the gathered throng asked Thorpe his real Indian name, Thorpe hesitated, then laughed. With typical self-effacing humor, he told the reporters that back in Oklahoma everyone called him "Drag-His-Root." Warner jumped in quickly and explained to the befuddled reporters that Thorpe did not know his Indian moniker. Later, the story emerged that Thorpe's full Indian name was Wathahuk, meaning illumination that comes after lightning, Wemikoha, member of the Thunder Clan, Sauki, Sauk.

After the press conference, Thorpe, Warner, McGraw, Mathewson, and others from the Giants organization gathered at the bar in the Imperial Hotel. According to an article carrying the "Christy Mathewson" byline, Thorpe sat quietly, graciously accepting rounds of drinks offered by well-wishers. When Warner finally got up to leave, he told the Giants manager that he would come to see Thorpe work his first game.

As it turned out, McGraw was no Pop Warner. He did not know how to get the best performance from his temperamental star. He resented Thorpe's playfulness, his sense of humor, and his defiant attitude. Thorpe spent most of the 1913 season on the bench and hated it. He never did perform his best for McGraw or for any other manager after Warner.

John "Chief" Meyers, Thorpe's teammate and roommate, later claimed that McGraw tried to control Thorpe by taunting him with racist jabs, a tactic that only made Thorpe more defiant. And Thorpe began to feel the loss of his Olympic honors as well. According to Meyers, a tearful Thorpe once complained, "You know, Chief, the King of Sweden gave me those trophies, he gave them to me. But they took them away from me. They're mine, Chief. I won them fair and square."

On October 14, 1913, Thorpe was back in Carlisle for a special ceremony, his marriage to Iva Margaret Miller. Two motion picture companies recorded the celebrity wedding for audiences across the country. With Gus Welch as his best man, Thorpe and Iva stood before the priest at St. Patrick's Catholic Church and spoke their vows. Iva was brought up Episcopalian but converted to Catholicism at her husband's request. Superintendent Moses Friedman gave the bride away. After a Mass and a reception at Friedman's home, the newlyweds left on an exhibition baseball tour around the world. "When the King of Sweden gave me the medals and the trophy, he said, 'Sir, you are the greatest athlete in the world,'" Thorpe told his young bride. "Well, if he called me Sir, then that means I'm a Lord; and if I'm a Lord, then you are my Lady."

Iva and "Snooks," as she called her husband, traveled to Japan, China, the Philippines, Australia, Ceylon, Egypt, Italy, France, and England. Iva's diary entry for February 4 and 5, 1914, read in part, "My Snooks played some ball both days in Cairo—getting one home run and two hits the first day (bringing in other runs) and four hits (four times at bat) the second. Some ball playing alright."

Pop Warner coached the 1913 Carlisle Indians to another strong season. Joe Guyon and Pete Calac played on the team, as did Gus Welch, who was the team captain. "No Carlisle quarterback ever directed an attack with better judgment," Warner said of Welch, "and his inspiring leadership was a great factor in Carlisle's fine showing."

On November 15, they faced their toughest opponent, undefeated Dartmouth. At halftime, the Carlisle Indians were trailing the Big Green 10–7 at New York's Polo Grounds. Warner was particularly concerned because he had bet $300 on Carlisle to win, at odds of three to five. In the locker room, Warner did not just give a pep talk to his players, he also made them an offer: "If each of you wants to earn $5 apiece to have a little fun when we stop off in New York on the trip home," Warner told them, "all you have to do is to win this game." Carlisle came out of the locker room and scored four touchdowns to win the game 35–10. Warner won his bet and paid off his players.

Though the team ended the season with a 10-and-1 record and was ranked second in the country behind Harvard, resentment was building against the Warner system. Welch and others believed that Thorpe had not been treated honorably. They felt that Warner had made him a fall guy and should not have lied to protect himself. In addition, Welch and the other "athletic boys" were fed up with making money for the Carlisle Athletic Association. Just like Warner, they wanted a piece of the action. And they did not respect the aloof Friedman, who seemed to be nothing more than Warner's lackey.

The teachers at Carlisle were as discontented as the students. Unlike Pratt, who had paid his teachers well and added to their salary with funds raised from private sources, Friedman was unable to boost salaries and actually had to decrease salaries for some of his new staff members. Teachers, who received as little as $660 per year, the same amount they had been paid twenty years earlier, bitterly resented Warner's $4,000 salary and the athletic program's power over Carlisle's operation. The faculty was fed up with the lack of discipline at the school and the lack of leadership on the part of Friedman.

John Whitwell, the principal teacher at Carlisle, led the attack on the administration. Friedman's predecessor Mercer had recommended Whitwell for the job of superintendent. Once at Carlisle, Friedman went out of his way to make life difficult for Whitwell by making the teacher take charge of various duties such as cleaning the buildings and keeping statistical reports.

Whitwell did not approve of the Warner system or of Friedman's managerial style. He encouraged the Indian students to voice their opinions and to call for an investigation of the school. He appealed to the students' pride, convincing them that telling the truth about Carlisle was the honorable thing to do. One of the students who led the protest was Gus Welch. With Whitwell's support, Welch coauthored a petition complaining of mismanagement at Carlisle. The petition was addressed to Cato Sells, the commissioner of Indian Affairs.

After gathering 214 signatures, Welch took the petition to the home of Congressman A. H. Rupley, who lived in Carlisle. While Welch was showing the petition to Rupley, the Reverend C. M. Diffenderfer entered the room. Rev. Diffenderfer was a strong supporter of Warner and Friedman who had worked as a Carlisle recruiter out West and who was paid by Warner to hold Sunday services on campus. Welch left the petition at Rupley's house, assuming that the reverend would report to Friedman and Warner about what was going on.

Rev. Diffenderfer did indeed inform the Carlisle authorities about the student petition. In response, Warner invited Carlisle football player Elmer Busch and others to his home to sign a petition supporting Friedman. Nothing came of it. Meanwhile, other students stepped forward. Montreville Speed Yuda was a member of the Oneida tribe who applied to Carlisle from Atlantic City, where he was making a living selling baskets on the boardwalk. A close friend of Welch and Thorpe, Yuda was something of a class clown, who starred as Miles Standish in the much heralded Carlisle presentation of the musical revue *The Captain of Plymouth*. Yuda wrote a petition similar to Welch's, collected 276 signatures, and carried it to Washington, D.C. Although Yuda never had the chance to deliver the petition to the Secretary of the Interior, Franklin K. Lane, in person, the document did eventually reach his desk.

"Dad had a tremendous sense of honor and loyalty to Carlisle," Montreville Yuda's son George later recalled. "For him and for his classmates, the school came first. Above all else, they did not want the school to be disgraced. How many students think of that today?"

Calls for an investigation at Carlisle came from other sources as well. Discipline had gotten so bad at the school that in the fall of 1913, Friedman had expelled thirty-two girls for pregnancy and ten boys for "immorality" or drunkenness. The secretary of the YMCA in Carlisle, Robert D. Hall, complained in a letter to the Department of Interior about the Carlisle situation. "When sin is covered up and unnoticed," Hall wrote, "immorality will abound and friction arise."

Some boys stole items from the school and simply ran away. In October 1913, the *Harrisburg Patriot* ran an article reporting on the apprehension of several Carlisle runaways, an article that made it to the desk of Congressman Rupley and even the Secretary of the Interior, Franklin Lane. Fred Bruce was an Indian from Montana who worked at a steamfitter at the Carlisle school. Bruce was living in the athletic dormitory during the Olympic scandal and knew Thorpe and Welch quite well. Bruce sent several letters detailing the situation at Carlisle to the Indian Rights Association, a Quaker public interest group based in Philadelphia that had been opposed to the management of the Carlisle school ever since Pratt's forced resignation in 1904.

In a letter dated November 18, 1913, Bruce wrote, "I am sure if you take up James Thorpe's case that it will be proved to you that Mr. Friedman and Mr. Warner knew that James Thorpe was paid and that it was for baseball before he went to Stockholm to win victory in the Olympic games. I am just writing this letter to show you how when an Indian is in trouble that they will have him shoulder all the blame and keep themselves clear. I say that is rotten business." Bruce stated that James Thorpe did not write his confession letter but copied in his own hand a letter that Warner had given him. "The reason I didn't make any noise at the time," Bruce explained, "was that I wanted to get in the Indian Service and I knew that if I said anything that they would knock me out of anything they had influence in."

M. K. Sniffen, the secretary of the Indian Rights Association, took Bruce's accusations seriously. He expressed his concerns in a letter written to the Commissioner of Indian Affairs, Cato Sells, who was no friend of Carlisle. "At present," Sniffen wrote, "there are rumors afloat reflecting seriously upon the moral atmosphere of the school, and unless something is done to 'clear the air,' so to speak, it may be difficult to properly maintain the institution."

Sniffern's ten-page letter listed numerous troubles at Carlisle, including accusations of fornication and drinking by students and the misappropriation of athletic funds. "The main thing is to direct a thorough and searching investigation of Supt. Friedman's entire administration of the Carlisle school," Sniffen wrote, "by such a man as Inspector E. B. Linnen, whose report would carry great weight because of his exceptional record for honesty and efficiency."

Enough was enough. Carlisle had enemies. Friedman had enemies. Warner had enemies. The Carlisle students demanded justice and had powerful friends. Gus Welch no doubt contacted Oklahoma Congressman Charles D. Carter, whom he had met in Washington, to tell him about the affair. Finally, the U.S. Senate and House passed a joint resolution establishing a joint commission of the Congress of the United States to investigate the situation at Carlisle. The Department of the Interior sent an inspector to Carlisle, the same E. B. Linnen whom Sniffen had recommended.

Linnen, the chief inspector of the Indian Service, arrived in late January 1914 to conduct a preliminary investigation of the U.S. Indian School at Carlisle. Linnen quickly realized that Carlisle was in "a state bordering on insurrection." A group of students approached Linnen and complained to him of brutal, unjust punishments, bad food, unfair expulsions, financial irregularities, and many other concerns. Congressman Rupley presented Linnen with Welch's petition, explaining that he had not sent it to Washington to protect Welch and the other signatories.

Linnen's investigation was met with hostility by many on the Carlisle staff, including Friedman and Pop Warner. When Linnen asked to inspect the books of the Carlisle Athletic Association, Warner refused to turn them over. Warner claimed that since the athletic association was a private corporation, it was outside the purview of Linnen's investigation. Linnen pointed out to Warner that according to regulations of the Indian Office approved by the secretary of the interior on June 14, 1910, funds received from athletic events at federally funded Indian schools were to be collected by the school superintendent and disbursing agent. Linnen further explained that since Warner had not incorporated the Carlisle Indian School Athletic

Association until April 11, 1911, his athletic association was subject to regulation by the U.S. Department of the Interior.

Within a very short time, Inspector Linnen had collected sufficient data and witnesses for the hearings at Carlisle to begin. Joe T. Robinson, a democratic senator from Arkansas and the chair of the joint congressional commission, and two Democratic congressmen, John H. Stephens from Texas and Charles D. Carter from Oklahoma, traveled to Carlisle in the first week of February 1914. According to the *New York Times*, "Without notifying Supt. Friedman of the Carlisle Indian School of their presence, they pre-empted quarters, and, with E. B. Linnen, Indian Officer Inspector, conducted an investigation of the school and its management."

Upon their arrival, the officials from Washington made a quick inspection of Carlisle and were shocked to find seven students incarcerated in the school jail, the old Hessian barracks, for drunkenness. The commission began its hearing on February 6, 1914, at 4:30 P.M. at the YMCA in downtown Carlisle.

The resulting 632 typewritten pages of testimony are an ugly epilogue to the triumph of Pop Warner and Jim Thorpe. The senators and congressmen heard brutal stories from sixty-one witnesses, including staff members, teachers, Carlisle residents, and a group of students selected by the student body. While the male students testified using their own names, many female students spoke anonymously because of the sensitive nature of their testimony.

The witnesses described Friedman's failure as an administrator, the "fornication" and corporal punishment at Carlisle, and the excesses of Warner's athletic program. They spoke in detail about the beating of an eighteen-year-old Potawatomi student named Julia Hardin. When Hardin stubbornly refused to go on her "outing," the bandmaster and sometime disciplinarian Claude Stauffer entered her room, where, according to Hardin, "[he] jerked a board down from one of the window sills and he punched me down on the floor and two of the matrons held me down." One of the matrons testified that the beating Stauffer administered "was not half enough." According to other testimony, Iva Thorpe reported for a lesson from the same bandmaster, Claude Stauffer, who instead told her "a very immoral story" about sisters and priests "living an immoral life."

Wallace Denny, Warner's longtime trainer and the disciplinarian for the younger boys, admitted that he disciplined students by hitting them "in the face with his fist" and whipping boys with a baseball bat. Denny told the commission that after students threw chairs at him he had thrown one student down a flight of stairs.

The commissioners heard testimony about female students who returned from their outing pregnant and who were kept in the hospital until they gave birth. One girl was reported to have had a liaison with an Indian boy in the Warner home when the Warners were out of town. Other witnesses told of a boy and a girl who spent seventy days in the county jail for fornication, even though fornication in the state of Pennsylvania was a misdemeanor punishable only by a fine. Another student, who stole pies from the school kitchen, was forced to serve thirty days in the county jail.

While unjustly severe punishments were handed out to some students, the commissioners heard that many of the athletic boys were not punished for getting drunk and/or breaking into the girls' dormitories. According to John Whitwell, "If we sent them [the "athletic boys"] all home that have gotten drunk I am afraid we would not have many left." There was testimony that Gus Welch was caught drinking with the school's assistant quartermaster. According to Angel Dietz, "The boys have told me they can get whisky any time they want it."

According to the affidavit of E. K. Miller, who ran the school print shop, "Warner's power . . . was absolute." Miller said that Warner served beer to the "athletic boys." "It was no uncommon thing for the boys of the athletic teams to be drunk and cause trouble," Miller testified. "Thorpe was among them."

The commission heard Warner explain the evolution of the athletic fund, describe payments to players and Friedman, and detail his investments in companies that supplied Carlisle with food. Warner described a scene in which he watched another Carlisle employee give each of four boys who had "gotten a hold of some liquor" fifty lashes with a trunk strap. "We thought it was a case where there was nothing else that would do as good," Warner told the commission, "and it did have a wholesome effect upon those boys."

After the chairman thanked him for his testimony, Warner added a lengthy commentary in which he said, "This thing has all been worked up by Whitwell and his crowd and a few of the students."

Fred Bruce submitted an affidavit in which he said that James

Thorpe and Gus Welch drank beer at the school and were not punished. Bruce also restated his accusation that Jim Thorpe's confession was actually written by Coach Warner.

Affidavits submitted by various "athletic boys" were equally revealing. Elmer Busch, the newly elected captain of the 1914 football team, wrote, "Mr. Warner is kind of rough to the football players, using profane language to them. I heard him curse a boy named William Hodge; called him a son of a bitch."

Welch's brother in Wisconsin fell ill before the hearings. Welch wanted his other brother, who also was at Carlisle, to travel back to Wisconsin to help with the family, but according to his affidavit, "Superintendent Friedman and Coach Warner were insistent that I should go, and they paid my expenses home out of the athletic fund, my idea being that they wanted to get rid of me during this investigation and not have me appear, as I am now doing."

Welch hit his coach hard. "In each large game we have fifty to seventy-five complimentary tickets which he is supposed to issue to the patrons of the school, and we have seen him sell these tickets outright in the hotel lobbies, and I think he kept the money. I regard him as being dishonest, and so do the other boys."

Welch testified that "Mr. Warner is a good football coach, but a man with no principle." Welch declared that his coach had no moral authority over his players and should be removed from his job. Welch also testified that the confession letter signed by James Thorpe about being a professional "was prepared by Coach G. S. Warner and Superintendent M. Friedman."

Overwhelmed by details of brutality, immorality, and financial malfeasance, the commissioners failed to pursue a line of questioning that would have revealed much about the Thorpe controversy. During his testimony, the following interchange took place between Friedman and Senator Joe T. Robinson, the chairman of the commission:

> The Chairman: You are a member of the executive committee or board of directors of the athletic association, are you, Dr. Friedman?
>
> Dr. Friedman: Yes, sir.
>
> The Chairman: Who are the other members of the board?
>
> Dr. Friedman: Mr. Warner and Mr. Miller, and there is an

advisory committee, composed of a number of gentlemen:
Walter Camp, Mr. McCormick, of the University of Pittsburgh;
James Sullivan, secretary and treasurer of the Amateur Athletic
Union; Dr. Noble; and one or two other gentlemen.

The commissioners followed up with questions about athletic association payments to Friedman but did not ask anything more about
Sullivan's involvement with the Carlisle Athletic Association and Pop
Warner. The fact that Sullivan served on the board of Warner's
athletic business enterprise is the smoking gun of the 1912 Olympic
scandal. As a member of the advisory board, Sullivan was in part
responsible for the actions of the association, actions that included
allowing Thorpe to compete in the Olympics. Sullivan and Warner
sold out Thorpe so quickly because they were actually in business
together, and their business was based in part on Jim Thorpe's
amateur status.

A few days after the congressional hearings at Carlisle, Warner
cleared out the bank account for the Carlisle athletic association
by writing a check for $25,640.08 to O. H. Lipps, who took over
as the interim supervisor of Carlisle. On March 21, 1914, fifty-five of
the "athletic boys" sent a letter to Cato Sells, the commissioner
of Indian Affairs, protesting the employment of Athletic Director
Glenn S. Warner.

The commission recommended that Superintendent Friedman be
suspended and tried. The *New York Times* reported that he was
indicted by a federal grand jury in Sunbury, Pennsylvania on January
14, 1915, for "embezzling money belonging to the students and of
burning receipts for students' money given to them by the financial
clerk of the institution."

In the press, Friedman claimed that the hearing was politically
motivated by Democrats who desired to oust as "many Republican
office holders as possible to make room for appointees of their own."
Friedman also accused Pratt of stirring up the whole affair to get his
old job back. In response, the school's founder, Captain Pratt, accused
Friedman of "a malicious, false and slanderous accusation unbecoming
a gentleman."

Friedman was acquitted five months later, but his career was ruined.
He served as the superintendent at the Anchor Ranch for Defective

Boys in Buckman, New Mexico, and the U.S. Vocational School in Pocono Pines, Pennsylvania, before fading from the documentary record.

In his autobiography, Warner blamed the scandal on the "Washington crowd," specifically legislators from the West who believed that federal funds should be going to schools in their areas and not to institutions in the East. "To my dying day I will maintain that Carlisle was a great and helpful institution, and that nothing was ever more cruel and stupid than its abolition," Warner later observed. "From its very inception, however, the school was fought by a type of politician who sees the Indian only as an opportunity for exploitation and plunder."

In May 1914, the *New York Times* reported that Warner might be removed because of "intimations of graft" unearthed in the investigation and involved in legal action proposed by the Department of Justice.

In that same month, Sullivan traveled to France for a meeting with Baron de Coubertin. The founder of the modern Olympics presented Sullivan with a trophy "as a token of appreciation . . . in promoting the Olympic Games." On September 16, 1914, Sullivan passed away. Though he received a trophy and an Olympic medal, Sullivan was never appointed to the most exclusive amateur sports club, the International Olympic Committee. Sullivan's business papers were destroyed shortly after his death.

Warner was never formally charged by the Department of Justice or forced to resign from Carlisle. He continued to coach at Carlisle through a disastrous 1914 season during which the Indians won four games and lost seven, their worst record since 1901. After six consecutive Carlisle losses, Welch showed remarkable team spirit and loyalty to the man he had testified against just months earlier. He agreed to play for Warner once again and took to the field during a brutal game against Notre Dame played in Chicago. In the third quarter, the Notre Dame fullback charged through a hole in the defense near the Carlisle goal line. Welch met the speeding ball carrier head on, literally. The fullback scored. Welch lay on the turf bleeding and unconscious until he was carried from the field and taken to a hospital. As the press reported, "His loyalty to his school may mean he will never don the moleskins again." Welch's willingness to play for Warner so soon after testifying against him was a glorious, tragic gesture. For Welch as well as for Thorpe, the honor of his team, his school, and his blood was more important than his feelings about his coach, or even his physical well-being.

The most important game of the season for Warner was Carlisle's 10–3 loss to the University of Pittsburgh. During that game, he began talking with the Pitt staff about a possible job with them. He liked the attitude at Pittsburgh, a school that had recently approved of summer baseball for its college athletes.

"The Pittsburgh authorities offered me a job after the game," Warner later recalled. "I accepted [the fact] that Carlisle's abolition was inevitable."

On February 25, 1915, the "C men," as the Carlisle lettermen were called, hosted a farewell reception for Pop Warner and his wife in the athletic quarters. Amid red and gold streamers, pennants, trophies, and photos of Carlisle's greatest athletes, speakers praised Warner's years at Carlisle, and Warner thanked the gathered students and faculty for their support. The mood was subdued but respectful. Since coming to Carlisle in 1899, Warner had coached the Indians in one hundred games and had won seventy-eight. From 1911 to 1913 the Carlisle Indians played thirty-eight games and lost only three.

A few months later, Warner took charge of the Pitt football program at a yearly salary of $4,500. During the 1915 season Warner's Pittsburgh squad defeated Carlisle 45–0, even though Gus Welch was on the field as one of Carlisle's assistant coaches.

Reeling from the Thorpe controversy and the congressional investigation, the U.S. Indian School at Carlisle struggled on for a few more years. During the 1917 football season, a weak Carlisle football squad won two games and lost seven, including a 98–0 shellacking at the hands of Georgia Tech, and a 26–0 loss against the University of Pennsylvania, the last game ever played by a Carlisle football squad.

In 1918, faced with an influx of wounded from the battlefields of France, the War Department revoked the transfer of the Carlisle Barracks to the Department of the Interior. Carlisle's students quietly transferred to other schools. The Carlisle administrators distributed the school's supplies and equipment to other federal schools. On September 1, 1918, J. F. Duran, a Pueblo Indian and a Carlisle employee, lowered the flag at Carlisle and presented it to Major A. C.

Backmeyer. The major raised the flag again over the War Department's newest medical facility, the U.S. Army Base Hospital No. 31. Later, the Carlisle Barracks became the Army Medical Field Service School. Finally, in 1951, the former U.S. Indian School became the U.S. Army War College and remains so to the present day.

19

Masters of the White Man's Game

On the banks of Lake Geneva in Lausanne, Switzerland, in a storeroom of the concrete and glass Olympic Museum, sits the gold, jewel-encrusted trophy that was presented more than ninety years ago to the world's most gifted athlete, Jim Thorpe.

In many ways, Jim Thorpe's athletic career suffered the same fate as his trophy. The Olympic scandal replaced his public image as the perfect athlete with the image of a shady operator. For the next twenty years, as he struggled to make a living from professional sports, Thorpe's exuberant, partying lifestyle embarrassed the sports establishment and the general public. Before the era of flashy, jewel-laden athletes with protective posses of lawyers, accountants, and hangers-on, before the era of professional football, before the era of televised sports and reality shows, there was really no place in America for Jim Thorpe. The press put him in a box marked "old Jim" and stuck him down in the American media's basement full of fallen and half-forgotten celebrities.

Jim played big-league baseball through 1919, bouncing from the Giants to the Cincinnati Reds, then back to the Giants and ending his career with the Boston Braves. In the early twenties, he played with triple-A teams—Akron, Toledo, and Portland. He was a good baseball player but not a great one. He played the game mostly for the paycheck, which shrank year by year. The game he truly loved was football, which he continued to play throughout his baseball career.

In 1915, Thorpe signed with John Cusack's barnstorming team, the Canton Bulldogs, for $250 per game. It was the biggest professional football money at the time, a hefty sum for a team in a league that did not even keep statistics. Thorpe played against so many college athletes that photographers hesitated to take pictures of the games, for fear that "amateur" athletes who did not want to lose their amateur status would rough them up and destroy their film.

Heavy betting often affected the outcome of the brutal games. During a championship contest between Massillon and Canton, fans had so much riding on the game that they swarmed into the end zone after the winning Canton touchdown and stripped the Canton player of the ball. Faced with an angry mob of Canton fans, the referee ruled that Canton had fumbled and declared the game a tie.

In another Canton Bulldogs game, Thorpe faced off against a young player named Knute Rockne. As Rockne told the story, he tackled Thorpe for a loss. "You mustn't do that, Rock," Thorpe said to the future Notre Dame coaching legend. "These fans paid to see old Jim run. Be a good boy and let old Jim run." On the next play, Thorpe's knee smashed into Rockne's head as Thorpe broke for a touchdown. "That's a good boy, Rock," Thorpe said, coming back to check on his would-be tackler. "You let old Jim run."

The Chicago bookmaker and professional footballer George Halas also recalled playing against Jim Thorpe. "He was a great defensive player. His tackling was as unusual as his running style—he never tackled with his arms and shoulders. He'd leg-whip the ball carrier. If he hit you from behind, he'd throw that big body across your back and damn near break you in two."

On September 17, 1920, Halas, who owned the Decatur Staleys football team, met with representatives from Hammond, Muncie, Akron, and other football towns at Ralph Hay's automobile agency in Canton, Ohio. The assembled promoters, gamblers, car salesmen, and sports hustlers formed the American Professional Football Association, the organization that eventually became the National Football League. The man they chose to be the first president of the future NFL was the greatest football player in America, Jim Thorpe.

Thorpe served as president of the rough and ruthless league for only a year. Like McGraw, the football promoters used Thorpe for his name recognition. Thorpe was a terrible administrator. He just did not give a rat's ass about finances or the social niceties necessary to grease the wheels of commerce. Thorpe liked to have fun on his own terms, and his own terms meant drinking, fighting, and carrying on. After he left the presidency of the league he formed his own team: "Jim Thorpe's Oorang Indians."

The team took its name from its sponsor, the Oorang Kennels in La Rue, Ohio, which supplied Jim with his favorite Airedale hunting dogs. Thorpe attracted Indian players from across the country, including Joe Guyon, Pete Calac, Elmer Busch, and other Carlisle alumni. Taking comic names such as "Wrinkle Meat" and "Bear Behind," Thorpe's Indians played reasonable football but mostly enjoyed themselves. Occasionally, at halftime, Thorpe and his teammates dressed up like "wild Indians," threw tomahawks and knives, and re-created a World War I battle scene in which Indians fought Germans and Airedales raced across the gridiron with packets of medicine to heal the wounded warriors.

The Oorang Indians disintegrated after the 1923 season. Thorpe then played for the Rock Island Independents, the New York Football Giants, and for various other clubs. In May 1928, the forty-two-year-old Thorpe was playing with the Chicago Cardinals when he announced his final retirement from sports. When Grantland Rice asked Thorpe if he had ever been seriously injured during his quarter century of gridiron battles, Thorpe shook his head and said, "Who in hell can get hurt playing football?"

Too old for sports, Thorpe tried Hollywood. With his well-known name and "Indian look," he got the chance to appear in a number of Hollywood productions. He played Chief Black Crow in the serial *Battling with Buffalo Bill*. In 1932, he starred with Tom Mix and Mickey Rooney in *My Pal, the King*, a comedy about a Wild West show stranded in the Balkans. In 1935 he appeared with Helen Gahagen in *She*. The next year, he played opposite Mae West in *Klondike Annie*. He played a white man in *Northwest Passage* with Spencer Tracy in 1940, and wore a feathered headdress as an extra in the Deanna Durbin 1944 wagon train musical *Can't Help Singing*.

But even the most famous athlete in the world had a hard time making a living from sports and entertainment in the days before World War II. Thorpe took odd jobs as a security guard, a laborer, a bartender. For a time he got involved in Indian politics and campaigned for the abolition of the Federal Bureau of Indian Affairs. He briefly became a lecturer, touring the country in a Buick, his hunting dogs sitting in the backseat for company. When he got too pinched for cash, Jim borrowed money from old friends such as Gus Welch and more recent acquaintances such as the Hollywood personality Chief Long Lance.

Jim's personal life was as chaotic as his professional life. In 1914, he and Iva had a son, James Jr., who died three years later of infantile paralysis. The loss of his son was a brutal emotional blow to Thorpe, who later had three daughters with Iva: Charlotte, Gail, and Grace. When he was home, he was loving and strict with the girls but mostly he was just absent. "Dad did not try to set himself up as an example for others to follow," wrote his daughter Charlotte Thorpe in her biographical portrait of her father, *Thorpe's Gold*. "Young and old loved him for what he was—a big, warm, fun-loving boy-man."

Thorpe and Iva divorced in 1923. In 1925, the thirty-eight-year old Thorpe married Freeda Kirkpatrick, a seventeen-year-old office worker for the Oorang Indians football team. Jim and Freeda had four boys: Carl Phillip, William, Richard, and John, whom Thorpe affection-ately called "the four little horsemen" in honor of Knute Rockne's 1924 Notre Dame backfield.

John "Jack" Robert Thorpe, who served as the principal chief of the Sac and Fox Indian tribes in Oklahoma from 1980 to 1987 and who spent more than thirty years working in Indian affairs, best remembers his father's laughter, hugs, and sheer physical strength. "One time we got a flat tire," Jack recalled. "He couldn't find the jack and finally said, 'You boys, loosen the lug nuts and when I lift up the car, change the tire.' So we loosened the nuts. Dad grabbed that 1942 Hudson by the rear bumper and when he lifted it up, we changed the tire. He was just that strong."

When he was home, Thorpe enjoyed hunting with his boys. "He'd sit under a tree with a short bow," Jack recalled, "and knock squirrels out of that tree. He was that good with it."

Jack remembers his dad as a disciplinarian who was constantly harassed by guys out to pick a fight. "Dad took my brother and me into a bar one time, we were just little boys, and this fellow started to give him a hard time, you know, about being a tough guy. Well, Dad put up with it for a while, then he put a hundred-dollar bill on the counter. 'Look,' he told the guy, 'I'll give you one punch. If you can knock me down, I'll give you this hundred dollars. But if you can't knock me down, I get your hundred dollars and a punch of my own.' The fellow agreed to the bet. I was scared, you can imagine. Well, the fellow slugged Dad, and Dad didn't move. He just smiled. Then he reared back and clocked that fellow, knocked him down. Dad picked up the hundred-dollar bill from the bar and said to us, 'Come on, let's get out of here.'"

Thorpe's son Bill claimed that his father liked to drink but never drank in front of his children. "Dad was not an alcoholic. Much of the time he wasn't drunk. He was a disciplinarian. He was a really happy-go-lucky individual. He was never mean and vicious. He set an example for us and other young people, to be a great athlete you have to work hard. It's not something you can do just a little bit."

Though he protected his children, Thorpe was unable to protect himself from his hard partying ways. On one occasion, he was fined for drunk driving. On another, police had to restrain him before taking him to jail for being drunk and disorderly. On some occasions, Thorpe's reputation kept him out of trouble. "Dad took us to a carnival one time, and he went up to this shooting gallery," Jack Thorpe recalled. "He picked up the gun, and instead of moving as close to the target as he could, he took a couple of steps back and started shooting. Bang! Bang! Bang! Each shot was dead on. But when the guy took down the target, he claimed that there was a little bit of the bull's-eye left. He refused to give Dad the prize money. Well, Dad took the gun in both hands, and bent it, like a horseshoe, which caused quite a disturbance. A policeman came along and asked for Dad's ID. The policeman looked at it, then looked at the guy in the booth and said, 'Goddamit, if Jim Thorpe said he shot out the circle, he shot out the circle. Give him the prize money.'"

Over the years, Freeda Thorpe had few things to say about her marriage to the world's greatest athlete. According to Jack Thorpe, "My mother once told me, 'I just didn't understand him.' And I told her, 'Of course you didn't understand him. He was an Indian. He had a different way of thinking.'"

Freeda and Jim divorced in 1941. He took a job along with other aging athletes as a security guard at a Ford plant in Dearborn, Michigan, before he sailed with the Merchant Marine in 1943.

Thorpe, still a celebrity, attended the China-Burma-India Theater Invitational Volleyball Tournament in Calcutta, India, and joked with the press, telling them that he was a member of the FBI, a "full-blooded Indian."

On June 2, 1945, Thorpe married for a third time, to Patricia "Patsy" Gladys Askew, who took over management of his business affairs. Once again, Thorpe hit the small-time-celebrity trail. In 1948, he appeared at a U.S. Olympic soccer team match against Israel in New York City. The sixty-one-year-old Thorpe drop-kicked three out of ten field goals from the fifty-yard line.

A few years after displaying his old form in the Polo Grounds, Thorpe was working as a bouncer in Suey Welch's Sports Club, a working-class watering hole in downtown Los Angeles. With his thick arms folded, the fleshy, sixty-two-year-old Thorpe explained to the sportswriter Al Stump that he had known Suey, the club owner, since his days playing football with the Oorang Indians. "Guess you could call me the bouncer here," Thorpe told Stump. "Not that we have much trouble. But if we do, I settle it."

Stump described the aging champion as "not a complex man . . . pliable, irresponsible, and sometimes unruly" whose talk was "unadorned and honest as his character." Thorpe did not complain about the men Stump described as "the sharpies, the parasites, the doubletakes, the chiseling promoters" who had surrounded him for decades. Instead, Thorpe talked about the "missus," his third wife, and looked toward the end of his long, hard run. "The old warhorse is all through," he joked. "One of these days, they'll take me out and shoot me."

Thorpe returned to the headlines in 1951, with the opening of the film *Jim Thorpe—All American*. The project had been in the works since 1929, when MGM paid Thorpe $1,500 for the rights to his life story. Warner bought the rights for $35,000 from MGM, then paid Thorpe an additional $15,000 to be an adviser on the film. "They really didn't know what to do with him," Burt Lancaster, who portrayed Thorpe, recalled about the great athlete's appearance on the set, "which is generally the case when you do anyone's life who happens to be alive." The film featured Nestor Pavia as Hiram Thorpe, Al Mejia as Louis Tewanima, and Charles Bickford as Pop Warner. It was a Hollywood version of the "old Jim" story, a fantasy that portrayed

Warner as a soft-spoken, kindly uncle figure and laid the blame for Thorpe's Olympic downfall and subsequent struggles solely on his stubborn, proud, and hard-partying nature.

The film boosted Jim Thorpe's public profile enough to bring him back to the fringes of show business. He became the handler for Suni Warcloud, a professional wrestler, and headed up an all-Indian song and dance troop, "The Jim Thorpe Show," organized by his manager/wife. He made the rounds of interviews with top sports reporters. According to Jack Thorpe, one sportscaster asked Jim Thorpe, "What was the greatest moment in your athletic career?"

"Well," Thorpe said, spreading his hands apart, "I caught this fish that was this big, the biggest fish you ever saw—"

"No, seriously," the reporter interrupted, "what was the greatest moment in your athletic career?"

Thorpe looked at the reporter right in the eye. He paused, then spread his hands apart again. "You see, I caught this fish . . ."

Thorpe's humor never failed him, but his body finally began to wear out. He suffered a heart attack in 1943 and underwent surgery for lip cancer in early 1952. In August of that year, Thorpe suffered a second heart attack in Nevada, where he ran a small bar. Living in a modest trailer home in Lomita, California, Thorpe suffered a third heart attack, this time fatal, on March 28, 1953.

According to Thorpe's grandson Michael Koehler, "He [Jim Thorpe] spent his last days reminiscing . . . about carefree days fishing with his twin brother, Charlie, along the red clay banks of the North Canadian River in southwestern Oklahoma. . . . Jim Thorpe's satisfactions, therefore, were found in the simplicity of his pleasures, not the magnificence of his gifts. His life is a lesson for all of us."

After Thorpe's death, members of his Sac and Fox clan honored him in a funeral ceremony back in Oklahoma. "We were honoring him in the traditional manner, when his wife showed up in a car and took his body away," recalled Jack Thorpe, who was at the ceremony. "The folks at the ceremony were furious." On April 13, 1953, Thorpe was buried in a Catholic service in Shawnee, Oklahoma. When the town of Shawnee refused to erect a memorial for her husband, Patsy Thorpe moved his body to Tulsa. She lobbied hard to get the state of Oklahoma to approve $25,000 for the construction of a memorial, but her efforts were in vain.

Still searching for a fitting memorial, the third Mrs. Thorpe traveled to Carlisle, Pennsylvania, to talk with officials and then went to Philadelphia to meet with NFL commissioner Bert Bell. Watching TV news in her hotel room, Patsy Thorpe noticed that the towns of Mauch Chunk and East Mauch Chunk were creating an industrial development board and considering changing the names of their towns. Patsy called Mauch Chunk officials, who agreed to rename their town Jim Thorpe and envisioned a sports complex, a cancer research center, a Jim Thorpe museum, and the Jim Thorpe Teepee Motel, all built around an elegant memorial to Jim Thorpe. Patsy agreed to move her husband's body back East and buried her husband in the newly renamed town of Jim Thorpe, Pennsylvania, in 1954. Nothing but a $15,000 gravesite memorial ever materialized. One civic leader in Jim Thorpe later commented on the deal, "All we got was a dead Indian."

The first president of the NFL, the man whom the Associated Press declared the Greatest All-Around Male Athlete and Football Player of the Half Century in 1950, the man named the Greatest American Football Player in History in a 1977 *Sport* magazine national poll, the man declared the greatest athlete of the twentieth century in a 2000 ESPN/ABC Internet poll, the only American to play professional football and baseball and win Olympic medals in track and field, rests eternally in a town he never knew. As Grantland Rice once observed, "Looking down on it all, old Jim must be chuckling an ironic chuckle."

Throughout his hard later life, Thorpe cherished his Carlisle experience. He stayed in contact with Warner, Welch, and others from Carlisle and even sent his children to Indian boarding schools. Thorpe figured that if the education was good enough for him, it was good enough for his children as well.

Although Warner once commented that "coaching is a very uncertain and precarious calling and I do not advise any young man to enter it," many of the young men he coached at Carlisle went on to coaching careers. Charles Albert Bender pitched twelve seasons for the Philadelphia Athletics and later coached baseball at the U.S. Naval Academy at Annapolis and for the White Sox, the Giants, and the Philadelphia Athletics. Frank Mt. Pleasant coached at Indiana and

West Virginia Wesleyan University and also taught French. William "Lone Star" Dietz, who claimed "I think I have Warner's system down better than any other man," coached the State College of Washington, later Washington State University, to an undefeated season in 1915 and defeated Brown 14–0 on New Year's Day 1916 in the second Rose Bowl. In 1932, Dietz coached the Boston Braves in the National Professional Football League. Four years later, the team moved to Washington and was renamed the Washington Redskins.

Albert Exendine earned a law degree at Dickinson College and coached at Otterbein College in Ohio, Occidental College, and elsewhere. Joe Guyon continued to play professional baseball and football through the 1920s. At quarterback, Guyon led the New York Giants to a world championship in 1926.

Gus Welch recovered from his grave injury in the 1914 Notre Dame game and returned to school. He graduated from the Dickinson School of Law in 1917 and volunteered for the army. During his training, Welch played football for the Seventy-ninth Division Team at Camp Meade and played a few professional games with Jim Thorpe and the Canton Bulldogs. During one game Welch ran through a member of the 1914 Notre Dame team for a touchdown. The former Notre Dame player thought, "Pretty good for a dead Indian."

Welch rose quickly to the rank of captain and was eager to see service in Europe. When white officers refused to lead a troop of black engineers, Welch volunteered for the job. He served with distinction in World War I, building roads for the American Expeditionary Force during the Meuse-Argonne campaign. In 1923, he married Julia Carter, the daughter of Oklahoma congressman Charles David Carter. The Welches had no children of their own, but they adopted a niece, Serena, who served as the model for the figure portrayed on the canning labels of Pocahontas Foods.

Welch coached and taught physical education at a variety of colleges and secondary schools, including Haskell Institute, American University, Washington State University, the University of Virginia, and Georgetown University. He introduced lacrosse as a varsity sport at the University of Virginia. He drew up plans for the Junior Athletic League of America and created a new sport that combined features of soccer, basketball, and football. Welch called the game "Honor Ball."

In 1929, he and Julia pooled their life savings, purchased a mountainside farm in Bedford County, Virginia, and opened Camp Kewanzee, named for Welch's grandfather, a Chippewa elder. In the late 1930s, the National Park Service decided to extend the Blue Ridge Highway directly through Welch's property. The road threatened to destroy Welch's camp and ruin him financially since the government was offering to pay him $14 an acre, much less than he had paid for the property.

As he had at Carlisle, Gus Welch stood his ground. He launched a letter-writing campaign that generated a good deal of publicity. Welch pointed out that the proposed highway would run directly through a rare poplar tree, one of the environmental landmarks of the area. "I told them I thought the Parkway was to be installed to enhance scenic beauty and the wonders of nature, not to destroy it," Welch told the press. "Why, it took centuries for that tree to grow."

The feds agreed to save the tree but refused to spare Welch's land. "The white man has been taking land from the Indian for so long that it has become a habit with him," Welch said after the court ruled against him. "There's nothing an Indian can do about changing the white man's habits." In his declining years, the honorable Gus Welch coached public school sports in Bedford, Virginia, and claimed, "I should have done this years before as it is the finest work a coach can do."

Pop Warner coached at the University of Pittsburgh from 1915 to 1924 and led his teams to three undefeated seasons. In 1921, Warner's Pitt team played West Virginia in one of the first football games broadcast live over the radio. The following year, Pitt administrators were furious when they discovered that Warner had signed a contract to coach at Stanford. They refused to let him out of his contract, so he continued to coach at Pitt, traveling to Stanford to oversee spring practices in 1922 and 1923 and sending two of his assistants to coach during the season. Warner eventually moved to Stanford, where he coached full-time from 1924 to 1932 and turned out three Rose Bowl teams. In 1933, he left Stanford for Temple University in Philadelphia, lured by the record-breaking salary of $100,000 a year. "Warner was an outcast of sorts, somewhat of a rogue," observed Mike Bynum, who edited Pop Warner's autobiography. "If a big paycheck was on the line, he'd usually go."

In April 1934, Warner led a clinic for kids and coaches sponsored by a local Philadelphia youth football league. Renamed the Pop Warner Conference and later Pop Warner Football, the organization thrived. Today, more than 350,000 young people in thirty-five states and two foreign countries participate in the football and cheerleading programs sponsored by Pop Warner Little Scholars, Inc. According to the official rules of the organization, "The general objectives of Pop Warner Football are to inspire youth, regardless of race, creed, religion, or national origin, to practice the ideals of sportsmanship, scholarship, and physical fitness, as reflected in the life of the late Glenn Scobey 'Pop' Warner." If the drinking, smoking, profane, gambling Pop Warner were alive today, he would probably not be allowed to coach Pop Warner football. When Warner died of throat cancer on September 7, 1954, in Palo Alto, California, he left behind an estate of more than $500,000 and a record as one of the winningest coaches in college football history.

"Looking back," Warner said, "I have estimated that in the long run I would probably have made more money while practicing law than in coaching football. Still, I have never regretted making this decision, although at times it has been rather difficult on the nerves."

Warner never admitted that he lied about Jim Thorpe to protect his own career. Jim Thorpe never blamed Pop Warner for the 1912 Olympic scandal and always stuck to his story—that Warner had not known about his days playing summer ball in North Carolina. Thorpe even did some assistant coaching for Warner at Pittsburgh and made several public appearances with his former coach over the years.

The closest Thorpe ever got to blaming Warner was in comments to friends such as Jack Cusack, Thorpe's coach while he played for the Canton Bulldogs. "Jim explained to me that after returning from the Olympics, being unmarried at the time, he turned the medals over to Pop Warner for safe keeping," Cusack told the author Robert Wheeler. "When the charge of professionalism was made, Warner advised that they be returned. Jim regretted the action later and told me if he had it to do over, he would have kept them. In my opinion, he was ill-advised by Pop Warner."

"I never heard anything bad about Pop Warner from Dad," recalled Thorpe's daughter Grace. "I did hear Momma say that Pop Warner knew all that time that Dad had played baseball." According to Grace, her father never complained to the family about the Olympic injustice. "He never tried to get those medals back for himself. He was very philosophical about it, he wasn't bitter at all."

Though Thorpe himself never fought to clear his name, his family and friends lobbied to restore the Olympic honor that he clearly deserved. Damon Runyon began the push for justice in 1914. Franklin D. Roosevelt, Branch Rickey, and Gerald Ford also joined the pro-Thorpe cause. The sportswriter Grantland Rice became one of Thorpe's greatest supporters. "If ever an individual was pilloried by the shabby treatment he received from most of the press and the public, Jim Thorpe is that man," Rice wrote. "What right did the AAU have to Thorpe's private gifts, fairly won in those 1912 Olympics? They merely robbed the Indian in cold-blooded fashion."

Avery Brundage, who had finished sixth behind Thorpe in the 1912 Olympic pentathlon, became the head of the U.S. Olympic Committee in the 1930s and the head of the International Olympic Committee from 1952 to 1972. An aloof, wealthy patrician who protected his power over athletics as ferociously as James E. Sullivan had protected his, Brundage enforced amateurism to such an absurd extent that sportswriters dubbed him the "meanest man in sports," the "apostle of hypocrisy," and "slavery Avery."

While he was head of the IOC, Brundage stonewalled any pro-Thorpe movement. In 1973, a year after Brundage's retirement, the AAU finally restored Thorpe's amateur status. Nine years later, Robert Wheeler and his wife, Dr. Florence Ridlon, who had established the Jim Thorpe Foundation, collected 250,000 names on a petition to return Thorpe's gold medals. In their research, the Wheelers uncovered the hard evidence they needed to prove that Thorpe's medals had been taken away illegally. They found a copy of the rulebook for the 1912 Olympics in which was stated the regulation that protests concerning individual athletes had to be made thirty days after the presentation of the medal. In Thorpe's case, the protests had been made five months too late.

Presented with the evidence and the petition, members of the U.S. Olympic Committee set up a meeting with the IOC president, Juan Antonio Samaranch. Samaranch agreed to support Thorpe's cause. On October 3, 1982, the IOC executive committee unanimously passed a resolution to give Thorpe back his honors. On January 13, 1983, Samaranch presented reproductions of Jim Thorpe's gold medals to two of his children in Los Angeles. The real medals had been lost long ago, stolen from museums.

In 1997, students at Cossack High School in Wisconsin did some Internet research and discovered that the AAU had never given the Thorpe family back his national championship medals for his post-Olympic victory as the American champion in the decathlon, although the AAU had restored his amateur status. "It was an oversight," explained AAU official Keith Noll after he presented the Thorpe family with copies of the medals. "It was the last thing the AAU had to do to make things right for Jim Thorpe." Looking back on the scandal, Noll believed that everyone from Pop Warner to James Sullivan and the AAU officials at the time made mistakes in the way they handled the Thorpe case. "They did things for a reason at the time, and maybe not for the right reason," Noll said. "It was a case of everybody using an individual who was a phenomenal athlete."

In a former bank building in Oklahoma City, W. Lynne Draper serves as the director of the Jim Thorpe Foundation. "Jim Thorpe was the greatest all-around athlete in history," Draper maintains. "Any truly objective analysis of sports history shows this. Nobody could match him. Nobody has come close to doing what he did." Draper, who heads the foundation that operates the Bright Path athletic programs for children and presents the Jim Thorpe Award to the best defensive back in college football every year, believes that Thorpe was one of America's greatest heroes. "I think in a way he represents the highs and the lows of all of us. He accomplished so many great things. . . . He wasn't perfect by any means, but he cared about people, especially young people."

At the NFL Hall of Fame in Canton, Ohio, a life-size bronze statue of Thorpe greets visitors. The award given every year to professional football's most valuable player is the Jim Thorpe Trophy. But like the glittering Viking ship from the last czar of Russia that resides in the storeroom of a Swiss museum, the name of Jim Thorpe lies hidden in the basement of America's athletic memory. Today, few people remember the first modern football running back or the historic moment when the world of sports honored a true champion without regard for blood, money, or politics, and Jim Thorpe stood beside Pop Warner bathed in the glory of international athletic achievement. As Thorpe later told Grantland Rice, "I played with the heart of an amateur—for the pure hell of it."

Afterword

The Continuing Problem of "Amateur" Athletics

Today, the Warner system of coaching, fund-raising, and promotion dominates the world of amateur athletics. On the positive side, Warner perfected the forward pass, introduced the single- and double-wing formations, the three-point stance, lightweight pads, tackling dummies, and blocking sleds. He engineered the first transcontinental schedule in football history. He was a coach, an administrator, a publicist, an accountant, and a one-man precursor of the multibillion-dollar college and Olympic athletics establishments that have followed in his wake.

Unfortunately, the downside of the Warner system also continues to dominate the world of amateur sports.

The problem of amateurism continues to plague college and Olympic athletics. In 1971 the IOC struck the word amateur from the Olympic charter. Fifteen years later, the organization adopted rules permitting the international federations controlling each sport to decide whether to allow professionals into Olympic competition. When Congress finally passed the Amateur Sports Act of 1978, the AAU's involvement in Olympic sports came to an end. The act wrested control of the United States' participation in the Olympic games from the AAU and placed it under the aegis of the U.S. Olympic Committee (USOC).

Today many of the thirty-nine USOC-affiliated organizations that control individual sports have moved to allow professionals to compete in the Olympic games, a trend that is helping to solve the amateur dilemma at least in regards to Olympic competition.

Unfortunately, even with the loosening of amateur regulations and the expulsion of the AAU, the management of amateur athletics by the

USOC is in some ways as bad as it was in 1912, when Sullivan and Warner betrayed Jim Thorpe. The main difference is the huge amount of money at stake due to mushrooming revenue from the sale of television rights. In 1960, CBS paid $394,000 for the rights to broadcast the Rome Olympics. Broadcasting rights for the 2012 Olympics cost NBC $1.18 billion. The USOC budget has mushroomed along with the broadcasting revenues. From 2000 to 2004, the USOC's quadrennial budget was $495 million. The human side of the organization has grown proportionately. At the beginning of 2003, the USOC included a paid CEO, a volunteer president, a paid staff of about 550, and a 125-member board of directors.

With big money and big overhead, infighting and inefficiency have found fertile ground at the USOC. USOC officials paid more than $1 million in inducements to members of the International Olympic Committee to secure the 2002 Winter Olympics for Salt Lake City. A subsequent investigation resulted in the firing or resignation of 10 members of the IOC. The U.S. courts held American Olympic officials not guilty of fraud. This kind of situation was so common in the Olympic site selection process that the American officials were just conducting business as usual.

On a micro level, USOC staff members fought over the money related to the "amateur" games. Norm Black, the fifth CEO of the USOC in six years, served for only nine months before resigning in 2000. According to Black, the motto of the USOC had become "What's in it for me?"

"After extravagant severance packages and allegations of nepotism, after senatorial sleuthing and suspect expense reports," wrote Selena Roberts in the *New York Times* on March 2, 2003, "the Olympic committee is recognized in every home in the nation. So is Enron, so is Tyco, so is WorldCom."

"This has been a nightmare for us," said Evan Mergenstein, an agent for more than fifty Olympians. "The Olympic movement is turning into the laughingstock of the sports marketing world." Senator Ben Nighthorse Campbell, Republican of Colorado, who is Native American and a 1964 judo Olympian, has been one of the leaders in calling for reform of the USOC. Campbell claims that the recent track record of the USOC "makes me sick to my stomach."

Drastic changes have indeed been recommended for the USOC,

including cutting the board of directors from 125 to 11. Actual restructuring of the organization will probably require congressional action and a thorough revision of the Amateur Sports Act of 1978.

Like the USOC, the NCAA clings to the amateur ideal. In 1952, the NCAA began regulating television broadcasts of college football games, at first in order to protect game attendance. Like the USOC, in recent years the NCAA has become the beneficiary of ballooning revenues from the sale of broadcasting rights, money that goes into the pockets of sports administrators but not the "amateur" athletes who actually play the games. "College System Still Benefits Coaches, Not Players" ran the headline in the *New York Times* "Sports of the Times" column by William C. Rhoden on April 6, 2003. The article read in part:

> Major collegiate sports functions like a plantation. The ath-
> letes perform in an economic atmosphere where everyone
> except them makes money off their labor. In the revenue-
> producing sports of football and basketball, athletes are the
> gold, the oil, the natural resource that makes the NCAA
> engine run and its cash register ring. Coaches climb the ladder
> on the shoulders of players. Too often the only thing players
> get are sore shoulders.

Problems involving violations of NCAA rules and the rules of other amateur athletic rule-making bodies have become so common-place that only the most exceptional controversies make the head-lines. In early 2003, the high school basketball phenomenon LeBron James was stripped of his amateur status by the Ohio High School Athletic Association for accepting two free sports jerseys. The NCAA prohibited the Ohio State University football running back Maurice Clarett from playing because he had taken a $500 check and payment of $1,000 in phone bills from a booster. Clarett then sued the NFL over a rule prohibiting football players from signing with the NFL until they have been out of high school for three years. According to Clarett's lawyer Alan C. Milstein, "I see Maurice's case as a league trying to make certain players, young players, who are often poor, wait on earning a living, while the NFL and colleges, either directly or indirectly, make millions off them. To me, his situation is about another huge entity trying to take advantage of a smaller group of people who don't necessarily have powerful voices like themselves." Clarett eventually lost his case.

On August 1, 2003, the *New York Times* published an article written by the University of Colorado sophomore Jeremy Bloom titled, "Show Us the Money." Bloom claimed that the NCAA "not only rules college athletics, it also limits the opportunities of the 360,000 student-athletes it purports to serve. . . . As the organization has smoothly adapted to the big-money era of sports, it has kept the student-athletes themselves from benefiting from the changes. . . . And not only do the student-athletes not share in the wealth, the NCAA has plenty of rules to keep us from making money on our own. It prohibits us from having sponsors or appearing in advertisements even if the products have no relation to the collegiate sports we play. In my case, to be allowed to play wide receiver for the University of Colorado football team, I had to give up endorsement opportunities I had garnered as an Olympic moguls skier."

In the article, Bloom cited the example of Aaron Adair, a third baseman for the University of Oklahoma and a brain cancer survivor who wrote an inspirational book about his recovery, only to have the NCAA terminate his college baseball career because his name was attached to a "corporate product."

Bloom drafted the "Student-Athletes' Bill of Rights," which is now circulating in state legislatures across the country. The bill of rights would allow students to "secure bona fide employment not associated with his/her amateur sport" and collect money from certain categories of merchandise. "My goal is to improve the circumstances of the next generation of student-athletes," Bloom wrote. "That seems to be a goal the NCAA has forgotten."

State legislators have recently taken action against the NCAA. The Nebraska legislature, whose flagship university belongs to the Big 12 Conference, recently adopted a law that would allow the university to pay student-athletes a cash stipend. The bill will take effect when two other states in the Big 12 pass similar legislation. Texas and other universities are responding favorably.

In May 2003, the California State Senate approved a bill calling for the expulsion of the NCAA from the state unless universities increased their payments to student athletes. "If you just take a look at what goes on," says Kevin Murray, a coauthor of the California bill, "it [the current amateur system] is completely designed to keep the student under the thumb of the NCAA for the NCAA profit."

Myles Brand, the current president of the NCAA, has expressed sympathy toward the efforts to update the amateur concept. "Amateurism was borrowed from the English during the early nineteenth century," Brand said with a slight misread of history, "and it never fully carried over to America." He described athletics in America as the "collegial model" that permits enhanced financial aid for athletes but no salaries.

"There are certainly plenty of things wrong with college athletics," observed Bob Bowlsby, the athletic director of the University of Iowa and the President of the NCAA Division I-A Athletic Directors' Association. "Some of these conversations sound an awful lot like what was being said about athletics and education at the beginning of the twentieth century. It's all the same issues. It has always been a multiheaded monster."

More than ninety years after Pop Warner lied about Jim Thorpe to protect his "amateur" sports program, some NCAA coaches continue to play with the truth. In June 2003, Patrick Dennehy, a basketball player at Baylor University in Waco, Texas, was murdered. To forestall an investigation of Baylor's "amateur" sports program, Dennehy's coach, Dave Bliss, deliberately misled police investigators by spreading the lie that his murdered player was involved in drug dealing. "I think the thing we want to do—and you think about this—if there's a way we can create the perception that Pat may have been a dealer," Bliss said on a tape to one of his assistant coaches. "Even if we have to kind of make some things look a little better than they are, that can save us." Bliss lost his job, but Robert B. Sloan, Jr., the President and CEO of Baylor, did not step down.

"Like anything else that gets twisted or manipulated, college athletics can also be the source of failure and even evil," President Sloan wrote in the editorial pages of the *Los Angeles Times* on August 26, 2002. "The system can and must be improved."

A good first step toward improvement of the amateur sports system would be to make sports administrators accountable for the excesses of their athletic programs. When a sports program goes bad, university presidents, conference administrators, Olympic officials, and NCAA bureaucrats should be held to the same standards of accountability as corporate executives and punished according to the severity of the transgression. Making sports bureaucrats accountable for the organizations they lead will insure that no athlete will ever again suffer the fate of Jim Thorpe, the greatest All American.

Acknowledgments

I nvestigating the story of Jim Thorpe and Pop Warner has led me to fascinating documents, rich archives, and wonderful people. The writing process began more than ten years ago, when I first started researching the story of Louis Tewanima and the tradition of Indian athletics. Since that time, I have had the privilege of traveling to Arizona, Oklahoma, Pennsylvania, Kansas, New York, and Connecticut to collect the threads of what I consider to be the greatest American sports saga of the twentieth century.

My research efforts began with several key books. *Indian Running: Native American History and Tradition* (Santa Fe: Ancient City Press, 1981) by Peter Nabokov first brought me into the world of the Indian athlete. John Steckbeck's impeccably researched sports history, *Fabulous Redman: The Carlisle Indians and Their Famous Football Teams* (Harrisburg, Penn.: J. Horace McFarland Company, 1951) provided scores, dates, and other vital statistics that form the skeleton of this work. John Newcombe's *The Best of the Athletic Boys: The White Man's Impact on Jim Thorpe* (New York: Doubleday, 1975) is simply one of the best books I have ever read—clearly written, richly detailed, and brilliantly nuanced.

Jim Thorpe: World's Greatest Athlete (Norman, Okla.: University of Oklahoma Press, 1979) by Bob Wheeler is by far the most complete treatment of Thorpe's athletic career. A fanatic researcher whose efforts led directly to the restoration of Jim Thorpe's gold medals in 1983, Wheeler is a true gentleman, as generous as he is professional. Robert Whitman also was generous with his time and information regarding the stunning photographs included in his book, *Jim Thorpe: Athlete of the Century: A Pictorial Biography* (Oklahoma City: Robert L. Whitman and the Jim Thorpe Association, 2002). John Bloom's *To*

Show What an Indian Can Do: Sports at Native American Boarding Schools (Minneapolis: University of Minnesota Press, 2000) provided much information on Carlos Montezuma and the politics of Indian schools.

Pop Warner's autobiography, *Pop Warner: Football's Greatest Teacher: The Epic Autobiography of Major College Football's Winningest Coach, Glenn S. (Pop) Warner* (Birmingham, Ala.: Gridiron Football Properties, 1993) edited by the football historian Mike Bynum is an eye-opening account of Warner's side of the story. Warner wrote at least two versions of his autobiography: a series of fifty-nine newspaper articles distributed by the Christy Walsh syndicate from 1927 to 1928 and a series of articles published in *Collier's* magazine in 1931. In several instances where different versions of the same Pop Warner story have emerged, I have chosen Bynum's variant, which has the endorsement of Pop Warner Little Scholars.

Early in my investigations, the California-based filmmaker Michael Rhodes provided inspiration and a hard copy of a key document: *The Carlisle Indian School, Hearings Before the Joint Commission of the Congress of the United States, Sixty-Third Congress Second Session to Investigate Indian Affairs, February 6, 7, 8 and March 25, 1914, Part II* (Washington, D.C.: Government Printing Office, 1914). Although I was unable to locate part I of the hearings, part II was both riveting and revealing.

In Arizona, Scott Thybony graciously introduced me to the land of the Hopi while Wendy Holliday of the Hopi Cultural Preservation Office put me in touch with a promising young Hopi runner, Juwan Nuvayokva. Best wishes to the members of the Tewanima Memorial Footrace Committee for leading new generations of runners in the footsteps of Louis Tewanima.

The National Archives and Records Administration is the starting point for all researchers of the federally funded Indian school system and its Native American students. Thanks to Glen Siple and the other staff members for providing me with copies of their extensive files in a timely and professional manner. And thanks to Genevieve Bell. In the process of writing her 1998 Stanford University doctoral dissertation, "Telling Stories Out of School: Remembering the Carlisle Indian Industrial School, 1879–1918," Ms. Bell helped organize and catalogue the NARA files, a service that will greatly benefit future generations of relatives, writers, and historians. Thanks also to other

Thorpe researchers whom I have contacted along the research trail, including David Thomas at the American Museum of Natural History and Kate Buford, whose forthcoming biography of Jim Thorpe will undoubtedly reveal new, fascinating information beyond the scope of my humble effort.

Bill Welge, director of the research division, and the staff at the Oklahoma Historical Society in Oklahoma City provided me with great assistance in accessing the society's rich collection of material on Jim Thorpe, the Sac and Fox tribe, and local Oklahoma history. Also in Oklahoma City, W. Lynne Draper, president of the Jim Thorpe Foundation, took time out from his busy schedule to talk with me about the heart of the Thorpe tradition and the many athletic programs now being carried on in Jim Thorpe's name.

Jellene Factor introduced me to the archives at the Sac and Fox National Public Library, located at the Sac and Fox tribal complex south of Stroud, Oklahoma, and pointed me to the oral history of Walter White as well as other invaluable items in the collection. The staff at the Jim Thorpe Home in Yale, Oklahoma, was equally generous with their time and energy in helping me reconstruct elements of Thorpe's boyhood.

At the University of Tulsa, Department of Special Collections and University Archives at the McFarlin Library, Gina L. B. Minks and Timothy Anderson assisted in my investigation of the Gus Welch Papers. In Lawton, Oklahoma, Towana D. Spivey, director of Fort Sill National Historical Landmark, generously shared his insights into the career of R. L. Pratt and other military men on the post–Civil War frontier. The staff at the Yale University Beinecke Rare Book and Manuscript Library, Yale Collection of Western Americana in New Haven, Connecticut, made my lightning examination of the Richard Henry Pratt Papers efficient and worthwhile.

In Lawrence, Kansas, Jessica James, museum assistant, and Shelby Palmer, administrative assistant, spent a day with me combing through the archives at the Haskell Cultural Center and Museum on the campus of the Haskell Indian Nations University. I am grateful for their patience and their sharp eyes.

In western New York state, Margaret S. Mayerat, the Town of Concord historian, took me on a day-long tour of Pop Warner's hometown, including a visit to the fascinating Warner Museum in Springville. Ms. Mayerat's insight, patience, knowledge, and sense of humor provided me with a thorough understanding of Pop Warner's background and an appreciation for the wonders of Springville, Concord Township, and Erie County. And a special thanks to Lee Luss for her help in processing documents at the Concord Historical Society offices.

Close to home, Michael Granof, the Ernst and Young Professor of Accounting at the University of Texas at Austin, provided a former student with real-world insight into the politics of big-time college sports. Jan and Terry Todd took the time to introduce me to the Todd-McLean Collection at the University of Texas at Austin, a fantastic resource for the study of the history of physical culture. The Todds also introduced me to the historian Wayne Wilson, the vice president of research at the Amateur Athletic Foundation in Los Angeles. Mr. Wilson's encyclopedic knowledge of Olympic history was the key to my understanding the controversy surrounding the Thorpe Olympic trophies. Thanks also to Keith Noll at the Wisconsin Amateur Athletic Union. Keith has a great attitude and a hunger for truth that should serve as an example for all administrators in the world of sports.

In Carlisle, Pennsylvania, the site of the U.S. Indian School where much of this story took place, the former Carlisle campus, now the U.S. Army War College, is sacred ground. The playing fields, Warner's home, the "athletic boys" quarters, and many of the other historic buildings remain almost exactly as they were when the events chronicled in this story took place, at least from the outside. To walk across the campus is to walk in the steps of Jim Thorpe and Pop Warner. Thanks to the staff at the United States Army Military History Institute on the grounds of the college who pointed me to the Glenn Warner box, which included priceless sporting memorabilia and "Memories of the Indian School," a fascinating account of sports at Carlisle, written in Pop Warner's own hand. Jay A. Graybeal, the photo archivist at the institute, provided me with unexpectedly generous assistance and access to one of the most fascinating and workable photo archives in the United States.

Equally fascinating was the time I spent at Wardecker's Men's Wear in downtown Carlisle with Fred Wardecker. It was magical to hang around the store and talk sports, just like Jim Thorpe, Gus Welch, and so many other players, coaches, and writers have done over the past century. Fred was generous enough to provide several photos for this book and to lend me rare volumes from his fascinating collection of Carlisle material. I owe Fred several cold beverages, and I look forward to reading his buddy Tom Benjey's book on William "Lone Star" Dietz.

Fred has donated many of his images to the great collection of U.S. Indian School material housed at the Cumberland County Historical Society (CCHS). Thanks to Richard L. Tritt, the photo curator at the CCHS, for his diligence and taste in tracking down, selecting, and processing many of the photos included in this book. And a special thanks to the author Robert Whitman for donating his collection of Thorpe photos to the historical society.

For more than a decade, I have been in touch with Barbara Landis, the Carlisle Indian School Biographer at the CCHS. Ms. Landis is a dedicated, talented, and hardworking professional who has done more than any other individual to preserve the history and the dignity of the students who passed through the U.S. Indian School at Carlisle. With the help of Ms. Landis, David Smith, the librarian, and the rest of the staff at the Cumberland County Historical Society, I was able to unearth, examine, and appreciate a number of documents that have literally changed history. Among the greatest finds at the CCHS was the Johnson Collection, a group of papers saved from destruction by the former janitor at the U.S. Indian School and the Miller Box, which contained material from Hugh Miller, one of Carlisle's primary publicists. In addition, the oral histories of former Carlisle employees collected and transcribed by the CCHS provided invaluable insight into the history of Carlisle. Barbara Landis also introduced me to George Yuda, the son of Jim Thorpe's classmate Montreville Speed Yuda. It was an enlightening pleasure to visit with Mr. Yuda and his wife and talk about his father's relationship with his alma mater. Mr. Yuda helped teach me the true meaning of loyalty.

Although I was not able to speak to all the descendants of Jim Thorpe, the people I did talk with, Bill Thorpe, Jack Thorpe, Grace Thorpe, and Dagmar Thorpe, all exhibited a generosity of spirit and a vibrant interest in their father's legacy that was truly inspirational. My prayers and blessings go out to the entire Thorpe family and to the future generations to come.

Publishing a book is a lot like playing a football game, a team effort requiring talent and patience on the part of all concerned. Thanks to the key players of my All-American team: Lori Borden, my editor and friend with writing skills honed in her legendary Newton High School English classes; Cynthia Prescott, who braved the elements to visit the Worcester Public Library; Cliff Farrington, my indefatigable researcher (thanks for the sabal palm); and Tom Miller, my editor at John Wiley & Sons, who went the extra mile to get this project on the market in a timely fashion. Finally, thanks to my agent, Jim Hornfischer. More than a deal maker, Jim is a great writer and a great friend.

Notes

Introduction

1 *"Watching him turn . . . flesh and blood"* Percy Haughton as quoted in Al Stump, "Jim Thorpe: Greatest of Them All," *Sport*, December 1949, 49–54.

1: American Airedale

5 *"What do you think you're doing out there?"* The story of Pop Warner and the football tryout is based on two sources: Mike Bynum, ed., *Pop Warner: Football's Greatest Teacher: The Epic Autobiography of Major College Football's Winningest Coach, Glenn S. (Pop) Warner* (Birmingham, Ala.: Gridiron Football Properties, 1993) 121–122; and Robert W. Wheeler, *Jim Thorpe: World's Greatest Athlete* (Norman: University of Oklahoma Press, 1979), 55 ff.

6 *Captain Richard Henry Pratt* founder of the U.S. Indian School at Carlisle. A lieutenant in 1879 when he founded the school, Pratt was promoted to captain in 1893, then major, colonel, and finally brigadier general in 1903. Most of the Carlisle students referred to the then superintendent as Captain Pratt.

8 *Jim Thorpe had been running* Sources on Jim Thorpe's family background include William T. Hagan, *The Sac and Fox Indians* (Norman: University of Oklahoma Press, 1958); Jack Newcombe, *The Best of the Athletic Boys: The White Man's Impact on Jim Thorpe* (New York: Doubleday; 1975); Dagmar Thorpe, "Ancestors of Jim Thorpe: An Annotated Genealogy and Bibliography (1700—1887)," 2003; Grace F. Thorpe, "The Jim Thorpe Family: From Wisconsin to Indian Territory, Part 1," *The Chronicles of Oklahoma*

59 (1981): 91–105 and "The Jim Thorpe Family: From Wisconsin to Indian Territory, Part II," *The Chronicles of Oklahoma*, 59 (1981): 179–201; and Wheeler, *Jim Thorpe*.

9 *"Grandpa was a horse breeder"* Interview by the author with Grace Thorpe, Prague, Oklahoma, on April 27, 2003.

10 *"Hiram walked in"* Interview by the author with Jack Thorpe, Kickapoo Reservation, Kansas, on February 5, 2004.

2: An Incorrigible Youngster

13 Sources on Thorpe's youth include The Prague Historical Museum, *Prague, the First 100 Years* (Prague, Okla.: Prague Historical Society and Museum, 1991); and Wheeler, *Jim Thorpe*. Sources on Keokuk Falls include Blake Gumprecht, "A Saloon on Every Corner: Whiskey Towns of Oklahoma Territory, 1889–1907," *The Chronicles of Oklahoma* 74, no. 2 (Summer 1996): 146–173; and Charles W. Mooney, *Localized History of Pottawatomie County, Oklahoma to 1907* (Midwest City, Okla.: Thunderbird Industries, 1971). Sources on the history of Indian education include Myriam Vuckovic, "Onward Ever, Backward Never: Student Life and Students' Lives at Haskell Institute, 1884–1920s" (Ph.D. diss., The University of Kansas, 2001).

18 *"Many were transferred"* Thomas Wildcat Alford, *Civilization, as Told to Florence Drake* (Norman: University of Oklahoma Press, 1936).

20 *"The superintendent was very ill."* Harriet Patrick as quoted in Harriet Patrick Gilstrap, "Memoirs of a Pioneer Teacher," *The Chronicles of Oklahoma* 38, no. 1 (Spring 1960): 20–34.

20 *"I'm a twin."* Jim Thorpe as quoted in Grantland Rice, *The Tumult and the Shouting: My Life in Sport* (New York: Barnes, 1954), 234.

21 *Sometimes Thorpe attended powwows* Walter White, *The Greatest Athlete*, unpublished manuscript, The Sac and Fox National Public Library.

3: Men Born Shaggy

23 Sources on Warner's boyhood include Bynum, *Pop Warner;* Glenn S. Warner, "Autobiography," 59 chapters, distributed 1927–1928 by the Christy Walsh newspaper syndicate; Glenn S. Warner, "The Indian Massacres," *Collier's*, October 17, 1931, 7–8, 61–63; "Heap

Big Run Most Fast," *Collier's*, October 24, 1931, 18–19, 46; "Red Menaces," *Collier's*, October 31, 1931, 16–17, 51; "Battles of Brawn," *Collier's*, November 7, 1931, 10, 45–47; "What's the Matter with Football?" *Collier's*, November 14, 1931, 26, 57–58; "Here Come the Giants!" *Collier's*, November 24, 1931, 20, 34.

26 "*I will not permit*" in Ronald A. Smith, *Sports and Freedom: The Rise of Big-Time College Athletics* (New York: Oxford University Press, 1988), 74.

26 "*Johanson took one look at Pop*" Dr. Ralph W. Waite as quoted in Maury May, "Dr. Waite Remembers Pop's Daring, Love of Horses and His Snoring," September 11, 1954, from the Concord Historical Society, Springville, N.Y.

28 "*The organizer wins in athletics*" Walter Camp as quoted in Smith, *Sports and Freedom*, 157.

32 "*I even let my youthful gambling spirit*" Bynum, *Pop Warner*, 62.

4: Oklahoma Buckaroo

37 Sources on Warner's early coaching career include Bynum, *Pop Warner*; and Warner, "Autobiography."

39 "*Work is the most necessary*" Dr. Carlos Montezuma as quoted in *The Indian Leader* (Haskell Institute weekly publication), January 12, 1900.

39 "*If you should*" Richard Henry Pratt as quoted in Newcombe, *Athletic Boys*, 64.

Sources on the Haskell Institute include Vuckovic, "Onward Ever."

43 "*Can you teach the boy anything?*" White, *Greatest Athlete*.

5: The "Hunchback" Play

46 "*Tom O'Rourke, the old prize-fight promoter*" Warner, "Battles of Brawn."

47 "*The Indians gathered*" Warner, "The Indian Massacres."

48 "*Some plays you make up*" Pop Warner quoted in Edwin Pope, *Football's Greatest Coaches* (Atlanta: Tupper and Love, 1955), 300.

48 Stories about Jim Thorpe at the Garden Grove School from White, *Greatest Athlete*.

6: "White Man Bathed in Red"

53 Sources on Carlisle, Pennsylvania, include "The Carlisle Indian Industrial School," R. Christopher Goodwin and Associates (U.S. Army Construction Engineering Research Laboratory); Landis, Barbara, "Carlisle Indian Industrial School History," published online at home.epix.net/~landis/histry.html, site visited on February 2, 2002; Robert L. Whitman, *Jim Thorpe: Athlete of the Century, A Pictorial Biography* (Oklahoma City: Robert L. Whitman and the Jim Thorpe Association, 2002); and Linda F. Witmer, *The Indian Industrial School, Carlisle, Pennsylvania, 1879–1918* (Carlisle, Pa.: Cumberland County Historical Society, 2002).

53 Sources on Richard Henry Pratt include Elaine Goodman Eastman, *Pratt: The Red Man's Moses* (Norman: University of Oklahoma Press, 1935); and W. S. Nye, *Carbine and Lance: The Story of Old Fort Sill* (Norman: University of Oklahoma Press, 1937).

58 Sources on Thorpe's early experiences at Carlisle include Genevieve Bell, "Telling Stories Out of School: Remembering the Carlisle Indian Industrial School, 1879–1918" (Ph.D. diss., Stanford University, 1998); Carmelita S. Ryan, "The Carlisle Indian Industrial School" (Ph.D. diss., Georgetown University, 1962); and Luther Standing Bear, *My People the Sioux* (London, Neb.: University of Nebraska Press, 1975).

58 *"In 1900, only one out of"* Cynthia Crossen, "In 1860, America Had 40 Public High Schools; Teachers Chopped Wood," *Wall Street Journal*, September 3, 2003.

61 *"It was not a flattering salary offer"* Bynum, *Pop Warner*, 112.

61 *"When one of Warner's recruits, Frank Beaver"* David Wallace Adams, *Education for Extinction: American Indians and the Boarding School Experience, 1875–1928* (Lawrence: University of Kansas Press, 1995), 185.

7: "Athletocracy"

63 Sources on Francis E. Leupp and William Mercer include Bell, "Telling Stories"; and Robert M. Kvasnicka and Herman J. Viola, eds., *The Commissioners of Indian Affairs, 1824–1977* (Lincoln, Neb.: University of Nebraska Press, 1979).

64 *"By force of both"* Francis E. Leupp as quoted in Bell, "Telling Stories," 83.

64 *"Every Commissioner and Secretary"* Francis E. Leupp as quoted in Wallace, *Education for Extinction*, 323.

66 Sources on President Theodore Roosevelt's reaction to football include Guy M. Lewis, "Theodore Roosevelt's Role in the 1905 Football Controversy," *The Research Quarterly* 40, no. 4 (December 1969), 717–724.

68 *Warner ran into Mercer,* Newcombe, *Athletic Boys*, 94.

8: "Run Fast Good"

69 *"I stopped to watch"* Jim Thorpe as quoted in Wheeler, *Jim Thorpe*, 50.

70 *"I immediately sent for Jim"* Pop Warner as quoted in Bynum, *Pop Warner*, 120.

70 Sources on Louis Tewanima include Peter Nabokov, *Indian Running: Native American History and Tradition* (Santa Fe, N.M.: Ancient City Press, 1981); John Steckbeck, "From Hopi Indian Hogan to the Waldorf: The Louis Tewanami [sic] Saga of Footracing," *The (Harrisburg, Penn.) Evening News*, Oct. 12, 1954; and Peter Whiteley, *Bacavi: Journey to Reed Springs* (Flagstaff, Ariz.: Northland Press, 1988).

73 *"No one who does not know these Indians"* Francis E. Leupp in *Annual Reports of the Department of the Interior 1906. Indian Affairs: Report of the Commission and Appendixes* (Washington, D.C.: Government Printing Office, 1906).

73 *To demonstrate their transformation* Newcombe, *Athletic Boys*, 96–97.

9: A Perfect Football Machine

75 Sources on Albert Exendine include Frank Lankard, "Exendine—A Walking Football History Book" UPI (n.d.), Oklahoma Historical Society, Thorpe vertical file; and Newcombe, *Athletic Boys*.

77 Description of Pop Warner's coaching technique is based on Glenn S. Warner, *A Course in Football for Players and Coaches* (Carlisle, Pa.: 1912).

78 *"They [the Carlisle athletes] did not manifest"* Pop Warner as quoted in David Wallace Adams, "More Than a Game: The Carlisle Indians Take to the Gridiron, 1893–1917," *Western Historical Quarterly* 32, no. 1 (Spring 2001): 47.

78 *"The Carlisle ends wore white"* Ford Park as quoted in Newcombe, *Athletic Boys*, 113.

10: Spreading the Wealth

86 *"Every cent spent on track"* Glenn Warner, "Memories of the Indian School," handwritten notes, U.S. Army Military History Institute, Carlisle, Pa.

86 *"The sort of things"* Witmer, *Indian Industrial School*, 78.

86 Sources on Angel de Cora and William Lone Star Dietz include John C. Ewers, "Five Strings to His Bow: The Remarkable Career of William (Lone Star) Dietz," *Montana: The Magazine of Western History* 27 (January 1977): 3–12; and Witmer, *Indian Industrial School*.

87 Sources on Warner finances include *The Carlisle Indian School, Hearings Before the Joint Commission of the Congress of the United States, Sixty-Third Congress Second Session to Investigate Indian Affairs, February 6, 7, 8 and March 25, 1914, Part II* (Washington, D.C.: Government Printing Office, 1914); Newcombe, *Athletic Boys*; and Records of Wardecker's Department Store.

88 Sources on Arthur Martin include Arthur Martin, Carlisle Indian School Oral History Project, Cumberland County Historical Association.

88 Sources on Hugh R. Miller include Miller Box, Cumberland County Historical Association.

89 Frank Hudson and embezzling, Bell, "Telling Stories," 86.

89 Sources on Moses Friedman include Bell, "Telling Stories," 88.

90 Sources on Carlos Montezuma include Peter Iverson, *Carlos Montezuma and the Changing World of American Indians* (Albuquerque: University of New Mexico Press, 1982); and John W. Larner, Jr., *The Papers of Carlos Montezuma, M.D.* (Wilmington, Del.: Scholarly Resources, 1984).

90 W. G. Thompson allegations are from John Bloom, *To Show What*

an Indian Can Do: Sports at Native American Boarding Schools (Minneapolis: University of Minnesota Press, 2000), 28.

91 *"Three or four years ago we"* Myriam Vuckovic, "Onward Ever," 314.

91 *"Athletics at the school are financed"* from Glenn S. Warner, "Athletics at the Carlisle Indian School," *The Indian Craftsman: A Magazine Not Only About Indians But Mainly By Indians*, February 1909.

93 Letter from J. Frank Ridenour is from *The Arrow*, Sept. 20, 1907.

94 *"Jim was a natural athlete"* Henry Roberts as quoted in Bill Kirch, "Tepee Topics," *Pawnee Chief*, Oct. 13, 1966.

11: The Olympic Idea

95 Sources on the early Olympics include *Encyclopedia Britannica Online*; Allen Guttman, *The Olympics: A History of the Modern Games* (Urbana: University of Illinois Press, 1992); John Lucas, *The Modern Olympic Games* (South Brunswick, N.J.: A. S. Barnes, 1980); Bill Mallon and Ian Buchanan, *The 1904 Olympic Games: Results for All Competitors in All Events, with Commentary* (Jefferson, N.C.: McFarland & Co., 1999); Bill Mallon and Ian Buchanan, *The 1908 Olympic Games: Results for All Competitors in All Events, with Commentary* (Jefferson, N.C.: McFarland & Co., 2000); Bill Mallon and Ture Widlund, *The 1912 Olympic Games: Results for All Competitors in All Events, with Commentary* (Jefferson, N.C.: McFarland & Co., 2002); *The Olympic Review*; Kay Schaffer and Sidonie Smith, eds., *The Olympics at the Millennium: Power, Politics and the Games* (New Brunswick, N.J.: Rutgers University Press, 2000); and Alfred Eric Senn, *Power, Politics, and the Olympic Games* (Champaign, Ill.: Human Kinetics, 1999).

96 *"No person shall be considered"* as quoted by Ronald Smith, *Sports and Freedom*, 166.

96 *"As defined by another influential sporting group"* S. W. Pope, *Patriotic Games: Sporting Traditions in the American Imagination, 1876–1926* (New York: Oxford University Press, 1933), 22.

97 *"Oh, what a stupid old business Olympic amateurism is"* Pierre, Baron de Coubertin as quoted in Robert Parienté, "Jim Thorpe: What a Storybook Life!" *Olympic Review* (May 1983): 285.

97 *"the most knotty, elusive and exasperating"* William Milligan Sloane, "The Olympic Idea," *The Century Magazine*, 3, no. 84 (July 1912), 410.

97 Sources on James Edward Sullivan include Melvin Adelman, *A Sporting Time: New York City and the Rise of Modern Athletics* (Urbana: University of Illinois Press, 1986); *Dictionary of American Biography* 5-9 (New York: Charles Scribner's Sons, 1936); Guttman, *The Olympics*; Henry Beach Needham, "The College Athlete: How Commercialism Is Making Him a Professional," *McClure's* 25, no. 2 (June 1905); Pope, *Patriotic Games*; and "Obituary," *New York Times*, September 17, 1914.

99 "*The practical point is that under*" William B. Curtis as quoted in Adelman, *A Sporting Time*, 90.

99 Sources on A. G. Spalding include Allen Guttman, *Essays on Sport History and Sport Mythology* (College Station: Texas A & M University Press, 1990); and S. W. Pope, *Patriotic Games*.

100 "*vermin,*" "*the great unwashed*" Whitney as quoted in S. W. Pope, *Patriotic Games*, 30.

101 "*no longer [has] any power to name*" Sullivan as quoted in Lucas, *Modern Olympic Games*, 67.

104 "*a horrible, sickening sight of*" Gustavus Kirby as quoted in Mallon and Buchanan, *1908 Olympic Games*, 401.

12: Starting Halfback

107 "*a hard name*" Report concerning Frank Thorpe from the U.S. Farmer at Shawnee to Horace J. Johnson, Superintendent, Sac and Fox Indian School, Stroud, Okla. May 26, 1914. Sac and Fox Archives, Oklahoma Historical Society.

108 "*The boys can't run*" Wheeler, *Jim Thorpe*, 41.

109 "*Warner believed in no more than*" Press release from Hugh R. Miller, November 22, 1902. From the Miller Box, Cumberland County Historical Society.

112 "*Bill Hollenback of Penn*" Thorpe as quoted in Wheeler, *Jim Thorpe*, 68.

114 "*Still, Warner distributed*" *The Carlisle Indian School*, 1127.

117 "*The little Hopi*" Pop Warner as quoted in *The Arrow*, May 19, 1911.

13: Rocky Mount Railroader

121 Sources on the Eastern Carolina League include Chris Holaday, *Baseball in North Carolina's Piedmont* (Charleston, S.C.: Arcadia, 2002) and *Professional Baseball in North Carolina: An Illustrated City-by-City History, 1901–1996* (Jefferson, N.C.: McFarland & Co., 1998); Robert W. Reising, *Jim Thorpe: Tar Heel* (Rocky Mount, N.C.: Communique, 1974); and Jim C. Sumner, *Separating the Men from the Boys: The First Half-Century of the Carolina League* (Winston-Salem, N.C.: John F. Blair, 1994).

121 *"Libby and Youngdeer were fair"* Jim Thorpe as quoted in Wheeler, *Jim Thorpe*, 78.

127 *"Friedman was eager for positive"* The James Wheelock incident from Bell, "Telling Stories," 91.

131 *"Okay, you're going to spend a nickel"* Francis L. Fugate and Roberta B. Fugate, *Roadside History of Oklahoma* (Missoula, Mont.: Mountain Press Publishing Company, 1991), 188.

14: Marvel of the Age

134 *"According to Thorpe"* Stump, "Jim Thorpe."

134 *"I never made any"* Thorpe as quoted in Wheeler, *Jim Thorpe*, 151.

134 *"A lot of people think"* Bill Newashe quoted in Roy Angel, "City Man Recalls Days At Carlisle," *Shawnee-Oklahoma News-Star* (n.d.), Sac and Fox National Public Library.

134 Sources on Gus Welch include Newcombe, *Athletic Boys*, 67, 68; and Roulhac Teldano, "Serena, A Recollection, Felt in the Bones." October 1991. Unpublished memoirs in the Gus Welch Papers, University of Tulsa, Tulsa, Oklahoma.

136 *"cough medicine"* Edwin Pope, *Greatest Coaches*, 293.

137 *"He [Thorpe] wouldn't exert"* L. J. Fitzpatrick, Jr., "They Remember Jim Thorpe," *The Carlisle Shopper's Guide*, Oct. 30, 1968.

139 *"They'd sit there starting"* Arthur Martin, Carlisle Indian School Oral History Project, Cumberland County Historical Association.

139 *"We didn't have any huddles"* Gus Welch as quoted in Roland Hughes, "Teammate of Jim Thorpe Now Retired," *Roanoke World-News*, May 12, 1960.

140 *"Harvard was the Indian"* Glenn S. Warner, "Heap Big Run Most Fast."

142 *"On fourth down I called for a place kick"* Gus Welch from a handwritten manuscript in the Gus Welch Papers, University of Tulsa, Tulsa, Okla.

15: The Greatest Athlete in the World

161 *"The people in town"* Bell, "Telling Stories," 144.

162 *"He [Thorpe] was my classmate"* Fannie Kennerly as quoted in Ed Kelley, "Commerce Woman Remembers Jim Thorpe," *The Daily Oklahoman*, Nov. 22, 1977.

162 Sources on Iva Miller include Grace Thorpe, News Release, "Iva Thorpe Davies Obituary," June 7, 1981, Sac and Fox National Public Library.

163 Sources on Marianne Moore include Bonnie Costello, *The Selected Letters of Marianne Moore* (New York: Alfred Knopf, 1997); Charles Molesworth, *Marianne Moore: A Literary Life* (New York: Atheneum, 1990); and Marianne Moore, "Ten Answers, Letter from an October Afternoon, Part II," *Harper's Magazine*, November 1964, 92.

165 *"The first event I"* Abel Kiviat as quoted in Brad Steiger and Charlotte Thorpe, *Thorpe's Gold: The Inspiring Untold True Story of Jim Thorpe—World's Greatest Athlete, An American Tragedy and Triumph* (New York: Quicksilver Books/Dell Publishing, 1984), 167.

168 Sources on the 1912 Olympics include Erik Bergvall, ed., *The Fifth Olympiad: The Official Report of the Olympic Games of Stockholm 1912* (Stockholm: Wahlström and Widstrand, 1913); Bynum, *Pop Warner*; Guttman, *Olympics*; Mallon and Widlund, *1912 Olympic Games*; and Jim Thorpe, in collaboration with Thomas F. Collison, *Jim Thorpe's History of the Olympics* (Los Angeles: Wetzel, 1932).

168 *"Louis, go out and win"* Story reprinted in *The Carlisle Arrow*, Sept. 13, 1912.

168 *"Thorpe did little training"* Rice, *Tumult and Shouting*, 229.

169 *"At night we went girl-hunting"* Abel Kiviat quoted in Steiger and Thorpe, *Thorpe's Gold*, 174.

171 *"In addition to having every physical asset"* Pop Warner quoted in Rice, *Tumult and Shouting*, 233.

172 "*It answers the charge*" James Sullivan as quoted in Wheeler, *Jim Thorpe*, 107.

175 "*All through the meet*" Warner, "Red Menaces."

16: All-American

177 Sources for Thorpe's post-Olympic celebrations include Mallon, *1912 Olympic Game*, 406., Rice, *Tumult and Shouting*, 230., *Jim Thorpe*, Wheeler, 112.

179 "*He [Thorpe] was a hell of a nice*" Abel Kiviat as quoted in Lewis H. Carlson and John J. Fogarty, *Tales of Gold* (Chicago: Contemporary Books, 1987), 8–9.

179 Coverage of Thorpe's return home from *The Arrow*, September 13, 1912.

180 Sources on Louis Tewanima include Nabokov, *Indian Running*; John Steckbeck, "Hopi Indian Hogan"; and Edwin McDowell, "Memories of a Forgotten Olympian," *Wall Street Journal*, July 11, 1972.

184 "*By golly*" Jim Thorpe quoted in Whitman, *Jim Thorpe*, 12.

185 "*He had terrific*" Dr. Joseph Alexander as quoted in Wheeler, *Jim Thorpe*, 121.

185 "*Well, Elmer, how did you enjoy*" George H. Greenfield, "Coaches Parry with Humorous Tales When Queried on Technical Points," *New York Times*, Dec. 28, 1932.

186 "*The Carlisle School Appropriation Bill*" Welch's handwritten memoirs, Gus Welch Papers, University of Tulsa, Tulsa, Oklahoma.

188 "*When playing against college*" Pop Warner as quoted in Adams, "More Than a Game," 188.

193 "*The ground was covered*" Warner, "The Indian Massacres."

194 "*Thorpe, in physical equipment*" Warner, "Here Come the Giants!"

17: The Swindle

197 Sources on the Thorpe scandal include Mallon and Widlund, *1912 Olympic Games*; Newcombe, *Athletic Boys*; *New York Times* (January—February 1913); *New York Tribune* (January—February 1913); Wheeler, *Jim Thorpe*; and *Worcester Telegram* (January—February 1913).

18: A Man with No Principle

211 Sources on the federal investigation of Carlisle include: Bell, "Telling Stories"; *The Carlisle Indian School*; and George Yuda, interview with author, November 12, 2003.

216 *"I am sure if you"* Fred Bruce letter from Johnson Collection, Cumberland County Historical Society.

220 *"The Chairman: You are a member"* The Carlisle Indian School, 1261.

19: Masters of the White Man's Game

225 Sources on Thorpe's later years include Brad Steiger and Charlotte Thorpe, *Thorpe's Gold*; Stump, "Jim Thorpe"; Bill Thorpe, interview with author, January 16, 2004; Jack Thorpe, interview with author, January 17, 2004; and Wheeler, *Jim Thorpe*.

226 *"You musn't do that"* Knute Rockne story in Whitman, *Jim Thorpe*, 90.

227 *"Wrinkle Meat"* from Michael Koehler, "Pawns in the Game: Today's Student Athletes and the Tragedy of Jim Thorpe," *The College Board Review* 172 (Summer 1994).

232 *"All we got was a dead Indian"* Wilbur J. Gobrecht, *Jim Thorpe— Carlisle Indian* (Carlisle: Cumberland County Historical Society, 1969), 20.

Afterword: *The Continuing Problem of "Amateur" Athletics*

239 Sources on recent developments with the International Olympic Committee and the NCAA include the *New York Times* and the *Wall Street Journal*.

243 *"There are certainly plenty of things"* Bill Pennington, "Unusual Alliance Forming to Rein In College Sports," *New York Times*, January 17, 2003.

244 *"I think the thing we want to do"* Vic Bernstein, "On Tape, Ex-Coach Told Players to Lie About Slain Teammate," *New York Times*, August 17, 2003.

Selected Bibliography

Unpublished Manuscripts

Bell, Genevieve. "Telling Stories Out of School: Remembering the Carlisle Indian Industrial School, 1879–1918." Ph.D. diss., Stanford University, 1998.

Lehr, Robert E. "The American Olympic Committee, 1896–1940: From Chaos to Order." Ph.D. diss., Pennsylvania State University, 1985.

Ryan, Carmelita S. "The Carlisle Indian Industrial School." Ph.D. diss., Georgetown University, 1962.

Thorpe, Dagmar. "Ancestors of Jim Thorpe: An Annotated Genealogy and Bibliography (1700–1887)," 2003.

Vuckovic, Myriam. "Onward Ever, Backward Never: Student Life and Students' Lives at Haskell Institute, 1884–1920s." Ph.D. diss., The University of Kansas, 2001.

Warner, Glenn. "Memories of the Indian School." Unpublished notes, Pop Warner Box, U.S. Army Military History Institute, Carlisle, Pa.

Welch, Gus. Unpublished memoirs. Gus Welch Papers, University of Tulsa, Tulsa, Okla.

White, Walter. *The Greatest Athlete*. Unpublished manuscript. The Sac and Fox National Public Library, Stroud, Okla.

Key Periodicals

Annual Report of the Commissioner of Indian Affairs to the Secretary of the Interior. Washington: Government Printing Office, 1880–1896, 1899–1905.

Publication of the Haskell Institute
  The Indian Leader (weekly, 1899–1901)

Publications of the U.S. Indian School, Carlisle, Pa.
  The Red Man (monthly, 1910–1017)
  The Indian Helper (weekly, 1885–1900)
  The Arrow (weekly, 1904–1908)
  The Carlisle Arrow (weekly, 1908–1918)

New York American
New York Evening Journal
New York Herald
New York Journal
New York Times
New York Tribune
New York World
Philadelphia Enquirer
Raleigh News and Observer
San Francisco Examiner
Wall Street Journal
Washington Post

Noteworthy Articles

Adams, David Wallace. "More Than a Game: The Carlisle Indians Take to the Gridiron, 1893–1917." *Western Historical Quarterly* 32, no. 1 (Spring 2001): 25–53.

Angel, Roy. "City Man Recalls Days at Carlisle." *Shawnee-Oklahoma News-Star*. Sac and Fox National Public Library.

Barney, Robert Knight. "Born from Dilemma: America Awakens to the Modern Olympic Games, 1901–1903." *Olympika: The International Journal of Olympic Studies* 1 (1992): 92–135.

Camp, Walter. "The New Football." *The Outing Magazine* 57 (Oct. 1910): 17–25.

———. "The New Football." *The Outing Magazine* 57 (Nov. 1910): 205–208.

Connolly, James B. "The Capitalization of Amateur Athletics." *Metropolitan Magazine* 32 (1910): 443–454.

Deming, Clarence. "Athletics in College Life: 1. The Money Power in College Athletics." *Outlook* 80 (July 1905): 547–576.

Dyreson, Mark. "America's Athletic Missionaries: Political Performance, Olympic Spectacle, and the Quest for an American National Culture, 1896–1912." *Olympika: The International Journal of Olympic Studies* 1 (1992): 70–91.

Ewers, John C. "Five Strings to His Bow: The Remarkable Career of William (Lone Star) Dietz." *Montana: The Magazine of Western History* 27 (January 1977): 3–12.

Fitzpatrick, L. J. Jr. "They Remember Jim Thorpe." *The Carlisle Shopper's Guide*, Oct. 30, 1968.

Fulton, Bob. "A Frank, Open-hearted Gentleman." *IUP (Indiana University of Pennsylvania) Magazine* 10, no. 3 (Fall-Winter 1992–1993), 4–5, 25.

Gilstrap, Harriet Patrick. "Memoirs of a Pioneer Teacher." *The Chronicles of Oklahoma* 38, no. 1 (1960): 20–34.

Gumprecht, Blake. "A Saloon on Every Corner: Whiskey Towns of Oklahoma Territory, 1889–1907." *The Chronicles of Oklahoma* 74, no. 2 (1996): 146–173

Heisman, John W. "Signals." *Collier's*, October 6, 1928.

———. "The Thundering Herd." *Collier's*, October 13, 1928.

———. "Fast and Loose." *Collier's*, October 20, 1928.

———. "Hold 'em." *Collier's*, October 27, 1928.

———. "Signals, Rules Rush In." *Collier's*, November 10, 1928.

———. "Between Halves." *Collier's*, November 17, 1928.

———. "Their Weight in Gold." *Collier's*, November 24, 1928.

Howell, Reeta, and Maxwell L. Howell. "The Myth of Pop Warner: Carlisle Revisited." *Quest Monograph* 30 (Summer 1978): 19–27.

Hughes, Roland. "Teammate of Jim Thorpe Now Retired." *Roanoke World News*, May 12, 1960.

Jordan, Edward S. "Buying Football Victories." *Collier's*, November 11, 1905.

———. "Buying Football Victories." *Collier's*, November 18, 1905.

———. "Buying Football Victories." *Collier's*, November 25, 1905.

Kashatus III, William C. "A King Crowns the World's Greatest Athlete." *Pennsylvania Heritage* 22, no. 4 (Fall 1996): 32–39.

Kelley, Ed. "Commerce Woman Remembers Jim Thorpe." *The Daily Oklahoman*, Nov. 22, 1977.

Kirch, Bill. "Teepee Topics." *Pawnee Chief*, Oct. 13, 1966.

Koehler, Michael. "Pawns in the Game: Today's Student Athletes and the Tragedy of Jim Thorpe." *The College Board Review* 172 (Summer 1994).

Lambert, Craig. "First and 100: Harvard's Stadium with Its Storied Past, Is Football's Edifice Rex." *Harvard Magazine* 106, no. 1 (September-October 2003): 42–53.

Lankard, Frank. "Exendine—A Walking Football History Book." UPI (n.d.).

Lewis, Guy M. "Theodore Roosevelt's Role in the 1905 Football Controversy." *The Research Quarterly* 40, no. 4 (December 1969): 717–724.

Lucus, John A. "Caspar Whitney." *Journal of Olympic History* (May 2000): 30–38.

Matthews, George R. "The Controversial Olympic Games of 1908 As Viewed by the *New York Times* and the *Times* of London." *Journal of Sport History*. 7, no. 2 (Summer, 1980): 40–53.

McDowell, Edwin. "Memories of a Forgotten Olympian." *Wall Street Journal*, August 11, 1972.

Moore, Marianne. "Ten Answers, Letter from an October Afternoon, Part II." *Harper's Magazine*, November 1964, 92.

Needham, Henry Beach. "The College Athlete: How Commercialism Is Making Him a Professional." *McClure's* 25, no. 2 (June 1905).

———. "The College Athlete: The Amateur Code: Its Evasion and Administration." *McClure's* 25, no. 3 (July 1905).

Parienté, Robert. "Jim Thorpe: What a Storybook Life!" *Olympic Review* 187 (May 1983): 281–287.

Peterson, James A. "Thorpe of Carlisle." Written and compiled for the Nineteenth Annual Hinckley and Schmitt Football Luncheon. Undated pamphlet. Oklahoma Historical Society.

Sloane, William Milligan. "The Olympic Idea." *The Century Magazine* 3, no. 84 (July 1912): 410.

Smith, Jane R. "Triumph and Tragedy." *American History*, May/June 1997.

Smith, Ronald A. "Harvard and Columbia and a Reconsideration of the 1905–1906 Football Crisis." *Journal of Sport History* 8, no. 3 (Winter 1981): 5–19.

Steckbeck, John. "From Hopi Indian Hogan to the Waldorf: The Louis Tewanami [sic] Saga of Footracing." *The (Harrisburg Penn.) Evening News*, Oct. 12, 1954.

Stump, Al. "Jim Thorpe: Greatest of Them All." *Sport*, December 1949, 49–54.

Thorpe, Grace F. "The Jim Thorpe Family: From Wisconsin to Indian Territory, Part I." *The Chronicles of Oklahoma* 59 (1981): 91–105.

———. "The Jim Thorpe Family: From Wisconsin to Indian Territory, Part II." *The Chronicles of Oklahoma* 59 (1981): 179–201.

Warner, Glenn S. "Autobiography." 59 chapters. Distributed 1927–1928 by the Christy Walsh newspaper syndicate.

Warner, Glenn S. "The Indian Massacres." *Collier's*, October 17, 1931.

———. "Heap Big Run Most Fast." *Collier's*, October 24, 1931.

———. "Red Menaces." *Collier's*, October 31, 1931.

———. "Battles of Brawn." *Collier's*, November 7, 1931.

———. "What's the Matter with Football?" *Collier's*, November 24, 1931.

———. "Here Come the Giants!" *Collier's*, November 24, 1931.

———. "Athletics at the Carlisle Indian School." *The Indian Craftsman: A Magazine Not Only About Indians but Mainly by Indians*, February 1909.

Books

Adams, David Wallace. *Education for Extinction: American Indians and the Boarding School Experience, 1875–1928*. Lawrence: University of Kansas Press, 1995.

Adelman, Melvin. *A Sporting Time: New York City and the Rise of Modern Athletics*. Urbana: University of Illinois Press, 1986.

Alford, Thomas Wildcat. *Civilization, as Told to Florence Drake*. Norman: University of Oklahoma Press, 1936.

Anderson, Dave. *The Story of Football*. New York: William Morrow, 1985.

Benson, Lee. *From Athens to Atlanta: 100 Years of Glory*. Salt Lake City: Commemorative Publications, 1993.

Bergvall, Erik, ed. *The Fifth Olympiad: The Official Report of the Olympic Games of Stockholm 1912*. Stockholm: Wahlström and Widstrand, 1913.

Bernotas, Bob. *Jim Thorpe: Sac and Fox Athlete*. Philadelphia: Chelsea House Publishers, 1992.

Bernstein, Mark F. *Football: The Ivy League Origins of an American Obsession*. Philadelphia: University of Philadelphia Press, 2001.

Bloom, John. *To Show What an Indian Can Do: Sports at Native American Boarding Schools*. Minneapolis: University of Minnesota Press, 2000.

Bynum, Mike, ed. *Pop Warner: Football's Greatest Teacher: The Epic Autobiography of Major College Football's Winningest Coach, Glenn S. (Pop) Warner*. Birmingham, Ala.: Gridiron Football Properties, 1993.

The Carlisle Indian School, Hearings Before the Joint Commission of the Congress of the United States, Sixty-Third Congress Second Session to Investigate Indian Affairs, February 6, 7, 8 and March 25, 1914, Part II. Washington, D.C.: Government Printing Office, 1914.

Carlson, Lewis H., and John J. Fogarty. *Tales of Gold*. Chicago: Contemporary Books, 1987.

Cope, Myron. *The Game That Was: The Early Days of Pro Football*. New York: World Publishing, 1970.

Costello, Bonnie. *The Selected Letters of Marianne Moore*. New York: Alfred Knopf, 1997.

Daley, Arthur. *Pro Football's Hall of Fame*. Chicago: Quadrangle Books, 1963.

Danzig, Allison. *Oh, How They Played the Game: The Early Days of Football and the Heroes Who Made It Great*. New York: Macmillan, 1971.

———. *The History of American Football: Its Great Teams, Players, and Coaches*. Englewood Cliffs, N.J.: Prentice Hall, 1956.

Danziger, Jr. Edmund Jefferson. *The Chippewas of Lake Superior*. Norman: University of Oklahoma Press, 1978.

Dictionary of American Biography 5–9. New York: Charles Scribner's Sons, 1936.

Eastman, Elaine Goodman. *Pratt: The Red Man's Moses*. Norman: University of Oklahoma Press, 1935.

Espy, Richard. *The Politics of the Olympic Games*. Berkeley: University of California Press, 1979.

Flath, Arnold William. *A History of Relations Between the National Collegiate Athletic Association and the Amateur Athletic Union of the United States (1905–1963)*. Champaign, Ill.: Stipes Publishing, 1964.

Fugate, Francis L., and Roberta B. Fugate. *Roadside History of Oklahoma*. Missoula, Mont.: Mountain Press, 1991.

Gobrecht, Wilbur J. *Jim Thorpe—Carlisle Indian*. Cumberland County Historical Society, 1969.

Green, Harvey. *Fit for America: Health, Fitness, Sport and American Society*. New York: Pantheon, 1986.

Guttman, Allen. *The Olympics: A History of the Modern Games*. Urbana: University of Illinois Press, 1992.

———. *Essays on Sport History and Sport Mythology*. College Station: Texas A&M University Press, 1990.

Hagan, William T. *The Sac and Fox Indians*. Norman: University of Oklahoma Press, 1958.

Heuman, William. *The Indians of Carlisle*. New York: G. P. Putnam's Sons, 1965.

Holaday, Chris. *Baseball in North Carolina's Piedmont*. Charleston, S.C.: Arcadia, 2002.

———. Professional *Baseball in North Carolina: An Illustrated City-by-City History, 1901–1996*. Jefferson, N.C.: McFarland, 1998.

Iverson, Peter. *Carlos Montezuma and the Changing World of American Indians*. Albuquerque: University of New Mexico Press, 1982.

Kieran, John, and Arthur Daley. *The Story of the Olympic Games, 776 B.C. to 1972*. New York: J. B. Lippincott, 1973.

Kvasnicka, Robert M., and Herman J. Viola, eds. *The Commissioners of Indian Affairs, 1824–1977*. Lincoln: University of Nebraska Press, 1979.

Larner, J. W., ed. *The Papers of Carlos Montezuma* (microfilm). Wilmington, Del.: Scholarly Resources, 1983.

Lipsyte, Robert. *Jim Thorpe: 20th-Century Jock*. New York: HarperCollins, 1993.

Lucas, John. *The Modern Olympic Games*. South Brunswick, N.J.: A. S. Barnes, 1980.

Mallon, Bill. *The 1908 Olympic Games: Results for All Competitors in All Events, with Commentary*. Jefferson, N.C.: McFarland, 2000.

Mallon, Bill, and Ian Buchanan. *The 1904 Olympic Games: Results for All*

Competitors in All Events, with Commentary. Jefferson, N.C.: McFarland, 1999.

———. *The 1908 Olympic Games: Results for All Competitors in All Events, with Commentary*. Jefferson, N.C.: McFarland, 2000.

Mallon, Bill, and Ture Widlund. *The 1912 Olympic Games: Results for All Competitors in All Events, with Commentary*. Jefferson, N.C.: McFarland, 2002.

Mathewson, Christy. *Pitching in a Pinch or Baseball from the Inside*. Lincoln: University of Nebraska Press, 1994.

Molesworth, Charles. *Marianne Moore: A Literary Life*. New York: Atheneum, 1990.

Mooney, Charles W. *Localized History of Pottawatomie County, Oklahoma to 1907*. Midwest City, Okla.: Thunderbird Industries, 1971.

Nabokov, Peter. *Indian Running: Native American History and Tradition*. Santa Fe, N.M.: Ancient City Press, 1981.

Newcombe, Jack. *The Best of the Athletic Boys: The White Man's Impact on Jim Thorpe*. New York: Doubleday, 1975.

Nye, W. S. *Carbine and Lance: The Story of Old Fort Sill*. Norman: University of Oklahoma Press, 1937.

Oriard, Michael. *Reading Football: How the Popular Press Created an American Spectacle*. Chapel Hill: University of North Carolina Press, 1993.

Oxendine, Joseph B. *American Indian Sports Heritage*. Champaign, Ill.: Human Kinetics Books, 1988.

Pfaff, Tim. *Paths of the People: The Ojibwe in the Chippewa Valley*. Eau Claire, Wisc.: Chippewa Valley Museum Press, 1993.

Pope, Edwin. *Football's Greatest Coaches*. Atlanta: Tupper and Love, 1955.

Pope, S. W. *Patriotic Games: Sporting Traditions in the American Imagination, 1876–1926*. New York: Oxford University Press, 1997.

Powers, Francis J. *The Life Story of Glen [sic] S. (Pop) Warner: Gridiron's Greatest Strategist*. Chicago: The Athletic Institute, 1969.

Prague Historical Museum. *Prague, the First 100 Years*. Prague, Okla.: Prague Historical Society and Museum, 1991.

Reel, Estelle. *Uniform Course of Study*. Washington, D.C.: U.S. Government Printing Office, 1901.

Reising, Robert W. *Jim Thorpe: Tar Heel*. Rocky Mount, N.C.: Communique, 1974.

Rice, Grantland. *The Tumult and the Shouting: My Life in Sport*. New York: Barnes, 1954.

Roufs, Timothy G. *The Anishinab of the Minnesota Chippewa Tribe*. Phoenix, Ariz.: Indian Tribal Series, 1975.

Schaffer, Kay, and Sidonie Smith, eds. *The Olympics at the Millennium: Power, Politics and the Games*. New Brunswick, N.J.: Rutgers University Press, 2000.

Schoor, Gene, and Henry Gilfond. *The Jim Thorpe Story: America's Greatest Athlete*. New York: Julan Messner, 1951.

Senn, Alfred Eric. *Power, Politics, and the Olympic Games*. Champaign, Ill.: Human Kinetics, 1999.

Smith, Ronald A. *Sports and Freedom: The Rise of Big-Time College Athletics*. New York: Oxford University Press, 1988.

Standing Bear, Luther. *My People the Sioux*. London, Neb.: University of Nebraska Press, 1975.

Steckbeck, John S. *Fabulous Redmen: The Carlisle Indians and Their Famous Football Team*. Harrisburg, Pa.: J. Horace McFarland, 1951.

Steiger, Brad, and Charlotte Thorpe. *Thorpe's Gold: The Inspiring Untold True Story of Jim Thorpe—World's Greatest Athlete, An American Tragedy and Triumph*. New York: Quicksilver Books/Dell Publishing, 1984.

Sullivan, George. *Pitchers: 27 of Baseball's Greats*. New York: Aladdin, 1999.

Sullivan, James E. *Olympic Games, Stockholm, 1912*. New York: American Sports Publishing, 1912.

Sumner, Jim C. *Separating the Men from the Boys: The First Half-Century of the Carolina League*. Winston-Salem, N.C.: John F. Blair, 1994.

Thorpe, Jim in collaboration with Thomas F. Collison. *Jim Thorpe's History of the Olympics*. Los Angeles: Wetzel, 1932.

Updyke, Rosemary K. *Jim Thorpe: The Legend Remembered*. Gretna, La.: Pelican, 1997.

Warner, Glenn S. *A Course in Football for Players and Coaches*. Carlisle, Pa.: 1912.

Warner, Glenn Scobey. *Football for Coaches and Players*. Stanford, Calif.: Stanford University Press, 1927.

Watterson, John Sayle. *College Football: History, Spectacle, Controversy*. Baltimore: The John Hopkins University Press, 2000

Wheeler, Robert W. *Jim Thorpe: World's Greatest Athlete*. Norman: University of Oklahoma Press, 1979.

Whiteley, Peter. *Bacavi: Journey to Reed Springs*. Flagstaff, Ariz.: Northland Press, 1988.

Whitman, Robert L. *Jim Thorpe: Athlete of the Century, A Pictorial Biography*. Oklahoma City: Robert L. Whitman and the Jim Thorpe Association, 2002.

Witmer, Linda F. *The Indian Industrial School, Carlisle, Pennsylvania, 1879–1918*. Carlisle, Penna.: Cumberland County Historical Society, 2002.

Index

Page numbers in italics refer to illustrations and photographs.